(continued)

SUPERVISION IN EARLY CHILDHOOD EDUCATION

A DEVELOPMENTAL PERSPECTIVE

THIRD EDITION

Joseph J. Caruso
with M. Temple Fawcett

TEACHERS
COLLEGE
PRESS

Teachers College, Columbia University
New York and London

Published by Teachers College Press, 1234 Amsterdam Avenue, New York, NY 10027

Library of Congress Cataloging-in-Publication Data

Caruso, Joseph J., 1943–
    Supervision in early childhood education : a developmental perspective / Joseph J. Caruso with M. Temple Fawcett. — 3rd ed.
        p. cm. — (Early childhood education series)
    Includes bibliographical references and index.
    ISBN-13: 978-0-8077-4731-5 (pbk : alk. paper)
    ISBN-l0: 0-8077-4731-9 (pbk : alk. paper)
    1. School supervision—United States.   2. Early childhood education—United States.   3. Child development—United States.   4. Educational surveys—United States.   I. Fawcett, M. Temple, 1928-   II. Title.   III. Series: Early childhood education series (Teachers College Press)

LB2822.7.C37   2006
372.12'03—dc22

                                                        2006017816

ISBN-13: 978-0-8077-4731-5 (paper)   ISBN-10: 0-8077-4731-9 (paper)

Printed on acid-free paper
Manufactured in the United States of America

14   13   12   11   10   09   08   07   8   7   6   5   4   3   2   1

Contents

16.   Staff Evaluation and Learning   214

PREFACE

E VERY EARLY CARE AND EDUCATION program deserves a qualified and competent supervisor. This book, about supervising staff in early care and education, is for directors, principals, educational coordinators, mentors, head teachers, consultants, and others currently working in programs for young children who recognize a need to expand and improve their supervisory skills. Instructors of courses or workshops preparing persons for early childhood supervisory and leadership positions may wish to consider it as their principal text.

We believe that the personal and professional development of the adult is basic to formulating supervisory strategies. Through supervision, staff members can receive continuing support in their development as professionals and paraprofessionals. As supervisors and staff investigate, learn about, and reflect on their practice, they become better providers of care and education for children. Although supervision encompasses more than staff development and support, we have chosen to focus this book on that aspect of the role. We also stress the importance of the supervisor's ongoing development and learning.

The content of this third edition continues to be descriptive and practical. We provide the reader with specific suggestions for improving supervisory skills when working with individual staff members and with groups. The book has four major sections. In Part I, supervisory myths are challenged in order to ease the burden under which supervisors carry out their work. Then the various types of early childhood programs and the people who work in them are described from the perspective of the supervisor's role. Descriptive data to reflect changes in the field have been updated since our last edition.

In Part II, we explore the developmental framework upon which this book is based. These chapters focus on the development of supervisors and supervisees, their relationship to each other, and implications for planning supervisory approaches. A description of clinical supervision follows in Part III, with basic information and suggestions for holding reflective conferences with staff, and for observing within the context of a clinical supervision approach. Several significant issues that affect staff morale and effectiveness in early care and education programs, including staff emotional well-being, are also examined.

Part IV includes two new chapters, one on the career ladder/lattice and another on staff recruitment, selection, and orientation. The next chapter gives suggestions for designing various types of staff development experiences that emphasize staff learning, and some specific strategies for putting these plans into practice. Issues in staff evaluation are explored in the final chapter, including suggestions for a differentiated staff evaluation and learning plan.

Throughout this book, we use the term *supervisor* to mean those persons who do supervision as part or all of their job. These may be administrators, supervisors, consultants, or teachers. The terms *teacher, staff member, caregiver,* and *supervisee* are generally used interchangeably.

Since our second edition, the field of early care and education has made great strides in upgrading practitioner preparation and training through higher standards for licensure and certification, for program approval at the college level, and for the accreditation of early care and education programs. This edition of *Supervision in Early Childhood Education: A Developmental Perspective* is intended to support those efforts and the work of supervisors at the program level.

For example, in 2005 the National Association for the Education of Young Children (NAEYC) revised its process for accrediting early childhood programs. As a result, we have updated the relevant NAEYC accreditation standards and criteria included at the end of the appropriate chapters. Given the rapid progress made in the establishment of state early care and education career development programs and state registries that document the training of individuals, we have placed a greater emphasis in this edition on career ladders and lattices. And we continue to stress the importance of diversity issues within the supervisory context.

Finally, throughout this book we have made changes based on new understandings about effective supervisory and staff development approaches, particularly the importance of dialogue and collaboration among staff and between supervisors and staff members. We have stressed the importance of considering the characteristics of adult learners and linking staff development to staff learning. We have included a number of promising new staff development practices that encourage staff to take charge of their own learning, learn together, and construct their own knowledge. Staff evaluation approaches that emphasize learning, reflection, and collaboration are also included.

We hope that this book will contribute to the goal of having a competent supervisor in every early care and education program, and to the common mission that brings early childhood professionals together—that is, to support the growth and development of young children and their families.

SUPERVISION IN EARLY CHILDHOOD EDUCATION

PART I

THE SUPERVISORY CONTEXT

CHAPTER 1

MYTHS ABOUT SUPERVISION

M YTHS INFLUENCE AND SHAPE—and are often used to justify—behavior. Myths about supervision come from expectations that supervisors have about their jobs and from their past supervisory experiences, training, and education. Myths can also arise from the attitudes toward supervisors held by staff members and others. Some of these myths are simply not true. Others are partially true. Nevertheless, we have found that they can create internal stress for supervisors and bring about pressure from others.

What are some of the myths about supervision in programs for young children?

ALMOST ANYONE CAN BE AN EARLY CHILDHOOD SUPERVISOR

If the individual hired to be a director, educational coordinator, or head teacher of an early childhood program has had children, is a nice person, and has taught in the classroom, then few other qualifications are thought necessary to be a good supervisor. After all, parents have raised children for years without formal training, so why would a director need any special skills or knowledge to supervise babysitters? And anyone who has taught surely understands teachers' problems and can therefore supervise teachers effectively.

This kind of thinking—perhaps more prevalent in the minds of the public at large than in the child care field—certainly contributes to the feelings many supervisors have that their work is not valued. Such thinking, however, is based on a lack of knowledge about the process of working with adults and about the needs of young children and their cognitive, social, emotional, and physical development. It fails to recognize the importance of the environments in which children learn and of the interactions between children and adults in those environments.

Supervision cannot be carried out without careful thought, planning, and skill. Not all adults are competent to work with other adults or with children. Some who work well with children have to make many adjustments to work effectively with adults. Other adults work best alone, or with machines, or behind a desk. They may not have the stamina or sensitivity to interact with people daily in small settings.

Persons holding supervisory positions in early childhood programs usually have more than one role to fill and are responsible for working with all types of people. Those who strive to provide quality supervision to their staff members do so because they understand its positive effects on children. They carry on with conviction and determination despite the perceptions people may have about the nature and importance of their work. The myth that anyone can supervise tends to be held by those unfamiliar with early childhood programs, not by those who work in them.

THERE IS ONE BEST SUPERVISORY APPROACH TO USE WITH EVERYONE

Life would be easy for supervisors if they could read a book or take a course that would guarantee them one workable method of supervision that would always succeed. Such a panacea can be appealing to supervisors who are frustrated by many problems and desperate for immediate solutions.

Supervisors work with people. The problem with adopting a "package" to solve one's supervisory dilemmas or clinging to a homegrown method is the human factor: Caregivers are unique. They have varying personal and professional needs and different levels of ability and skill, which require various supervisory strategies.

Experienced supervisors know that some supervisees need to be shown what to do and how to do it in a direct and detailed way. Yet others can develop their own solutions to problems or take the initiative to do what needs to be done without direction. Some people prefer to interact with authority figures with whom they can establish a personal relationship; that is, they prefer supervisors who are warm, expressive, and sensitive, and who model appropriate behaviors for them. Others object to overly attentive supervisors. They prefer to develop their own solutions to problems and appreciate a supervisor who is formal, serious, and impersonal.

The reasons supervisees respond to one approach or to another may have to do with cognitive style, cultural background, intelligence, personality, experience, developmental level, or other factors. Supervisors need flexibility when working with caregivers: The size of the settings, the number of supervisees for whom they are responsible, the individual differences among their supervisees, and their own personality and style all affect the supervisory strategies to be considered.

Supervision is a process involving the many variables of human behavior. Negating this process by looking at supervision with tunnel vision and adopting a single supervisory method will not resolve the complex problems supervisors face and will not help change caregiver behavior.

SUPERVISORS HAVE ALL THE ANSWERS

The myth that supervisors have all the answers is one that creates continuous pressure on supervisors, who live in fear that someone might discover they don't have a solution to a problem or may not even know how to go about solving it. They fear that others will think less of them or will suggest that they are incompetent and shouldn't be in a leadership position if they cannot step in, take charge, and resolve a pressing problem in short order.

The assumption that supervisors are omniscient beings makes it difficult for supervisors to be honest with themselves and with their staff members. It fails to recognize that some organizational problems or people problems take time to resolve—sometimes several years. This myth also discourages collaborative problem solving between a supervisor and a staff member, for a collaborative mode acknowledges that others have expertise, perhaps in areas in which a supervisor is weak. Through the dialogue, interaction, and give-and-take of the problem-solving process, supervisors and supervisees can grow professionally.

This myth is reflected in behavior in which supervisors feel obligated to tell caregivers how to resolve a problem or how to teach better. Supervisors may feel guilty if they cannot do so and may tend to react too quickly to a supervisee's questions or doubts by continually talking and offering solutions. The youthfulness of early childhood supervisors and the turnover rate among them may increase pressure on supervisors to prove themselves. Providing all the answers is, after all, what an expert, a supervisor, is expected to do.

Learning to listen to a staff member and to ask questions takes practice. By thinking through problems and developing solutions with a supervisor instead of simply being told answers, supervisees can be encouraged to move toward greater independence. By relieving themselves of the burden of having quick remedies to complex problems at their fingertips, supervisors can relax and explore the subtle circumstances and details of an event.

Supervisors are human. They have strengths and limitations. Although they have control over some of the variables affecting their programs, they have little influence and control over others. Supervisors who can be honest and realistic about themselves can create a group spirit in a program without losing supervisory credibility.

DIRECT CONFRONTATION WITH STAFF IS NONSUPPORTIVE

Many supervisors, particularly those in the early childhood field, have great difficulty confronting employees about situations, behavior, and habits that may negatively affect a program. They are reluctant to "lay it on the line" with a caregiver who, for example, is always late or who is creating strife among staff members. A direct approach is deemed a nonsupportive one.

Avoiding explicit supervision, a supervisor may deal with a problem indirectly: by raising the issue in a delicate way during a conference, by hinting at possible new behaviors, or by manipulating other variables to reduce the tension a particular situation has created. These strategies make a supervisor feel better. After all, how can one be so petty as to confront a caregiver who is earning so little money or who really needs the job? Leveling with a supervisee seems so antihumanistic, so uncaring. The direct approach has not been given much credence in early childhood training.

Attempting to resolve a problem indirectly is often appropriate, but sometimes supervisees do not "hear" the message, or do hear the message but choose to ignore it, so that problems continue to multiply. In situations such as these, stating the problem openly in a factual and honest way permits the issue to be acknowledged and dealt with.

Such a direct approach is exactly what some supervisees need. Although a caregiver may have recognized a problem, he or she may not have adequate self-discipline to solve it or the courage to go to a supervisor or other persons for help. On occasion, a teacher may not even be aware that he or she is not performing appropriately. Getting the concern out in the open can be revealing and cathartic, often laying the foundation for a trusting, supportive relationship.

Caregivers appreciate honesty in supervisors; they don't like "beating around the bush." They want to know what they are doing right and what they are doing wrong. Airing concerns in a straightforward, fair, and sincere manner prevents problems from deepening and feelings from intensifying. It allows supervisor and supervisee to start fresh without resentments from lingering unaddressed concerns. Evading issues will not improve relationships among people or increase program effectiveness. Problems create tension for supervisors, but confronting problems is part of the job and can actually relieve tension.

SKILLED SUPERVISORS NEVER ENGAGE IN MANIPULATION

The notion of supervision as manipulation is a difficult one to discuss. No doubt there are supervisors who unfairly control staff members to satisfy their ego needs, to feel more powerful, or to serve their own purposes. Manipulation, for example, can take the form of paternalism on the part of supervisors who think they always know what's best for their supervisees and never permit them to voice opinions, feelings, or ideas about an issue. Such supervisors simply make major decisions about the work life of their teachers, "convincing" the staff and themselves that a particular action is best for a supervisee, even though sometimes it may really be best only for the supervisor. Often, issues of class, status, politics, and culture underlie this type of manipulative behavior.

Supervision as skilled management through which caregivers improve performance and grow professionally is distinct from that which is self-serving and paternalistic. Some supervisors fear that if they make use of skills that enable them to influence a supervisee's behavior, they are being manipulative. Concerned about disrespecting and controlling others, they question the ethics of using these techniques. Supervisory behaviors like praise might be considered manipulative in some situations, but such techniques that shape the behavior of staff members are often appropriate means for building self-confidence.

An example might be a beginning teacher who presents a lesson for the first time. The lesson has many flaws in it, but the teacher is fragile and insecure. In the follow-up conference, the supervisor's feedback may be positive, despite the many problems with the lesson, because the supervisor decides that the emotional state of the teacher requires positive feedback at this time so that he or she can gain confidence and continue to grow and develop professionally. In a sense, this is manipulation on the supervisor's part; yet the truth would have been damaging. In this case, the teacher was inexperienced and still in the process of developing teaching competencies. The supervisor's conscious means of guiding the teacher did not have a selfish motive, nor did it abuse supervisory power. If this had been an experienced teacher, the supervisor's strategy would have been straightforward. In critiquing the lesson with the teacher, most likely all of its flaws would have been openly discussed.

Let us acknowledge, then, that some supervisory situations can be interpreted to have manipulative overtones; however, assumptions that suggest that staff should not be trusted, that they must be constantly watched and controlled, that they need to have decisions made for them, or that they should be "used" to the advantage of the supervisor do not have validity as a basis for supervision.

GOOD TEACHERS DO NOT NEED SUPERVISION

Supervisors sometimes assume that those staff members who perform their duties in an excellent fashion or who are very experienced in their roles require little or no supervision. This myth may allow problems to go unresolved, may diminish team spirit among staff members, and may cause excellent staff to feel neglected, undervalued, or excluded from the group.

Effective teachers, however experienced, require supervision. Like all staff members, they appreciate attention. They like to be recognized and to receive positive reinforcement. They want to know that supervisors are interested in their work and are knowledgeable about the scope of outstanding work. To do an excellent job without a supervisor's being aware of it can be discouraging and can create anxiety and stress.

Good teachers sometimes have work-related problems with other staff or with particular children. Their competence as teachers does not mean that they always have the right answer or the skills to resolve every problem. Often, they need someone else to validate their instincts about how to resolve a problem.

Some good teachers burn out over time and become bored with their work and eventually uninterested. They may be stimulated by a supervisor who can give them new ideas, allow them to take a new role within a program if there is one available, or encourage them to take leadership roles in the field outside the program.

Effective teachers also value criticism. They want constructive feedback. One reason for their excellence may be their ability to analyze their performance and to accept input about their work so that it constantly improves.

Good teachers have expertise that can be shared with a supervisor and others. A supervisor who neglects competent staff has lost a valuable resource. Excellent and motivated teachers can be a great help to supervisors by modeling behaviors for other staff, by teaching colleagues, and by providing ideas and suggestions to supervisors.

Directors who fail to supervise highly competent staff members risk losing the very people who provide strength to their programs.

SUPERVISION IS AN OBJECTIVE PROCESS

Supervising is a complex activity that cannot be totally objective. Supervisors come to the educational arena with "colored glasses." The ways in which they view their staff members are affected by their own childhood, their education, their life and work experience, and the philosophy and values they have developed. Supervisors' beliefs and values cannot easily be set aside as they work with staff members— nor should they be set aside. They should, however, be recognized.

If, for example, a teacher doesn't implement a lesson the way the supervisor would have, then the supervisor may question whether it was done correctly. But the lesson may have achieved its goals even though it did not reflect the supervisor's values. Supervisors are caught in a balancing act. They have their own goals, philosophy, and values, which they would like to see reflected in their programs; yet they wish to respect caregivers' values without being heavy-handed or forcing their personal styles or approaches on teachers.

It is perfectly legitimate for a supervisor to direct a program toward a particular philosophical orientation, but this does not mean that all staff members must think the way their supervisor thinks. It does suggest that supervisors who operate with a high level of consciousness about self can strive to be aware of the "tinted lenses" through which they view their programs and can recognize how their biases might affect the supervisory process.

The process of observing teachers is one that can become more objective through the use of various tools for gathering data. These instruments bring focus to an observation, generate information about teaching behavior, and raise questions of purpose and philosophy (see Chapter 11). Evaluation, however, is judgmental and therefore inherently subjective. Supervisors are expected to judge the competency of teachers in their programs as fairly as possible. Because they have expertise and experience, supervisors are qualified to judge and should not feel guilty for doing so.

SUPERVISORS ARE ALWAYS CALM

Many people believe that teachers should always be calm, assuming that they do not experience strong feelings and emotions while working with children. This myth of calmness and moderation applies to supervisors as well. Supervisors are expected to be model educators. Despite the many pressures they face—frustrations due to working conditions and feelings of impatience with staff members, parents, or government officials—they are always expected to be cool, calm, and collected. They are supposed to be able to respond to pressure in a low-keyed, logical, and emotionless manner.

This myth can create a sense of fear and guilt in supervisors: fear that if they are caught off-guard and show emotion they will lose power and status and their supervisees will think less of them; guilt because they have demonstrated imperfection by losing control for a moment and revealed human weakness.

Supervisors who believe they must be "super" at all times carry a burden that rejects reality and denies their humanness. Teachers who see human qualities in their supervisors often gain greater respect for them. Supervisees respond to, empathize with, and demonstrate greater willingness and enthusiasm for following a leader when they realize that they share certain qualities with that leader.

EXERCISES

1. Discuss how one or more of these myths has affected your own view of supervision and your work as a supervisor.
2. Discuss how these myths might affect a staff member's expectations of the supervisory relationship.
3. Describe other myths that can affect the supervisory role or supervisor-supervisee relationships.

EARLY CHILDHOOD PROGRAMS: IMPLICATIONS FOR SUPERVISION

T HE DEFINITION OF EARLY CARE and education that is used by the National Association for the Education of Young Children (NAEYC) is "any group program in a center, school, or other facility, that serves children from birth through age eight" (Bredekamp & Copple, 1997, p. 3). Within this scope there is a great diversity of programs: those for infants as young as a few months and for schoolchildren as old as third graders; settings designed for children who are present for a few hours a day, 2 or 3 days a week, and ones that serve those who come for many hours every day; large centers or schools where children are grouped by age, or family child care homes with a few children of mixed ages. Goals may be limited to making social experiences available to children who have many advantages or may encompass a rich educational program together with health and social services for those who have very few advantages. And while many programs for young children are still found in traditional settings such as church parish houses, others are located on-site in businesses or public schools and have facilities especially designed for young children.

Good supervisory practices do not change with the setting nor do basic staff needs. However, a program's administrative structure and such factors as size, hours, staffing patterns, regulatory agency, source of funds, children and families served, and educational goals do affect both staff needs and the ways a supervisor functions.

FULL-DAY PROGRAMS

Probably the most complex setting for young children is one that is available year round, for 8 or more hours a day, 5 days or more a week, while parents are working or in school. Because these programs act as a supplement to, and to some degree a substitute for, parental home care, their quality is of special importance. The long operating hours in particular affect both program planning and the social-emotional needs of children and staff.

Center-Based Child Care

Center-based programs are usually licensed to provide full-day care (more than 30 hours per week) for six to eight or more children. Although both the program goals and the client population have changed a good deal in recent years, there continues to be a public image of such centers as providing only custodial care for low-income children. In reality, center-based full-day, full-year programs are also now very common in middle- and upper-middle-income communities, and the number is rapidly increasing. In addition, developmental, educational, and caregiving goals are now all generally considered to be of great importance, although not equally emphasized in all programs. In general, the differences between these and other preschools are mainly influenced by the length of the day.

Centers that serve low-income families are almost always nonprofit, receiving federal funds, administered through state social service departments in the form of direct grants or through vouchers for individual children, or funds from municipalities and states, churches, social service agencies, and the United Way. This funding supports children of families receiving public assistance who are in work or training programs and other families on a sliding fee scale. Children are also placed in centers for special services, as in cases of actual or potential abuse or neglect.

Small, individually owned centers are usually for-profit, with the "profit" principally being in the form of salary for the owner-director. The goals and policies of these programs depend almost entirely on the views of the individual owner.

Chains of child care centers are usually set up as corporations to be moneymaking enterprises. Although some are very large, with hundreds of individual centers, many have relatively few sites in a limited geographical area. These systems frequently have standardized buildings, equipment, and materials; and the goals, policies, and curriculum for each center are predetermined by the corporation, in some cases specified in great detail. The number of chains providing services, however, is subject to the ups and downs of the U.S. economy and to competition from the public schools.

Full-day programs may also be sponsored by businesses, hospitals, or universities, designed specifically to serve the needs of the people working or studying at these institutions. Companies usually consider them an employee benefit, although fees are commonly charged.

Infant and Toddler Care

The need for center-based infant and toddler care and the number of centers providing it have grown rapidly in recent years, and this trend will certainly continue.

Most centers for very young children are part of larger programs for older children. They may enroll children as young as 6 weeks, although some do not take babies younger than 5 or 6 months. The upper limit is 2 or 3 years, the age often influenced by licensing standards. Because the children are so young, group sizes must be small, and larger numbers of staff are needed to maintain desirable adult-to-child ratios. The NAEYC (2005) program standards and accreditation criteria include the following recommendations:

Infants. Staff–child ratio of 1:3 or 1:4; group size of 6–8
Toddlers. Staff–child ratio of 1:3 to 1:6; group size of 6–12 for ages 12 to 28
   months and 8–12 for ages 28 to 36 months

The higher ratios are applicable where the groups are smaller.

School-Age Child Care

These programs provide a place before and/or after the public school day for children of working parents. The children may take part in a varied program on a 5-day-a-week basis for as few as 2 hours or, for kindergarteners in half-day programs, as many as 8 hours per day. Some programs also provide services for school holidays and vacations. For-profit care may take place in family child care homes or in centers that are independent or part of a chain, while nonprofit services are often provided by public schools, religious institutions, Ys , Head Starts, and other social service agencies.

The ages of children in extended-day programs is from 5 to around 13, although the majority of children are in the younger range. With such an age span, it is not unusual to have several children from the same family in a program, and children may attend the same center year after year.

Implications for Supervision

With their long days and year-round calendar, full-day center-based programs present great challenges for supervisors. Because centers must be staffed for 10, 12, or more hours a day, staff members must work on staggered shifts, making it difficult for supervisors to find time for meetings. They often take place during nap time, thus excluding some people, or in the evening, creating extra burdens on caregivers. There is much evidence that feelings of continuity and cohesiveness among staff members are not easily reached when they are not able to meet together to work on common goals.

Routines such as eating, napping, tooth-brushing, and toileting can take a prominent place during the day, making it more difficult to create individual and family-like activities along with age-appropriate educational experiences. We believe that private time for both staff and children is especially important, but privacy and individual attention require flexibility, and there is not always enough staff available to achieve these goals. Communication with parents, of great importance in such centers, is also not easy to establish, since most parents are at work during the time their children are being cared for.

When a child care center is part of a larger system, such as a social agency, a business, or a multicenter operation, decisions that are made at a central office may reflect an order of priorities different from those of the local center. Administrators or boards, even of social agencies, may not understand the developmental goals or space and equipment needs of early care and education. Or the goal that a chain of child care centers maintains a uniform curriculum may stand in the way of flexibility or creative programming. On the other hand, central administrators can become sources of support and backup because of the resources at their disposal.

Nonprofit centers may have available to them supplemental employees from a number of government-funded sources, such as job training programs, the Foster Grandparents Program, and people fulfilling welfare-to-work requirements. These additional staff members must be integrated into classroom teams and offered training and support directed toward their special needs. In large day care programs, administrators are also likely to have responsibility for support staff including cooks, custodians, and health and social service personnel, calling for greater diversity of supervisory skills.

Another challenge for supervisors is to assist staff in recognizing the strengths as well as the needs of low-income or at-risk children, those with disabilities, or those who are culturally or linguistically different from the mainstream population. Although in many ways they do not differ from all young children, there are issues that are special to these populations (see NAEYC, 2005).

In infant and toddler centers, the issues confronting supervisors and staff are directly related to the developmental needs of very young children, about which supervisors themselves may have limited knowledge. With the demands of babies' cycles of sleeping and being fed and changed, caregivers may not easily see that their role has dimensions beyond that of responding to physical needs. Brain research has shown how neurological systems are rapidly being shaped by the quality of care in the earliest weeks and months of a child's life (Shore, 2003). Although this research reveals that the brain retains its capacity to grow throughout life, the most rapid growth occurs during the first three years. Risk factors such as malnutrition, prenatal exposure to drugs, alcohol, and nicotine, and stress caused by abuse and neglect can impede normal brain development (Education Commission of the States, 2004a). Also, there are sensitive periods in which the brain must have particular stimulation in order to grow properly. Different experiences during these "windows of opportunities" contribute to the development of such areas as language, thinking, and visual development. The absence of such stimulation can have long-lasting effects on young children (Newberger, 1997; Shore, 2003).

These new insights point to the importance of creating loving, nurturing, and healthy environments for children and the critical role that early intervention practices can play, especially with children who are at risk. Language, sensory, and social interactions with both adults and children (Shonkoff & Phillips, 2000), along with warm, loving, and consistent care, are the keys to making it possible for children to form secure attachments to those who care for them and to grow into curious, confident, competent learners. Web sites such as *Zero to Three* (http://www.zerotothree .org), *Charles A. Dana Foundation* (http://www.dana.org), and *I Am Your Child* (http://www.iamyourchild.org) provide caregivers and parents with information about brain research and ways to support early brain development.

Training and mentoring can help caregivers be able to see each baby as unique and learn to respond to subtle differences in a child's need for stimulation versus comfort, and to sleeping, eating, and other developmental patterns (Lally, Young-Holt, & Mangione, 1994). Providing a primary caregiver to each child over relatively long periods of time, though difficult, has a positive effect on a caregiver's sense of value and helps staff members become more productive as they gain control over their work environment (Bernhardt, 2000).

Toddlers, of course, are extremely active. They need both freedom to explore and limits, along with help in negotiating social exchanges with their peers and developing control over elimination. Staff often need help in dealing with their own feelings about discipline and about appropriate times and methods for toilet training.

As in all center-based programs, the group situation can obscure a young child's individuality. It can make it difficult to provide for the stimulation and active exploration that very young children require. We hold that course work in infant and toddler development, even though many states do not require it for licensing, is essential in equipping caregivers to provide an appropriate environment for their growth. Developing observation and recording skills also helps them be able to see and appreciate the differences in children and the ways they change in this period of fast growth.

Relationships between caregivers and parents is an issue that is important at any age, but may require even more nurturing by supervisors of infant and toddler center staff. Validation of a family's culture, language, and values is important even at this early age. Staff members are not immune to the feeling that parents should not place very young children in day care, especially if they believe the mother can afford to stay home with her child, and thus may play on the guilt often felt by parents.

The caregiver-parent relationship becomes particularly critical as a child grows toward toddlerhood and acquires greater self-control. Parents will have strong feelings about feeding, toilet training, and discipline, which become more important at this time. Supervisors may have to spend both individual and group staff development time helping caregivers deal with their feelings and find ways to develop a partnership, rather than a rivalry, with parents. Staff members who have developed skill in communicating with parents will be able to discuss such matters in an atmosphere of mutual respect, which encourages an exchange of ideas, feelings, and expertise about what the child is doing.

Among the important issues in school-age care are the range in age of the children served and the fact that the children have been (or will be) in a school setting for a good part of the day. In addition, split shifts for staff, using shared and often inadequate space, can create stress (Neugebauer, 1993). Creative accommodation to the different social, emotional, and intellectual needs of 5-, 8-, and 12-year-olds, as they become more autonomous and independent and as their peer-relationship needs and skills increase, is a major goal of staff. Another challenge for staff is to plan same-age and multiage activities for children of different ages who are in a common setting.

Helping staff organize for and feel comfortable with a program that is flexible enough to provide contrast to the structured school day is another issue for supervisors. A staff with many abilities is required for a program that includes recreational and arts activities, field trips and neighborhood excursions, along with homework assistance, tutoring, and language help for bilingual children. Special training is often necessary to help staff see the overall goals of a program for out-of-school time as a place to enhance children's socialization, relaxation, and informal learning, and to understand the developmental needs of school-age children. We recommend that programs build in staff time to meet and discuss the special needs of all the children cared for during these important periods of the day.

The out-of-school time (OST) workforce tends to be a mature, skilled, and educated group. Respondents to a study by the National Institute on Out of School Time (NIOST & Academy, 2003) had an average age of 37, and 87% were female. Almost 80% of them, which included program directors and managers, had at least a bachelor's degree. It is interesting to note that, on average, they had been in their current position for 4 years, while more than half viewed out-of-school child care as a viable career choice. These staff members may view school-age child care as a place where they can develop interesting, long-term relationships with children who come back year after year, and where creative programming can flourish.

There is still a need, however, for affordable and accessible training, ongoing support, and educational opportunities for staff. Since many programs are small, directors may also serve as teachers, working as colleagues alongside the staff for whom they are responsible. They may not have much contact with other after-school program administrators, and those whose programs are housed in school buildings frequently have little support from the regular school staff. The National Institute on Out-of-School Time (NIOST; 2003) offers a retreat for executive directors, directors, and coordinators that emphasizes the development of leadership and advocacy skills as well as a peer-support network. Also, the National Association of Elementary School Principals (NAESP; 1999) has established standards for K–8 principals involved in after-school programs, which our readers will find useful.

We recommend that administrators working in after-school programs periodically check the NIOST Web site (www.niost.org) for staff training opportunities as well as for recent developments and progress in the field in such areas as the career lattice, credentials, and core competencies. For information about accreditation, contact the National AfterSchool Association (http://www.naaweb.org/accreditation.htm).

Family Child Care

Family child care is defined as taking place in the home of a nonrelative for up to 12 hours a day, 5 or more days a week. In most states where such care is regulated, the number of children in one home is limited to about six, usually including the provider's own children. In some states group home care for 7–12 children is allowed with an assistant. Currently, 44 states have separate regulations for this type of child care, and an equal number of states have clauses which legally exempt some homes from licensing requirements (Children's Foundation, 2004). Subsidies are available from the Child Care Food Program to licensed providers who take care of children of parents on government assistance who work or attend school, and abused or neglected children.

The Family Child Care Licensing Study reported that there are 290,530 regulated family child care homes in the 50 states, District of Columbia, Puerto Rico, and the Virgin Islands (Children's Foundation, 2004). Although virtually all states now license child care homes or have a required or voluntary registration process, many homes are not licensed. Providers are often reluctant to go through the process of becoming licensed because of the limits imposed by the regulations or through fear of intrusion. However, the Study of Family Care and Relative Care found that being regulated has the strongest relationship of any factor to quality care (Kontos, Howes, Shinn, & Galinsky, 1995).

The ages of children cared for in home settings range from infants to elementary school children, although most are younger than school age. Infants and toddlers are more likely to be cared for in family child care, because the availability of center-based care for very young children is not widespread, and because many parents value a homelike atmosphere.

Approximately 650,000 caregivers are working in the family child care field (Burton et al., 2002). Family child care providers have many different backgrounds, income levels, and reasons for involvement. As of this writing, however, there is little recent national demographic data on these providers, particularly since so many of them are unregulated. Data collected since 2001 in a survey of selected states show that average annual salaries of family child care providers range from a high of $30,000 in Connecticut to a low of $6,039 in small homes in Monterey County in California. Average hourly wages for providers can be as low as $4.90 per hour for a starting wage in Utah or as high as a median hourly wage of $9.19 per hour for teacher assistants in Alameda County in California. Nevada has an average annual turnover rate of 22%, while the turnover rate in Maryland is 16% (Center for the Child Care Workforce, 2004).

Implications for Supervision

Because of the isolation of family child care providers together with licensing requirements that are generally less stringent than those for center-based caregivers, there are still many who have had little or no specialized training in child care. In 2002, only 11 states required preservice training for small family child care home providers, and 12 states had such requirements for large family child care home providers (NAEYC, n.d.). National studies have reported that 64% of regulated providers and 34% of nonregulated providers have had specialized training, although many more have probably attended some informal workshops (Kontos et al., 1995). It is probable, however, that a much lower percentage have had on-site supervision.

When training exists, it is usually provided by resource and referral agencies or licensing or other state training agencies. Formal and informal associations, including affiliates of the National Association for Family Child Care (NAFCC; see Appendix), and various community projects are becoming more common as vehicles for providing caregivers with support and self-help, as well as assistance and training from professionals. Some states have Family Child Care (FCC) systems which support and monitor providers who serve state reimbursed families. Partnerships among community colleges, state agencies, FCC systems, and professional associations are needed to develop training and support programs for providers (Modigliani, 2001).

The supervisory role in family child care is most likely to grow out of some form of group training. Workshop or course instructors, mentors, or coaches can build in on-site visits to get a sense of the physical environment of the homes, the kinds of children enrolled, and the caregivers' interactions with the children. Conducting baseline assessments with home providers in relation to the accreditation process of the NAFCC can become a key aspect of training, as can other activities which meet the individual needs of providers. Trainers or coaches might then be viewed as supporters for individual providers and can build more meaningful content into their workshop or course sessions. It is essential that these supervisors be knowledgeable about the special characteristics of home-based care and have experience in home-based care themselves. Of course training given in the first language of the provider is likely to be more effective. A knowledge of early childhood education and child development, good people skills that are essential in establishing trusting relationships, and cultural competence to work with a diversity of providers are other important baseline competency areas for mentors and supervisors (Modigliani, 2001).

All caregivers should have knowledge of child development and how to provide programs appropriate to the age and development of children, but family child care providers have some unique additional needs. First, they are probably the most susceptible of early childhood caregivers to society's view that child care is "only babysitting." Thus a major priority for some providers is to improve their self-image, so they can begin to see themselves as professionals who do indeed have, and can further develop, special skills for working with children and parents, and who are carrying out a socially valued job. As providers gain confidence and competence, supervisors can assist them in growing into the role of mentor for other providers.

Other provider needs are related to the fact that care is given in the provider's own home. The intimacy of the setting may affect parents' and caregivers' expectations about care. For example, a major area of need is to become aware of the importance of planning for the children's day (Kontos et al., 1995). Misunderstandings between parents and providers can develop, especially where there are differences in culture, standards, or values, unless open communication systems have been developed. Relationships with the provider's spouse and own children, too, can be strained by the presence of day care children.

Other issues not encountered by center-based caregivers include developing effective learning environments within the limitations of the physical layouts of their homes, and planning and choosing appropriate materials for a span of ages. As family child care providers are operating a child care business, managing a business and relating to the community are also important issues, as well as guaranteeing children's health, nutrition, and safety (Roach, Adams, Riley, & Edie, 2003).

Because of the large number of day care homes and the difficulties involved in setting up monitoring systems, supervisors will find a great deal of variation in the quality of care provided. Even when their level of education and training is not high, however, most providers are people who have great potential.

Some useful resources for trainers include *Provider's Self-Study Workbook: Quality Standards for NAFCC Accreditation* (2005; available online from http:// www.nafcc.org); *There's No Place Like Home* (Modigliani & Dombro, 1996; available from Family Child Care Project, 125 Brooks Ave., Arlington, MA 02474); and the *Family Child Care Rating Scale* (Harms, Cryer, & Clifford, 2006).

HEAD START

Head Start is a national program, funded to local agencies through the federal government. It provides comprehensive developmental services to low-income preschool children and their families, focusing on education, socioemotional development, physical and mental health, and nutrition. Although direct services to children have always been a major goal, health and nutrition, social services, and parent involvement all receive equal emphases in program goals and implementation.

Most Head Start children take part in a center-based preschool program for 3- to 5-year-olds, 5 hours per day, 4 or 5 days per week. A home-based option that provides comprehensive services to children in their own homes is usually available. Other Head Start options include full-day/school-year, full-day/full-year, Early Head Start (which serves low-income pregnant women and families with children from birth through 3 years of age), and Parent and Child Centers. At least 10% of the enrollment in Head Start must be children with disabilities. They receive both regular Head Start services and individualized special services.

Inclusion of Parents

One of the most important premises of Head Start is the significance placed on the role of parents, who must be included as paid workers or as volunteers in classrooms. They are also to be given opportunities to participate in program decisions through committees and the policy council or committee, which is the governing board of each Head Start program. Staff members are required to communicate with parents frequently, including making home visits.

The Head Start FACES 2000 Study, a national longitudinal study of Head Start programs and of the cognitive, social, and physical development of Head Start children, found that programs continue to be of good quality across a wide variety of indicators. When compared to the original 1997 sample, teachers were more qualified. More Head Start teachers in 2000 had bachelor's or associate's degrees (38.7%) and more had graduate degrees (10.9%); more teachers reported having studied early childhood education or child development in preparation for their highest degree (62%); and more were members of professional organizations. Teachers were on average 44.4 years of age; 48% were White, 33.7% African American, 15% Hispanic, and 1% Asian (Zill, McKay, & O'Brien, 2003).

Quality Assurance

The Head Start Act places a strong emphasis on staff qualifications, supervision, training, development, and appraisal. It was amended in 1998 to require that by September 30, 2003, "at least 50% of all Head Start teachers nationwide in center-based programs have an AA, BA, or advanced degree in early childhood education, or development, or a degree in a related field and experience teaching preschool children" (U.S. Department of Health and Human Services, 2004, p. 34). Programs must provide adequate supervision and pre- and in-service training to staff and volunteers. Individual training needs are to be assessed, and in-service training and college-based course work made available. All staff are encouraged to develop competencies that will enable them to move vertically (e.g., from aide to mentor teacher) or horizontally (e.g., from social service to education) within a program. Head Start also supports the development of mentor teachers whose role is to observe and assess the classroom activities of Head Start programs and to provide on-the-job guidance and training to program staff and volunteers.

Another distinctive feature of Head Start is its built-in system for ensuring that services based on Head Start goals are actually being delivered by each local program, while allowing for flexibility at the local level. Two procedures assist this effort:

1. The Head Start Performance Standards, which define "the objectives and features of a quality Head Start program in concrete terms; they articulate a vision of service delivery to young children and families; and they provide a regulatory structure for the monitoring and enforcement of quality standards" (U.S. Department of Health and Human Services, 2002). Grantee and delegate agencies must provide staff members, parents, members of councils and boards, and community partners with training on the standards and ways to implement them.
2. A mandated system through which grantees are required to evaluate their performance in relation to the Performance Standards. This yearly self-assessment, which includes parents, staff, and community representatives, uses the On-Site Program Review Instrument (OSPRI). Every 3 years this includes a weeklong on-site visit from an outside team. The local program's own self-assessment is "validated," and where it is found to be out of compliance with the Performance Standards, it is given up to a year to correct the deficiencies pursuant to a Quality Improvement Plan.

Implications for Supervision

Each of the elements discussed above has an impact on the supervisory process, both for program directors and for educational coordinators. First, administrators will find that program goals that are mandated and closely monitored by the funding source (in this case, the federal government) can have both advantages and disadvantages. Accountability through various levels of bureaucracy can be confusing and frustrating. Newcomers to Head Start are confronted with a dizzying array of terminology and acronyms. Paperwork can seem endless. Policies or their interpretation may change with little time for staff preparation, and questions about whether the local program is in compliance with the Performance Standards are not always easily answered. These concerns can be especially unnerving when it comes time for an OSPRI review.

On the other hand, the structures that Head Start has created provide supports within the system that can be very helpful to supervisors. The Performance Standards, which serve as the basis for all program decisions, provide clear goals within a developmental early childhood perspective. They serve as common reference points for all staff, from aides and volunteers through the director. Supervision, training, and curriculum development all start from this point, but enough flexibility is allowed so that staff and parent input can make a difference. In addition, the OSPRI, in spite of the tremendous amount of work it requires, furnishes valuable information on strengths and weaknesses on which to build for the future.

Other supports built into the Head Start system are funds for training and technical assistance and for college courses and Child Development Associate (CDA) training; state and regional organizations of Head Start directors and supervisors; and regional office personnel.

The emphasis on the involvement of parents has a number of implications for supervision and training. Staff members—and supervisors themselves—may find it difficult to adjust to untrained parents as decision makers or to find ways to work through differences of opinion on important issues. Staff development that emphasizes communication skills, cultural competence, and an understanding of the concerns and strengths of low-income parents can help teachers work sensitively with parents in the classroom, in conferences, and in home visits. Effective orientation and training programs for parent aides and volunteers also contribute to staff-parent understanding.

Finally, in any program with a predominantly low-income clientele, some staff members may find it difficult to deal with the very real problems facing some children, parents, and even other staff members. Racial, class, linguistic, and cultural differences can sometimes create barriers to communication and understanding. Young middle-class teachers with little or no experience with low-income or culturally different children may especially need training and supervisory assistance.

PART-DAY PROGRAMS

Until recently, half-day school-year programs for 3- and 4-year-olds have been the most widespread type of early childhood program, except for kindergartens. Nursery schools (now often called preschools or child development centers) are characterized by small size, attendance by different children and teachers in mornings and afternoons, and alternate-day attendance options. A number also include kindergartens. Full-day or school-day options for children of working parents are becoming more common.

Nursery Schools

Nursery schools are almost always either privately owned or sponsored by a church, synagogue, YMCA or YWCA, or similar organization, or are part of a private school, rather than being publicly funded. An individual school may be an independent enterprise for an owner-director, or it may be parent sponsored and managed.

Formally organized *parent cooperatives* usually are nursery schools where there is a paid director, who most likely also teaches, and sometimes one or more paid teachers. A large part of the responsibility for the teaching and care of the children, along with secretarial, maintenance, or other needed work around the school, is carried by the parents. In most co-ops parents both govern and manage the school as well.

Laboratory Schools

A *laboratory school* (or *lab school*), which is associated with a high school, vocational school, college, or university, is established primarily as a place for students to observe and practice working with children as part of early childhood training, and generally has a part-day format. Day care programs, increasingly available in colleges to provide care for children of faculty, staff, or students, may also be used as a laboratory setting, but usually training is a secondary rather than a primary objective of these programs. In both types of centers, major teaching responsibilities are borne by the students in training or by work-study students who serve as paid assistants. Child care centers that are part of teen parenting programs in high schools have some of the same characteristics as lab schools.

Implications for Supervision

Traditionally, nursery schools were thought of mainly as places for children to develop social skills. Today there is often at least an equal emphasis on providing a more comprehensive developmental and educational program. Pressure from parents to train children in academic skills sometimes makes it difficult for teachers to resist the inclusion of activities that are inappropriate for preschool children.

The small size of most nursery schools makes supervision an informal process. Directors may find it difficult to even think about "supervising" an assistant or a teacher whom they think of as a colleague or friend. In this intimate atmosphere, problems can be hard to deal with. It is also difficult for teacher-directors who have responsibility for a group of children to find ways to observe teachers who work in adjacent rooms. Even in small programs, however, staff members can benefit from opportunities for peer evaluation and from assistance in improving their teaching.

Since it is common for different teachers to work in the morning and in the afternoon, staff in nursery schools often have difficulty finding time when all can meet together. Supervisors may find it hard to convince owners or boards that it makes sense to pay teachers, or sometimes even the director, for time to attend staff and parent meetings, to set up classrooms before the school year officially begins, and to participate in staff development during the year. When funds must come out of an owner-director's own pocket, obtaining money for such "extra" time may be even more challenging.

In *parent co-ops*, training and coordination are major issues for supervisors. Not only are there likely to be many different individuals working with the children over the course of each week, even in a small school, but there also may be an almost entirely new group of parent-staff as well as board members each year, frequently with little or no training in early care and education. A clear understanding that staff development sessions are part of the parents' responsibilities helps to set a positive climate for such training.

Differences in philosophy about discipline and about curriculum and methods are bound to arise from time to time between parents and staff. As in Head Start programs, one of the supervisor's tasks is to work out processes for resolving such differences. Where parents are the owners and managers, it may be especially difficult to integrate parents' ideas about curriculum and other issues with the professional knowledge of the staff.

In a *lab school* setting, one of the most important supervisory issues is creating real learning situations and support for education students while at the same time ensuring that the children receive skilled care and teaching. Supervisors may find that their attention—and loyalty—is divided among children, students, and paid staff. Settings for the children of teen parents have the added issue of the need to nurture parenting skills while dealing with self-esteem and normal adolescent concerns.

Because lab schools are a part of a larger institution whose goals mainly focus on a different age group, sometimes support for funding and resources is difficult to obtain. Maintaining good communication and coordination with all those who teach and supervise students is more complicated when course instruction is the responsibility of a separate faculty, when a supervising teacher is not directly involved with the children, or when lab school staff do not have faculty status.

Ensuring adequate staff coverage can be another problem for lab school supervisors. Sometimes children may be overwhelmed by too many caregivers. At other times, class schedules of education students may conflict with periods when staff are needed the most, or students may want time off during exam weeks, even though student and faculty parents still need care for their children. Helping education students understand the importance of their presence to children's well-being, therefore, becomes a key task for the supervisor.

SCHOOL-BASED KINDERGARTENS AND PREKINDERGARTENS

Kindergartens

Although kindergartens may be part of nursery schools or day care programs, most are based in public, private, or parochial schools. Although half-day, 5-day-a-week schedules have been the norm for many years, full-day kindergartens are becoming more prevalent. Currently, nine states mandate full-day kindergarten programs, while forty-three states, the District of Columbia, Puerto Rico, and the Virgin Islands require that districts offer at least half-day kindergarten; however, many districts are exceeding the law and implementing full-day kindergarten programs. Fourteen states require age-eligible children to attend at least half-day kindergarten. Of those, only Louisiana and Virginia mandate that children attend for the full day (Education Commission of the States, 2006). Kindergarten has almost become a universal experience in the United States. In 2001, full-day kindergarten was more common than half-day kindergarten, with 60% of children between the ages of 4–6 attending full-day programs, while 40% attended half-day kindergarten (National Center for Education Statistics, 2004). Some kindergartens have extended-day programs, with a nonacademic focus for that portion of the day, or children of working parents may be transported to or from child care centers for before- and after-school care.

Teachers in public school kindergartens (and in some states, independent schools) must be state certified with bachelor's degrees and specific teacher training experiences. This training may or may not be at the early childhood level.

Many communities allow more children per class in kindergarten than they do in preschools. Often a paraprofessional is assigned when a class reaches a certain size. In contrast to many nursery schools, the same teacher usually teaches both morning and afternoon sessions of half-day programs. Many states have enacted legislation to reduce class size (pre-K to 12); however, some are finding the costs to be prohibitive and are having trouble finding qualified teachers (Education Commission of the States, 2004b). States using funds from the federal government's Class Size Reduction (CSR) program through Title II have been able to lower class size in kindergartens to 18 children, on average (U.S. Department of Education, 2004).

There is a great deal of variation in kindergarten goals and curriculum, even in public school systems. Some use a developmental, emerging-literacy model in which child-initiated experiences and play are considered major means of learning. Others are group-oriented and tightly scheduled, and focus on readiness activities, especially in reading, that begin early in the year. They may include using workbooks as a daily routine, and play is usually not seen as a major vehicle for learning.

Most kindergartens probably combine elements of both of these models, with some systems allowing greater flexibility than others. However, teachers are likely to feel considerable pressure to "get children ready for first grade," pushing them toward more academically oriented curricula and the teaching of specific skills, with expectations for achievement being set by the standards movement in the name of educational reform. Certainly, given the range of differences in experiences and skill and ability levels of kindergarteners, an appropriate curriculum is one that meets each child at his or her level.

Prekindergartens

There has been an upward trend in the numbers of children attending preschool in the United States. In 1965, only 5% of 3-year-olds and 17% of 4-year-olds attended some form of preschool. By 2002, this percentage had increased to 40% of 3-year-olds and 66% of 4-year-olds (Barnett, Hastedt, Robin, & Shulman, 2004). In order to meet the demand and need, early childhood programs at the prekindergarten level have become more common in public as well as nonpublic schools. Currently, more than half of states provide some form of prekindergarten with Texas, New Jersey, and New York leading the way in terms of funding (Education Commission of the States, 2002).

Programs range from "universal" prekindergarten to those for children at risk, migrant children, and bilingual children. Some states appropriate funds to supplement existing Head Start programs. Public funds, however, are subject to budgetary shortfalls. In 2002–2003, funding failed to keep pace with the increase in enrollments. Some states such as Louisiana, North Carolina, and Kansas did make gains in terms of access during this time period (Barnett et al., 2004). Although progress is being made, there continues to be a lack of high-quality, readily available, state-funded prekindergarten programs in the United States, with current prekindergarten initiatives reaching only 10% of our nation's 3- and 4-year-olds (Barnett et al., 2004), despite the positive effects of such programs.

In a study of high-quality prekindergarten programs in five states sponsored by the National Institute for Early Education Research, it was found that children attending state-funded pre-K programs made significant progress in mathematics and literacy, regardless of ethnic background or economic level. They showed gains in vocabulary, math skills, and print awareness that were respectively 31%, 44%, and 85% greater than children without prekindergarten (Barnett, Lamy, & Jung, 2005).

The Foundation for Child Development (2003) has been engaged in a multiyear effort to promote universal full-day, full-year, voluntary prekindergarten for all 3- and 4-year-old children. *Mapping the P–3 Continuum (MAP)* is part of its initiative to connect prekindergarten, kindergarten, and the first three grades of school in a coherent, seamless alignment of public education in the United States, which would offer planned, sequential learning experiences for children. The goal would be to level the playing field so that all children would have equal opportunity to succeed in school. Currently, 17 states have a standards framework that links kindergarten with the primary grades or beyond (Education Commission of the States, 2005).

The notion of publicly funded and publicly or privately delivered prekindergarten for all children raises a host of critical issues including the cost of such programs, the desired characteristics (curriculum, staff-child ratios, provider qualifications) that would produce the most beneficial outcomes for children, and the impact that universal prekindergarten would have on existing early childhood education services and child care systems for children (Ruden & McCabe, 2004). These and other questions are being addressed by researchers, child advocates, and policy makers.

Implications for Supervision

Teachers and aides in kindergartens in public schools always come under the jurisdiction of their school principal. Preschool staff members, on the other hand, may be supervised by a principal or by a systemwide early childhood supervisor, an in-house director, or, in the case of Head Start, by the director or educational coordinator of an area-wide Head Start program.

When elementary school principals do not have training or experience in teaching young children, they may be uncomfortable about supervising teachers at these levels. Some may have unrealistic scheduling or curricular requirements for pre-K and kindergarten, especially centering on the early formal teaching of reading and math, or they may not understand such things as the appropriateness of play in young children's education.

Principals are, however, becoming more knowledgeable about the needs of children and teachers at the early childhood level. The burgeoning preschools in public systems, the development of "early childhood centers" housing preschools through grades 2 or 3, and the greater number of states with special early childhood teacher certification have contributed to this trend.

The Web site of the National Association of Elementary School Principals offers excellent online resources in the form of recent publications about kindergarten and prekindergarten issues relevant to the public schools. Principals have wonderful opportunities for professional development through NAESP's offerings on developing quality early childhood programs, some in collaboration with NAEYC.

Principals can also take advantage of the widespread availability of such sources as *Developmentally Appropriate Practice in Early Childhood Programs* (Bredekamp & Copple, 1997); *Basics of Developmentally Appropriate Practice: An Introduction to Teachers of Children 3 to 6* (Copple & Bredekamp, 2005); *A School Administrator's Guide to Early Childhood Programs* (Schweinhart, 2004); *K Today: Teaching and Learning in the Kindergarten Year* (Gullo, in press); and *Leading Early Childhood Learning Communities: What Principals Should Know and Be Able To Do* (NAESP, 2005).

Systemwide early childhood supervisors or preschool directors usually have an early childhood background and have a good understanding of the developmental needs of children at these ages. With this knowledge they can directly develop and support teachers' efforts to lay conceptual foundations before moving on to specific skills, and to focus on child-initiated learning. These supervisors are also in a position to establish or support the continuation of the strong parent-teacher relationships that may have begun at the preschool level. On the other hand, they may need to spend a lot of time and energy interpreting and advocating such goals to other administrators, teachers at other grade levels, school boards, and parents. In terms of developing quality programs for young children, then, it would certainly be very desirable to have supervisors who are not only well grounded in early childhood education and child development but who are also skilled in communicating with other school personnel at all levels.

To help those who do not have this background understand the issues, the texts mentioned above can be especially helpful. Two other sources that can help in understanding early childhood principles from different perspectives are *The Creative Curriculum for Preschool* (Dodge, Colker, & Heroman, 2002; also available in Spanish and for family child care) and *Educating Young Children: Active Learning Practices for Preschool and Child Care Programs* (Hohmann & Weikart, 2002).

CONCLUSION

The programs we have described in this chapter are the broad categories that supervisors of early childhood staff are most likely to encounter. Program differences affect the way supervisors function because they form the context within which supervision takes place. Nevertheless, when it comes to the needs of children and staff members, the similarities are greater than the differences, for it is the individuals who are being supervised and the appropriate practices within each context that are the goals.

PROGRAM ACCREDITATION

NAEYC program accreditation is a voluntary procedure through which child care, preschools, and kindergarten programs can become accredited in accordance with the criteria for high-quality programs developed and recently revised by NAEYC (2005). At the end of many of the chapters that follow you will find accreditation standards and/or specific criteria for programs serving children from birth through kindergarten that apply to the issues that have been discussed in the chapter. Due to space and copyright limitations, we cannot include all relevant criteria in this text. We encourage you, as a supervisor, to consider these criteria in the development and ongoing assessment of your own program and to become accredited through this system or that of the National Association for Family Child Care or the National Institute on Out-of-School Time (formerly School Age Child Care Project). See Appendix for contact information.

The Ten NAEYC Early Childhood Program Standards

In *NAEYC Early Childhood Program Standards and Accreditation Criteria: The Mark of Quality in Early Childhood Education* (NAEYC, 2005), the following early childhood program standards are named (they appear here without the rationale provided for each by NAEYC):

Standard 1: Relationships. The program promotes positive relationships among all children and adults to encourage each child's sense of individual worth and belonging as part of a community and to foster each child's ability to contribute as a responsible community member.

Standard 2: Curriculum. The program implements a curriculum that is consistent with its goals for children and promotes learning and development in each of the following areas: social, emotional, physical, language, and cognitive.

Standard 3: Teaching. The program uses developmentally, culturally, and linguistically appropriate and effective teaching approaches that enhance each child's learning and development in the context of the program's curriculum goals.

Standard 4: Assessment of Child Progress. The program is informed by ongoing systematic, formal, and informal assessment approaches to provide information on children's learning and development. These assessments occur within the context of reciprocal communications with families and with sensitivity to the cultural contexts in which children develop. Assessment results are used to benefit children by informing sound decisions about children, teaching, and program improvement.

Standard 5: Health. The program promotes the nutrition and health of children and protects children and staff from illness and injury.

Standard 6: Teachers. The program employs and supports a teaching staff that has the educational qualifications, knowledge, and professional commitment necessary to promote children's learning and development and to support families' diverse needs and interests.

Standard 7: Families. The program establishes and maintains collaborative relationships with each child's family to foster children's development in all settings. These relationships are sensitive to family composition, language, and culture.

Standard 8: Community Relationships. The program establishes the relationships with, and uses the resources of, the children's communities to support the achievement of program goals.

Standard 9: Physical Environment. The program has a safe and healthful environment that provides appropriate and well-maintained indoor and outdoor physical environments. The environment includes facilities, equipment, and materials to facilitate child and staff learning and development.

Standard 10: Leadership and Management. The program effectively implements policies, procedures, and systems that support stable staff and strong personnel, fiscal, and program management so all children, families, and staff have high-quality experiences. (pp. 9–12)

EXERCISES

1. Using the specific program in which you work, or one in which you are interested, describe characteristics that affect supervision of the staff. Include all the factors that (1) give clues to the kinds of areas where staff are most likely to need help and (2) might have a positive effect on or make more difficult your ability to carry out effective supervision and staff development. Inter-

view the director and other supervisory staff to obtain as broad a view of these issues as possible.

2. Compare and contrast your perceptions with those of a group of teachers or supervisors from other—similar or different—programs. Discuss ways that problem areas might be alleviated.

CHAPTER 3

SUPERVISORS AND STAFF: ROLES AND RESPONSIBILITIES

T HE ROLES AND DUTIES of persons in supervisory positions and of those whom they supervise are as varied as the early childhood programs described in the previous chapter. Our purpose in this chapter is to describe the most common positions supervisors occupy, the responsibilities associated with these positions, and the roles and duties of the people they supervise.

SUPERVISORS

Practitioners with supervisory responsibilities range from executive directors in central administrative offices of large agencies to those whose main responsibility is to teach children but who also supervise other teachers, aides, and volunteers.

Representative Job Titles and Descriptions

Some of the most common positions involving supervision are executive director, program director, educational coordinator, head teacher, teacher, college supervisor, and consultant. These jobs, however, have many titles. Individuals in them often have more than one major role to perform. Rarely is supervision the sole component of their work. Positions that carry multiple roles and responsibilities, such as owner-manager, director-teacher, or supervisor-bookkeeper, create consequences not always foreseen. Supervisors may experience role ambiguity, conflicting expectations from staff members, and overload, stress, and disenchantment with their jobs as they discover that they do not have the time or the resources for all their roles.

Executive Director

The executive director is usually the chief administrator of a large child care agency and reports directly to a board of directors. Although the organizational charts of such agencies vary, the executive director may supervise an assistant, the coordinators of several social service programs within the agency, program directors at various sites, and all other employees through a central chain of command. Supervision is usually one aspect of an executive director's responsibilities, along with administrative and fiscal duties. The executive director is likely to supervise upper-level staff directly but may have little personal contact with the staff who are responsible for children in the agency's various centers.

Program Director

Program directors are administrators who are responsible for running a program. In large child care agencies, they work within the larger organization but do not administer the organization as a whole. Most Head Start directors and public school principals are in this category since a program or a school is one of several in the organization. In small, private, or nonprofit independent child care centers or nursery schools, directors manage programs that are somewhat more autonomous. Some program directors administer more than one center.

The responsibilities of program directors usually include administration, supervision, board relationships, and community relationships, and, for many, teaching as well. Among their duties are maintaining compliance with applicable laws, recruiting staff and children, budgeting and fund raising, supervising and evaluating staff, conducting annual program evaluations, working with parents and outside agencies and institutions, planning curriculum, reporting to and working with a board, overseeing the maintenance of the facility and of equipment, and planning meals with the cook.

Because program directors are on-site and work directly with classroom and nonclassroom staff, supervision is a larger part of the job than it is for executive directors. Program administration or teaching can take up much of their time, however, and can overshadow supervisory duties.

Directors come in regular contact with a host of people, each of whom has a set of expectations about what the director should do and how he or she should do it. These include the director's supervisor, employees, and others with whom the director works closely. Together these people make up what sociologists (Katz & Kahn, 1966) call a *role set* (see Figure 3.1).

Members of a role set communicate their expectations to the director, who responds in certain ways based on his or her understandings and perceptions of the messages received. For example, representatives of community service agencies may believe that the program director should be more active in dealing with families with serious problems. Or the executive director may think that the

Figure 3.1. Role Set of a Program Director

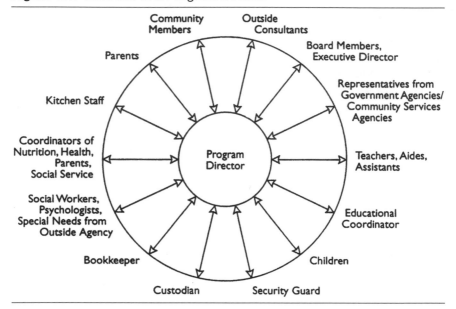

director should do a better job of linking with coordinators and other program directors and of completing paperwork on time. Teachers may feel that the director should give them more help in working with hard-to-manage children. And the cook may be unhappy because the director is too involved in weekly menu planning.

Thus members of the director's role set "push" and "pull" the director, competing for time and attention and creating multiple demands. This pressure may be more intense when the administrator fills more than one official role, a common occurrence. Program directors with clear priorities, goals, and philosophy of education will be better able to formulate realistic expectations for the job and for supervision.

As Figure 3.1 indicates, the program director is also a member of the role set of teachers, children, kitchen staff, and others, and has a responsibility to them. In reality, however, teachers may relate more often and sometimes more immediately to social service or other staff than to the director.

Educational Coordinator

The educational coordinator's role is narrower and more focused than the program director's. The coordinator's responsibility is to oversee the educational component of an agency or program to ensure that classrooms and staff are functioning according to the program's guidelines for the greatest benefit to children. The educational coordinator works in the areas of staff development, training, and curriculum, with time allotted for these purposes.

Supervision forms a large part of educational coordinators' work. In smaller programs, educational coordinators supervise staff who work directly with children and are also supervised by the program director. In large day care or Head Start agencies, educational coordinators provide emotional and technical support to program directors, as well as to classroom staff, often traveling to various program sites. The coordinator's duties may include observing teachers and children; planning and conducting staff training; conferring with staff; developing curriculum; serving as a liaison with health, nutrition, special-needs, and social service coordinators; modeling good teaching behavior; ordering classroom supplies and equipment; working with psychologists; and providing directors with guidance and support.

Coordinators, too, have a role set (see Figure 3.2). Those working in multiple settings are particularly susceptible to situations involving interpersonal conflicts. With their time divided between central office and various sites, they may not have the opportunity to build relationships to the extent they would like or to engage with staff in the process of clarifying and defining each other's roles and responsibilities.

Figure 3.2. Role Set of an Educational Coordinator

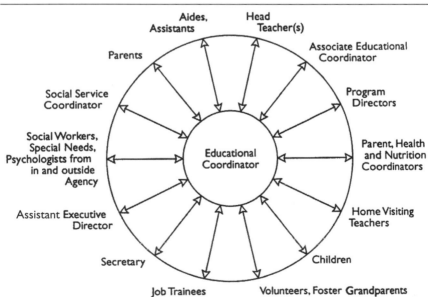

Educational coordinators are usually free from a daily routine and have some flexibility in organizing their day's work. The job of coordinator can be a lonely one, however, as there is usually no one else in the organization with the same role to share common problems and successes.

Head Teacher

Unlike program directors and educational coordinators, who work mostly with adults, head teachers have primary responsibility for working with children. Usually because of experience, education, training, and/or demonstrated expertise, classroom teachers become head or lead teachers. Head teachers usually oversee the functioning of several classrooms and, in some cases, even small centers. They supervise other teachers, and are supervised by the educational coordinator or program director (see Figure 3.3). As head teachers attempt to meet the dual responsibilities of teaching and supervising, they are likely to experience a certain degree of role conflict.

Among the specific duties of a head teacher are arriving before class to prepare and arrange materials for the day's activities, keeping daily attendance and observation records of children, assisting in planning parent programs, attending evaluation meetings with social service agency representatives, arranging yearly

Figure 3.3. Role Set of a Head Teacher

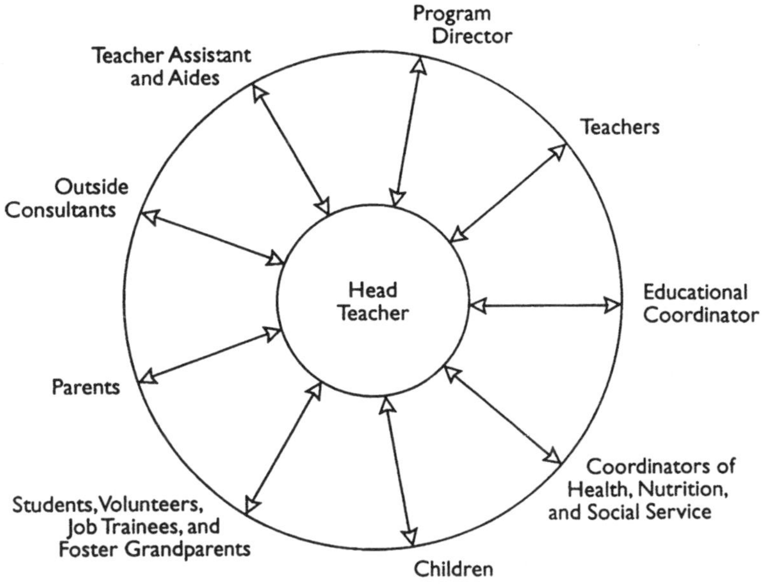

conferences with each parent, making special referrals, supervising other team members, teaching children, and planning and leading team meetings.

Teacher

Unlike public school teachers, who rarely supervise other adults in the classroom, preschool teachers often supervise an assistant, paid or volunteer, in addition to educating and caring for young children. Teachers are usually supervised by a head teacher, coordinator, and/or program director.

College Supervisor

The college supervisor is a faculty member of a college or university who is responsible for training and supervising those individuals aspiring to work in early childhood programs. Sometimes they supervise experienced caregivers who are working in a special program or for an advanced degree. More often, they supervise undergraduates who plan to work with young children.

Child Development Associate (CDA) Advisor

The CDA advisor may be part of a Child Development Associate training program or may work on a freelance basis with classroom staff who are preparing to be assessed for the CDA credential. A CDA advisor is often associated with a college, university, or resource and referral or training agency but may be a staff member from their own or another preschool. (See Chapter 15 for a description of CDA.)

Consultant

Consultants from training agencies, resource and referral programs, and cooperating colleges and universities, or who advise independently, sometimes work on-site with a program as a whole or with individual teachers. They may work with staff members through one-to-one or group supervision. This is a typical form of supervision for family child care.

Training and Experience

Many supervisors come into their roles directly from the classroom ranks. Some, particularly those in Head Start or other community-based programs, may have begun work as aides. After receiving on-the-job training, a high school equivalency degree, a Child Development Associate credential, or even an associate's or bachelor's degree while working in a program, they are good candidates for supervisory positions because of their understanding of the needs of children and families and their experiences in early childhood education.

Others, initially hired as teachers or even aides, move into coordinator's or director's roles because of their exceptional skills in working with children or sometimes because they are the only staff members with a degree in early childhood education or specific training in supervision. There are also early childhood supervisors with backgrounds in elementary or special education, or such related fields as counseling, nursing, social services, and recreation; still others have job experience in completely unrelated occupations.

Relatively few supervisors have had formal preparation specifically in supervision; of those who have, the great majority have had minimal amounts in the form of workshops and college-level course work. In the mid-1990s, 69% of center directors held a bachelor's or graduate degree, 27% had some college education, and 4% had high school education or less (Helburn, 1995). Although there has been progress in the last decade, as of August 2004, only 16 states require some administration-related training for licensure for center directors; the amount of this training varies from 3 clock hours to a 3 semester-hour course, usually in management, administration, or supervision (NCCIC, 2004). Only 9 states require some form of ongoing training in management, administration, or supervision in order to maintain a license (NCCIC, 2004). The current accreditation regulations of the National Association for the Education of Young Children require that program administrators hold a baccalaureate degree, with a minimum of 9 credit hours in management, leadership, or administration (NAEYC, 1995). Thus for many, their work with children and the model provided them by their own supervisors continue to be the most helpful experiences in preparing them for their jobs.

The Worthy Work, Unlivable Wages: National Child Care Staffing Study, 1988–1997, reported that the average length of tenure for directors in a program was 6.5 years in 1988 and 10.13 years in 1997 (Whitebook, Howes, & Phillips, 1998). In a large-scale, longitudinal study of child care centers, which examined three California communities at three points in time (1994, 1996, 2000), Whitebook and her colleagues (2001) found very high director turnover, even though a great many of the centers were accreditated or rated high on the Early Childhood Environmental Rating Scale (ECERS; Harms, Clifford, & Cryer, 2005). They report that 40% of participating centers in 1996 had a new director in 2000; centers that lost directors had higher rates of teacher turnover. Many of the directors who remained in their roles did so because of the gratification they received from their work, while many who left had experienced burnout, in part because of the stress created by staff turnover and the shortage of trained staff. The average tenure in centers of those directors who were studied in 2000 was 8 years; 30% had previous experience as director. The majority (77%) had bachelor's degrees, and 24% were pursuing a higher degree than they currently held. The latest available data on annual director turnover rate, collected in 2001 and 2002 in selected states, show a range from a low of 7% in Illinois to a high of 35% in Nevada (Center for the Childcare Workforce, 2004).

The Director Credential

Director credentialing refers to the awarding of a certificate, permit, or other type of document that certifies that an individual has acquired the knowledge, skills, and competencies to assume the role of director in any early childhood or school-age setting (Morgan, 2000). There are currently national, state, and private groups that offer director or administrator credentials. However, there is a wide range of differences in the number of hours or credits that these groups require as well as in their relationships with higher education, state licensing, and state early childhood career development initiatives.

The National Administrator Credential (NAC) sponsored by the National Child Care Association (www.ncca.org), for example, is a 5-day comprehensive course that focuses on a range of competencies from facility management to program marketing, to staff development and evaluation. The Professional Administrators National Credential offered by Professional Administrators for Worldwide Credentialing (PAC) provides a correspondence course based on clock hours, a weeklong or weekend training course, or training through colleges and universities covering a wide range of topics. PAC strives to establish ongoing relationships with licensing departments. Some states such as North Carolina, Mississippi, and Florida offer their own state director or administrator credential, while others such as Utah accept credentials from other agencies or organizations (National Child Care Information Center, 2004). And some national organizations such as Camp Fire, USA, offer an administrator credential, as do affiliates of national professional associations such as the New York Association for the Education for Young Children. It is interesting to note that the New York credential requires that the candidate submit a portfolio, with narratives and projects to document fulfillment of competency areas, in addition to coursework and a practicum or experience.

The differences in state licensing requirements for those in supervisory roles; the multiplicity of supervisory roles; the variability of background, experience, education, and training among supervisors; and the necessity of fulfilling duties outside of supervision are in a very real sense indicators of the evolving nature of early care and education. As early childhood professionals upgrade their skills and strive to make the field more professional, job qualifications, competencies, titles, and responsibilities are likely to become more uniform. With less ambiguity, some of the sources of stress may be removed, enabling supervisors to attain greater satisfaction from the job.

STAFF

Early childhood supervisors work with staff employed in a variety of jobs. These include providers of direct care, education, or services to children in classrooms, as well as nonclassroom staff who help the program run smoothly and/or support children by working with families or outside agencies. Program settings, the age levels of the children served, and the range of services provided influence the names used to identify early childhood staff.

Historically, practitioners have made a distinction between teacher and caregiver and between those in professional and auxiliary roles. Nursery schools have been viewed as serving mainly an educational function, while day care has been seen as having a caregiving or nurturing function. Thus practitioners in nursery schools have been thought of as teachers and those in day care centers as caregivers. Supervisors and teachers were considered professionals. Teacher aides, volunteers, and assistants have been viewed as auxiliaries (Spodek & Saracho, 1982). Today, as more is understood about the developmental, educational, and care needs of young children, many have come to refer to the early childhood field as "early care and education" and the terms *teacher* and *caregiver* have become more or less interchangeable.

Representative Job Titles and Descriptions

Classroom staff have a major responsibility for working with children and often have secondary obligations in other areas. Whitebook and her colleagues (1989) found that head teacher–directors, teachers, and aides all have the same range of duties, although head teacher–directors spent more time on parent communication and clerical and administrative work. All did curriculum planning and implementation, meal preparation, and maintenance.

Classroom Teachers

Responsibilities of all teachers usually include planning and carrying out the program for children indoors and outdoors, arranging classroom space for group and play activities, observing and recording children's growth in various skill areas, and preparing for snack and lunch. Those working with infants and toddlers spend a larger amount of their time feeding, changing, playing with, and observing children. Part of a caregiver's day also includes communicating with parents about the psychological well-being of their children, not only at the center but often in home visits. Sharing information and ideas with speech or physical therapists, nurses, social workers, and others is also a typical part of the regular routine when these specialists are available.

Although teachers may be supervised by a head teacher, director, or coordinator, as we noted earlier, they have supervisory responsibilities themselves. They usually have at least one aide or assistant, and many programs have parent and other volunteers, student teachers, foster grandparents, and job trainees. Classroom staff also informally supervise peers who are new to a program, providing emotional support and suggestions. Although the latter form of supervision often happens spontaneously, supervisors can support and train caregivers to work with other classroom staff who have little or no training.

Classroom Aides and Assistants

The job of aide or assistant in a classroom is also important but can be misused. The terms *aide* and *assistant* usually describe the same job, though there are sometimes both positions in a program. In general, the position of aide is an entry-level job, currently with few qualifications other than sensitivity to children and willingness to learn. In some programs, especially those for low-income families, aides may not be required to have a high school diploma, often beginning work as volunteers and later advancing to paid positions.

Aides assist and are supervised by the classroom teacher in carrying out such duties as teaching, performing clerical or housekeeping chores, preparing for snack time, and ensuring that the environment is sanitary and healthful. They are usually expected to attend staff meetings, training sessions, meetings with other professionals, and meetings with parents. Aides also provide general supportive help in family child care homes, allowing caregivers time for other duties.

Nonclassroom Staff

Sometimes taken for granted, nonclassroom staff are central to a program's efficiency and success. Nonclassroom staff come into contact with children and support and serve them and the program in peripheral yet important ways, but their responsibilities do not encompass the direct and ongoing care and education of children.

While some nonclassroom staff assist with the daily operation of a center, others support staff, families, and children. Cleaners, painters, and landscapers perform maintenance functions. Secretaries, bookkeepers, file clerks, purchasers, and office assistants are primarily involved with paperwork and administrative tasks. Cooks, custodians, and bus drivers may have more opportunities to interact with children, while community developers and outreach workers may get to know families. Some individuals, such as health coordinators, have supervisory functions with adults. Professionals who work on behalf of children and families on a consultant basis—for example, social workers, speech therapists, and psychologists—might also be considered part of the nonclassroom staff of a center, as well as individuals who are affiliated with centers but who spend most of their time working with children and families in their homes. As with supervisors and classroom staff, nonclassroom staff may be expected to carry out more than one role.

Nonclassroom staff members can be indispensable to supervisors and caregivers. They may orient a new director or teacher to a program, "be there" for a director to lean on when there is no one else with whom to discuss pressing problems, or fill in during an emergency. Nonclassroom staff should be considered integral members of the program "family."

Training and Experience

There have been a number of major studies of center-based early childhood programs during the past 15 years that have pointed to the importance of the relationship of training and education of staff members to better outcomes for young children. These studies include the National Day Care Study (Ruopp, Travers, Glantz, & Coelen, 1979), the National Child Care Staffing Study (Whitebook et al., 1989), The Children of the Cost, Quality and Outcomes Study Go to School (Peisner-Feinberg et al., 1999), and the Head Start FACES 2000 (Zill et al., 2003). When looked at as a group, these large-scale investigations strongly suggest that the presence of staff with bachelor's-level education with specialized training in early childhood education leads to higher quality preschool programs (Whitebook, 2003).

Although the National Day Care Study did not address the specific level of training and education associated with better quality and care, it did conclude that superior developmental effects for children were delivered by caregivers with education or training relevant to young children (Ruopp et al., 1979). Its other important finding was that smaller group size was consistently associated with better care and more socially active children. In the late 1980s the National Child Care Staffing Study examined services and personnel of 227 centers in five metropolitan areas in the United States and contrasted them with those of a decade earlier (Whitebook et al., 1989). The authors concluded that more sensitive and appropriate caregiving was provided by teaching staff if they completed more years of formal education and received early childhood training at the college level. Teachers with at least a bachelor's degree in early childhood education were more sensitive, less harsh and detached, and engaged in more appropriate caregiving than those with training at the vocational education level or less. Higher wages and better benefits were also associated with quality care.

Beginning in 1993, researchers in four states—California, Colorado, Connecticut, and North Carolina—worked together to examine the relationship between cost, quality, and child outcomes in child care centers (Cost, Quality, and Child Outcomes Study Team, 1995). They found that higher quality in preschool classrooms was associated with the lead teacher having a bachelor's degree or at least some college; quality was also linked to teachers earning higher wages and having a moderate amount of experience. The Children of the Cost, Quality and Outcomes Study Go to School is a study in which children from the original project were followed through to the end of second grade (Peisner-Feinberg et al., 1999). This was 4 years after initial contact was made with them, which was when they were in their next to last year of child care. The findings indicate that children who attended child care with higher quality classroom experiences scored better in math ability and language skills than children in low-quality care, and children with closer relationships with their preschool teachers had better classroom skills (e.g., attention, sociability) through second grade than children who had less close relationships. The study indicated that child care quality was related to specialized training of classroom teachers in early childhood education as well as formal education levels.

In the 2000 national sample of the longitudinal Head Start FACES 2000 study, researchers found that teachers in classrooms rated higher in quality tended to have more experience and higher levels of education, higher levels of knowledge of early childhood education practice, and more positive attitudes and knowledge about early childhood education practices (Zill et al., 2003).

These and other studies have fueled a trend toward raising requirements necessary for teachers to qualify for work in early childhood programs. NAEYC (2005), for example, has established the year 2010 for accredited programs' compliance with its teacher-qualification standards, which require that all teachers have a minimum of an associate's degree, and that at least 75% of teachers have a minimum of a baccalaureate degree or equivalent (for the timeline for compliance, see Table 6, NAEYC, 2005). The degree must include coursework in early childhood education, child development, or early childhood special education. (Note: Requirements vary according to the number of classes and number of teachers.) Teacher aides/assistants must have a high school diploma or GED, and 50% must have a CDA credential or equivalent.

Certification and Licensing

States set teacher qualification standards through licensing and certification requirements. The licensing process regulates teachers in nonpublic programs, while teacher certification is a process by which states certify individuals who work in public schools. As of August 2004 (NCCIC), 14 states have established some minimal entry-level education requirements for the licensure of child care teachers. These range from vocational child care training in secondary schools to the possession of a Child Development Associate Credential, to a specified number of clock hours of training. Forty-eight states require a specified number of clock hours of ongoing training (anywhere from 3–30) once an individual has been hired, in order to maintain a license. Seventeen states require that at least one teacher in a program be qualified at a higher level, often referred to as a head or master teacher. This position usually carries some staff supervision responsibility. Thirteen states have established minimal education requirements for teachers at this level, which range from a CDA credential in Alaska to a master's degree in early childhood education or related field plus 2 years of experience in Vermont. State education requirements for preschool teachers in publicly funded programs are much higher than those for child care teachers in nonpublic programs.

In 2002–03, more than two thirds of state preschool initiatives required teachers working in public school early childhood programs to have at least a baccalaureate degree, while less than half of state preschool initiatives had a similar requirement for teachers in nonpublic programs (Barnett et al., 2004). In a study of staffing and stability in preschool programs in five states, Bellm and his colleagues (2002) found that teaching staff in publicly funded programs had attained higher levels of education, and also received higher pay and more benefits, than those in private settings. In the five states they studied, teaching staff with bachelor's degrees ranged from a low of 76% in Georgia to a high of 100% in New York. In a large national survey of teachers of 3- and 4-year-olds working in for-profit and not-for-profit center-based programs, Saluja, Early, and Clifford (2002) found that 91% of teachers had some education beyond high school, with at least 50% of this group holding a bachelor's degree. Those in public schools were more educated than those in other settings, especially in for-profit programs.

Data from the National Prekindergarten Study, the first large-scale sample of publicly funded prekindergarten programs across all states, show that more than half of prekindergarten teachers (57%) hold a state department of education certificate for teaching preschoolers (Gilliam & Marchesseault, 2005). The highest education levels of prekindergarten teachers varied considerably, with 13% holding a high school diploma or GED, 14% an associate's degree, 49% a bachelor's degree, and 24% a master's degree or higher. Twenty-two percent held a CDA, usually working in Head Start programs. On average, teachers reported having 8.2 years of experience teaching preschoolers. Retirement (89%) and health benefits (80%) were offered to most of them. A majority of assistant teachers (59%) in this national sample held a high school diploma or GED, 17% had a CDA, and 24% had at least an associate's degree.

The difference in salary, benefits, and necessary teaching qualifications creates a two-tiered system between public and nonpublic early childhood programs and also affects the potential diversity of teaching staff through access to employment. Licensing rules tend to favor experience over coursework, making employment more accessible, while certification tends to value academic preservice preparation at the expense of early access to the profession. Neither licensing policies nor teacher certification requirements facilitate career mobility for early childhood practitioners.

Wages and Benefits

Requirements for the certification and licensure of early childhood staff and the stability of staff within programs are closely linked to the wages and benefits they receive. To what extent can the field raise minimum education standards, given the low wages paid to child care workers? The average hourly wage of a child care worker in 2003 was $8.37, similar to that of a parking lot attendant, while the $10.67 per hour paid to preschool teachers was only a few cents more than the average hourly wage of taxi drivers (Center for the Child Care Workforce, 2004). Neugebauer's (2004) Internet survey found that the typical lead teacher in North America has an average salary of $23,000 per year; with teacher aides earning on average less than $17,000 per year. Directors of single early childhood centers made $35,000 annually.

In their longitudinal study of three California communities mentioned earlier, Whitebook and her colleagues (2001) found turnover of teaching staff to be extensive even though staff were working in relatively high-quality programs. They found that three quarters (76%) of teaching staff who were working in centers in 1996 and 82% who were employed in the programs in 1994 were no longer on the job in 2000. A finding of particular interest to supervisors is that high turnover among colleagues negatively influenced staff members' job performance and contributed to the decision by some to leave their programs. The great majority of teaching staff, 88%, indicated that higher wages would reduce turnover.

Turnover was lower in a more recent study of child care workers in Alameda County, California (Whitebook et al., 2003); however, the authors point out that the turnover rate is still nearly three times that of K–6 teachers. Also, a little more than half of centers in their sample reported making a retirement or pension contribution for some of their employees.

Staff instability, then, due in large part to low wages and benefits and lack of respect from the public for the work that they do, creates a climate of low morale and stress and more turnover among teachers and directors, which in turn reduces the quality of the services that children and families receive. The solution to this staffing crisis lies beyond individual programs. It does point to the importance of the advocacy role of early childhood administrators and supervisors. Clearly, there is a need for teachers and directors to join with others in professional associations as well as in statewide political organizations to develop some creative solutions to change the job conditions that undermine their work. (We will continue this discussion of turnover in Chapter 12.)

Since more training and education does improve quality, a commitment by directors to professional development for all staff is essential. A range of professional development options for staff based on their individual needs and their levels of experience and training is critical to maintaining a climate and culture of professionalism and growth in a program (see Chapter 15). The notion of a career lattice or ladder, which represents steps of increased responsibility, based on increased qualifications and preparation that results in higher compensation, is one that can serve as a framework for staff recruitment, selection, development, and evaluation. (We will discuss this concept more fully in Chapter 13 of this text.) Of course, since staff members are likely to be more satisfied with their jobs if they are employed in quality programs, undertaking the process of program accreditation offered by NAEYC is a way to achieve staff collaboration and raise standards within programs.

CONCLUSION

Supervisors and administrators in early childhood programs often have more than one significant role associated with their jobs. Their preparation for supervision varies greatly as do the competency levels, ages, and stages of professional development of the staff members they supervise.

Because of the many demands for supervisor time, attention, and energy and because of possible insecurity about supervising, sometimes supervision may not take place at all unless it becomes a conscious goal with time set aside to confer with and observe staff on a regular basis. This is a point we would like to underscore.

Individuals who prefer certainty, predictable routines, and clarity of expectations may find the fluidity and complexity of early childhood settings overwhelming, in comparison with those persons who are more adaptable and enjoy challenges. Knowledge of early childhood development as well as an understanding of how adults grow and develop can make supervision more satisfying.

Finally, those who can analyze themselves in relation to their settings and who are realistic about what can be accomplished are likely to be more successful as early childhood supervisors.

EXERCISES

1. Write a job description for your present supervisory position.
2. Who are the members of your role set? What expectations do they have of you?
3. If you haven't already done so, join a local, state, or regional early childhood professional association or contact NAEYC and learn how to become a local volunteer assessor for program accreditation.
4. Review NAEYC's accreditation requirements for the educational qualifications of teaching staff and compare them to the qualifications held by staff members in your program. Use this initial assessment as a starting point for creating a long-range career ladder plan for your program (see Chapter 13, Exercises, Table 13.1).

PART II

A DEVELOPMENTAL PERSPECTIVE

CARING, KNOWING, AND IMAGINING

C ARING, KNOWING, AND IMAGINING are key and interrelated concepts associated with the notion of supervision as development. In this chapter, we explore supervisory issues related to these ideas as well as the roles of supervisors as caregivers, as helpers of others to become knowers, and as those who nurture imagination.

CARING

The word *care* is embedded in the names that we give to those who work with young children—*care*givers and child *care* providers—and to those places that house programs for young children—child *care* centers. If we consider various dictionary definitions of *care*, caregivers may be thought of as individuals who are in charge of the welfare of children, and child care centers as places where children are attended to, protected, and entrusted in care.

Noddings (2002) has proposed that the educational mission of schools be focused on matters of human caring, that we must teach our children how to receive and give care. Thinking of early childhood programs as "centers of care" might enable us to imagine them in different ways and broaden our conceptions of caring. Centers of care place an emphasis on caring not only for children, but also for adults who work with children, for other adults who enable centers to function, and for families who are associated with them. In addition to caring for people, educators in such centers also care for ideas, particularly about pedagogy and ways to support and nurture the growth of young children and their families and about principles and ideals, especially principles of social justice and policies that can put those principles into law and action.

But this is a book about supervision. What does supervision have to do with caring? Are those in supervisory positions caregivers? Can those who bear so much responsibility afford the risk of caring?

We believe that supervision is a caring process. Supervisors as caregivers strive to develop in their programs a culture of caring, a place where staff members and children grow in their capacity to care. Supervisors are also advocates for policies based on attitudes of caring.

A starting point for our discussion of supervision as caring behavior can be found in the following definition of *caring*:

> To care for another person, in the most significant sense, is to help him grow and actualize himself. . . . Caring, as helping another grow and actualize himself, is a process, a way of relating to someone that involves development. (Mayeroff, 1971, p. 1)

Mayeroff (1971) describes eight major ingredients of caring that have relevance for supervisors. The first of these is *knowing*. Caregivers, including supervisors, have to know themselves and those cared for, their needs, interests, and concerns, and they also have to know how to respond to them.

Second, caring involves the use of *alternating rhythms*. This concept involves reflecting on, learning from, and changing caring behavior. Caring may mean standing back sometimes and taking action at other times. The caregiver may address or ignore a specific incident or examine the larger context before modifying caring behavior. In many ways, using alternating rhythms is much like developmental supervision, in which the supervisor employs a range of strategies on a continuum, depending on the developmental characteristics of the supervisee, a concept we discuss in Chapter 5.

The third major ingredient of caring is *patience*, as giving time for the other to grow yet not waiting passively for something to happen. Caregivers must also be patient with themselves and give themselves a chance to care. Other ingredients of caring are *honesty* and *trust*—honesty in the sense of confronting and being open to oneself, and trust as encouraging the independence of another. A lack of trust is sometimes exhibited through dominance of the other or through overprotection. *Humility* is present in caring as we learn from the cared-for, as is *hope*, that is, excitement with a sense of the possible. Finally, as caregivers and the cared-for do not know where their journey will take them, they need *courage*.

Noddings (2002) believes that it is the relation between the cared-for and the one-caring that is essential, rather than personal attributes. She views a basic caring relation as an encounter in which there is genuine reciprocity; caring should not emphasize the actualization of one party over the other, nor should one be exploited for the sake of the other. The one-caring cares for the other. The other, the cared-for, recognizes and receives the caring and reacts in a way that shows it.

In Chapter 5, we emphasize the dynamic relationship between supervisor and supervisee because we want to underscore that staff members are not the object of supervision, but play an active role in the process, and that supervisors learn, change, and grow as a result of the process too. Caring as relation and reciprocity means that supervisors and staff members as caregivers and care-receivers are participants in and contributors to acts of caring.

Teachers, parents, and other caregivers lose energy when there is no response to their caring. Supervisors and administrators as caregivers of staff and children need a response too, for much of their work involves attending to others while seeing things as others see them.

Some staff members, engrossed in their own survival, may be less able to respond because they cannot "get out of themselves," but some response is necessary in order for caring to be complete. A teacher's response to a supervisor may take the form of showing natural excitement for an accomplishment, following through on a suggestion made by a supervisor, thinking out loud with a supervisor, revealing one's true thoughts and feelings with a supervisor, asking for advice, or simply letting one's supervisor know how things are progressing. In some cases, with supervisees who are at advanced stages of development, a response might take the form of a role reversal by attending to the needs of their supervisors.

In her discussion of moral education from the perspective of an ethic of care, Noddings (2002) describes four essential components that might be considered by supervisors who wish to create environments where caring can thrive. The first of these is *modeling*. Just as teachers need to model for children, supervisors have to show staff members how to care by fostering caring relations with them. As Noddings points out, the capacity to care may be dependent on having adequate experience in being cared for.

A second component is *dialogue*—dialogue in an open sense, without predetermined outcomes. Dialogue connects individuals to each other and develops in people the habit of acquiring information before making decisions. And as Freire (1972) states, only dialogue, "which requires critical thinking, is capable of generating critical thinking. Without dialogue, there is no communication, and without communication there can be no true education" (p. 81). Dialogue is really the heart of the supervisory process, yet sometimes honest dialogue is hard to achieve because of contextual issues, role definitions, or some of the personal background characteristics noted in Chapter 5 such as perceptions of authority figures and cultural values. The stage of development of supervisees and the skill levels of supervisors may also have an effect on the extent to which genuine dialogue is achieved. However, without dialogue there is no supervision. Caring between supervisors and staff will bring about more trust, which is the basis for honest and open dialogue.

Practice is a third component of moral education in which staff and children have experiences in acquiring skills in caregiving and in developing caring attitudes. A curriculum of caring makes space in the day for discussions about caring behaviors and provides opportunities for children to care for each other, for classroom plants and animals, for their environment, and their community neighbors.

Lastly, a person working toward a better self needs *confirmation*. This is an act of affirming and encouraging the best in others.

Supervisors, who spend a great deal of time encouraging staff, helping them to feel valued, and letting them know that their contributions are appreciated, also need to care for and nurture themselves. Caring can be exhausting. Sometimes supervisors care too much or feel guilty if caring seems to fail or if they don't want to care anymore. However, it is critical for supervisors to maintain their inner resources and to focus on their abilities in other areas, particularly outside the profession. Preserving oneself may take the form of participating in physical, intellectual, spiritual, and/or artistic pursuits that bring one into contact with new experiences and people outside the work setting and that permit one to be absorbed in creative or intellectual endeavors that actually can have the effect of restoring the energy that one needs for caring in the workplace each day.

KNOWING

A second objective in broadening our conceptions of early care and education programs is to facilitate knowing. Children and staff come to child care centers at different stages in perceiving themselves and in having confidence in themselves as knowers. It is not unusual for women with mothering skills, for example, to begin work as teacher aides and, with education and training, to move up the career ladder professionally. They blossom as individuals as they see themselves and gain confidence in themselves as knowers. Thus child care centers can be liberating learning environments for staff as well as for children.

In their classic book *Women's Ways of Knowing*, Belenky, Clinchy, Goldberger, and Tarule (1997) offer a framework of five categories of knowing that is a particularly helpful construct for supervisors and other facilitators as they think about their work in supporting the development of staff. The first category of knowing is *silence*. In their study, silent women viewed themselves as "deaf and dumb." They felt voiceless. As they were disconnected and isolated from others, they rarely had any dialogue with others. Growing up without experience in conversing and playing, they had difficulty understanding and using metaphors and symbol systems. They had little formal schooling and their experiences with schooling were negative; as a result, they had little confidence in their ability to learn. They tended to be passive, obedient, and subdued.

Silent women tended to blindly obey authority figures whom they saw as knowers. For some, a profound event, like the birth of a child and the responsibilities associated with mothering, forced them into the next category, *received knowledge*. Received knowers, who may also be educated, learn by listening to others. They are aware of the power of words, but keep their voices still in order to listen to others for direction and wisdom, for the "right answers." Unlike silent women, they see themselves as having the ability to absorb knowledge and even to reproduce it, but not as sources of knowledge.

Received knowers then may become *subjective knowers*, sometimes because of changes in their personal lives and/or crises of trust with authority figures. They become aware of their inner resources, perhaps out of protest, and take action on behalf of themselves such as moving out of their present circumstances or returning to school. As a small inner voice begins to emerge in them, they rely on intuition, feeling, and firsthand experiences as sources of knowledge.

The last two categories in women's perspectives on knowing are *procedural knowledge* and *constructed knowledge*. Procedural knowers are invested in learning. With their old ways of thinking challenged, procedural knowers move away from the personal and become more objective. They begin to learn in more formal and systematic ways. They carefully observe, learn to read between the lines, take another's perspective, and consider the opinions and expertise of others. They begin to become critical thinkers. Constructivists are passionate knowers who have found their voices. They carefully listen to and speak with others, and also listen to themselves. They believe that their own ways of knowing matter and that they can create knowledge. They pay attention to situation and context. Through empathy, they connect with what they are trying to understand. They wish to empower others and to integrate feeling and care into their work.

The comments below by a Head Start teacher we interviewed reflect some of the characteristics of procedural knowers as well as constructivists:

> I'm fairly open minded. I listen, see both sides. I like that I have my own set of beliefs that I have come to, that I can stand on. And if new information comes to me, I can turn it around and look at it in many different ways and hold it against my beliefs and see if I can make it fit, or disregard it if it doesn't and know why because of my beliefs. I can respect others because they've done the same kind of searching, but I can still disagree. . . . I like to sit and contemplate on what I've heard or read and run it through my mind and shadow wrestle with myself, take sides. I like to take what I've heard and put it into some sort of relevance, a real situation, relate it to some sort of experience I've had or have seen others have.

How can we as facilitators assist staff in finding their voices so that they can engage in dialogue with us, which is so central to coming to know and to growth and change? Freire (1972) reminds us that through dialogue the "teacher is no longer merely the-one-who-teaches, but one who is himself taught in dialogue with the students, who in turn while being taught also teach. They become jointly responsible for a process in which all grow" (p. 67).

In helping those who have been denied voice because of race, gender, social class, or culture to think of themselves as learners and knowers, relationship building is key, but this must be a relationship between two human beings that stresses a mutuality of trust, respect, and learning. Drawing out the concerns, questions, and ideas of those silenced can be achieved only if trust is developed.

As Child Development Associate (CDA) advisors in Native American Head Start programs, Katherine Greenough (1993) and David Beers (1993) encountered women who did not perceive themselves as knowers. Native Americans in particular were denied voice when government education policies replaced the use of their native languages with English in schools. Greenough and Beers helped these women come out of silence by building trusting relationships with them and in several other ways as well. They were good listeners and invited speech by encouraging the women to tell stories about their work with children, which eventually became the basis of training materials written in their own words rather than in the words of outside authorities. These CDA candidates also told their own life stories as autobiographical portfolio entries. Advisors encouraged one-on-one dialogue about observations of children and created opportunities for group problem solving. And they emphasized the strengths and competencies teachers already had. Gradually, these Native American teachers gained competence and confidence.

Teachers who are procedural and constructivist knowers also require support. They need to continually engage in dialogue with supervisors and colleagues as the challenge of dialogue, problem posing, and problem solving has the potential to push their thinking to new levels. Formal staff development in which they are confronted with new ideas to explore, reflect on, and critique can also have a major impact on their growth.

Persons come to know and to express what they know in different ways. Early care and education programs as centers of knowing are places where these differences are valued and fostered. Howard Gardner's (1993, 2003) theory of multiple intelligences has implications for supervisors as it helps them think of the varied abilities people have. He believes that human beings do not possess a single intelligence but a set of related intelligences. He has identified at least eight types of intelligence—linguistic, logical-mathematical, musical, spatial, kinesthetic, interpersonal, intrapersonal, and naturalistic—and suggests evidence for a possible existential intelligence. Daniel Goleman (1995) has added to this list with his work on emotional intelligence, and Albrecht (2006) directs our attention to the importance of social intelligence. Supervisors can strive to help staff develop their particular intelligences and use them in working with children by seeing staff members as unique and by making opportunities for them to display the different ways that they know. This is really an act of caring.

IMAGINING

Preschools and infant and toddler centers in the city of Reggio Emilia, Italy, are places where young children have opportunities to explore and communicate with the world through their strengths, with different "languages" or intelligences.

These schools have captured the attention of educators the world over because those who created them have imagined schools differently. Reggio Emilia educators have broken down the barriers of traditional pedagogy by creating liberating environments in which children's *imaginations* can flourish.

Children are encouraged to use their creativity in representing what they know or what they imagine. They represent their ideas in many ways, sometimes by constructing objects in clay or in paper, and/or by drawing them or building with blocks. A fascination with bridges, for example, may result in constructions of bridges in all of these media and then studying them from different perspectives and profiles. Shadow screens are often used so children can see images of subjects in a completely different light; they gain a "fresh eye." Observing the ordinary in a new way creates a sense of enchantment and wonder.

Constructing in various materials requires that particular problems be solved based on the medium used. Building a bridge with clay, for example, poses problems of equilibrium. Studying creations from multiple perspectives as part of a process of encouraging new ways of looking and representing is problem solving too. Reggio educators describe this process as *expressive research* (Vecchi, 1997).

The physical environment fosters an aesthetic atmosphere. Many kinds of materials and tools are available to children. The role of teachers is to encourage risk taking. Error is viewed as a natural part of the knowledge-building process. Children's courage is appreciated, sustained, and admired. Teachers observe, listen, and support exploration and encounter. Children work in groups where they discuss what they have seen or have constructed in common. They learn to listen, to respect each other, to take turns, to plan together, and to give suggestions and ideas.

We have described some of the elements of learning environments in Reggio Emilia preschools because we believe that many of the characteristics educators value for children's development are essential to adult learning as well. Adults in early care and education centers need to be lifelong learners. They also need the freedom to imagine, to explore, and to develop their ideas, and to think of things otherwise.

> To learn, after all, is to become different, to see more, to gain a new perspective. It is to choose against things as they are, to anticipate what might be seen through a new perspective or through another's eye. (Greene, 1988, p. 49)

The women in the Belenky et al. (1997) study described earlier could not have broken their silence if they were not able to think of themselves differently, in new situations. It is not unusual for those of us in supervisory and administrative positions to become frustrated because of the problems associated with daily routines or to feel bogged down because of increasing paperwork and bureaucratic requirements. Yet we need to persist in invoking our imaginations, to think of ourselves, staff members, and programs in new and different ways. Without imagination, we cannot move forward; we succumb to the press for conformity and accountability. Our vision becomes narrower, we lose our motivation, and we become numbed by the ordinary.

The multiple perspective taking that Reggio teachers foster in children is central to adult caring, knowing, and imagining. As staff work with children, with parents, and with each other, the ability to see things as others see them, to explore a problem from many different angles, and to generate alternative solutions is a critical one for them to possess. Through encounter with supervisors and each other, this ability can be nurtured.

> We have begun to understand that for children's experiences to be as wonderful as possible, teachers need to reacquaint themselves with the wonder of the world and begin to see and understand it through children's eyes. (Cadwell, 1997, p. 103)

Just as Reggio teachers encourage the development of multiple literacies in children, supervisors can assist staff in finding or expanding their voices by thinking of alternative ways for them to express what they know or are learning. Through different projects and particular responsibilities, staff can bring their special knowledge and competence to their everyday work and share them with others and also express their frustrations and difficulties. At the Toscanni Play Center, pedagogical coordinators, who are on-site supervisors, facilitate such discussions among small classroom groups of teachers and larger teams, share their own experiences and opinions, and promote overall planning and evaluation (Terzi & Cantarelli, 2001).

Maxine Greene (1995) points out that "All we can do . . . is cultivate multiple ways of seeing and multiple dialogues in a world where nothing stays the same" (p. 16). Preschools, child care centers, kindergartens, and the primary grades as centers of imagining create openings for children and staff to see in many different ways, to think of things otherwise. Greene adds, "Imagining things otherwise may be a first step toward acting on the belief that they can be changed" (p. 22).

CONCLUSION

In our exploration of child care programs as centers of caring, knowing, and imagining, we see several commonalities. An ethos of trust, respect, and openness is necessary in nourishing these characteristics. Dialogue is critical in the caring relationship, in bringing people out of silence and into freedom, and in developing different ways of seeing as well as learning about the perspectives of others. And lastly, it takes courage to care, to know, and to imagine.

EXERCISES

1. Set some time aside during a staff meeting to explore ways that you and your staff members can nurture and care for yourselves.
2. Make a list of your staff members. Think about their particular strengths or intelligences—the different ways that they express what they know. When working with them, try to recognize what they do well.
3. What are some additional ways that your program can encourage imagination in children and staff?

THE DEVELOPMENTAL DYNAMIC

S*UPERVISOR, SUPERVISEE,* AND THE *CONTEXT* in which they work are three components of a complex, dynamic process in which development occurs. Supervisor and supervisee grow and change in an environment that also changes. The interaction between these two individuals and the context in which it takes place can create energy, force, and power for continued professional and personal growth.

A major assumption of developmental supervision is that there is no single best method of improving the performance and facilitating the professional growth of supervisees. By assessing the developmental characteristics of staff members, supervisors can select and use an approach that best matches the individual with whom they are working and the specific problem or concern at hand. This diagnosis takes into account staff members' cognitive abilities, their level of professional development, and their stage in life. Basic to this view of supervision is the ability to "read" staff members to determine which strategies to use with them and to shift from one supervisory approach to another.

Knowledge of self is also fundamental to developmental supervision. By understanding ourselves and the impact of our early life experiences and cultural backgrounds, we increase the control we have over our own behavior and can more easily modify and redirect it when necessary. The literature on developmental supervision has focused primarily on changes in teachers. Yet supervisors' perceptions of self, life situations, and levels of competence change too, and these changes affect the supervisor and teacher development that takes place.

Supervisors and staff members interact within a context. They work with people; they confront problems; they feel pressures that affect the dynamics of the supervisory process. The situation and setting in which they work make up the third significant variable in the developmental dynamic. Figure 5.1 illustrates these three components, which will be discussed further in this chapter. Contextual issues are also addressed in Chapter 12.

Figure 5.1. Supervisor, Supervisee, and Context: Three Components of the Developmental Dynamic

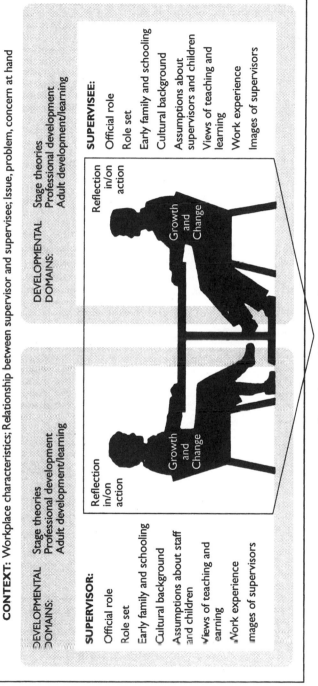

CONTEXT: Workplace characteristics; Relationship between supervisor and supervisee; Issue, problem, concern at hand

DEVELOPMENTAL DOMAINS:
Stage theories
Professional development
Adult development/learning

DEVELOPMENTAL DOMAINS:
Stage theories
Professional development
Adult development/learning

SUPERVISOR:
Official role
Role set
Early family and schooling
Cultural background
Assumptions about staff and children
Views of teaching and learning
Work experience
Images of supervisors

SUPERVISEE:
Official role
Role set
Early family and schooling
Cultural background
Assumptions about supervisors and children
Views of teaching and learning
Work experience
Images of supervisors

Reflection in/on action

Growth and Change

Growth and Change

Reflection in/on action

Supervisor and Supervisee Strategies
|
OUTCOMES

SUPERVISORS AND SUPERVISEES

As supervisor and teacher work together, each brings to the encounter an accumulated set of experiences, perceptions, beliefs, and values that make them who they are, shape their behavior, and influence supervisory outcomes. These include early childhood experiences, cultural perspectives, images of supervisors, previous work experiences, assumptions about people, and views about how individuals learn.

Early Childhood, Cultural Background, and Work Experiences

Supervisors and staff members live with emotional remnants from their early experiences with authority figures. Family training, education, culture, and socialization play a part in how they see themselves and how they express their own authority with others. A supervisor/teacher illustrates this point in describing her background and style of supervision:

> My father expected immediate action following a command. My parents usually fought in front of us over authority issues. Teacher was boss and unfair at times, not listening to my reasons. As a teacher and supervisor, I try to right the wrongs which were done to me; however, I often fall back into the pattern of wanting things done immediately from kids and of being didactic to staff.

Cultural background also has a particular impact on how supervisors and staff members view and carry out their authority. Cultural factors that may affect the supervisory dynamic are verbal and nonverbal language patterns, concepts of dependence and independence, cooperation and individuality, and the value placed on time and punctuality, as well as issues of gender and age. These factors are discussed further in Chapter 10.

Through employment in various settings, staff members and supervisors have had experiences with supervisors who have served as role models and who have left impressions about what it is that supervisors do and how they behave. Both supervisors and staff bring these lasting images with them as they interact with each other.

Assumptions and Philosophy of Learning

Assumptions about human nature also affect how supervisors and teachers work with children and adults. Supervisors who see staff members as basically good, honest, and trustworthy are likely to display behavior patterns that are quite different from those of supervisors who regard teachers/caregivers with distrust and suspicion.

Another significant factor in determining how supervisors or teachers inter-act with others is their point of view about learning. Some individuals believe that behavior is mainly caused and shaped by outside forces. Supervisors and teachers with this orientation select goals and objectives for learners, organize the material to be learned, and develop ways to reinforce learners as they strive to attain established goals. This *direct mode* of teaching can help learners organize skills and knowledge essential to specific tasks, and it can shorten learning time since learners do not have to go through the process of discovering new concepts. But direct teaching can foster a cycle of dependency between instructor and student (Brundage & Mackeracher, 1980) and does not encourage problem solving and reflective behavior.

However, some individuals learn best through a direct approach because of their personal learning style or because they come from cultural or class back-grounds that value and respect directness. They expect teachers and supervisors to be directive and may have little respect for them when they are not. Although some teachers and supervisors are uncomfortable with this style, it can be considered a starting point. A direct mode does not eliminate the need for listening to learners, and becoming familiar with who they are and how they think.

Other people believe that learners need the freedom to explore and discover knowledge through a natural self-directed process. Supervisors and teachers favoring this view work in a *facilitative mode.*

Facilitating helps learners discover and create new meanings, skills, and structures from experience. It requires that the facilitator be a catalyst, resource, reflective mirror, and coinquirer. The structure, objectives, and direction of the learning are negotiated, although the context, in the form of personal meanings, comes from the student (Brundage & Mackeracher, 1980).

Interaction between the individual and the environment is central to yet another view of learning, which emphasizes collaboration and mutual problem solving between teacher and student. A *collaborative mode* requires that learners and teachers jointly engage in the processes of discovering and developing new understandings, skills, and strategies. As colearners, they act interdependently, dividing tasks on a mutually acceptable basis, building a "community of learners" (Brundage & Mackeracher, 1980).

Views about how people learn and the connection between a supervisor's or a teacher's personal philosophy of learning and personal style of working with others are, of course, not quite as simple as described above or as distinct in practice. An underlying premise of developmental supervision, however, is the recognition that humans learn through self-exploration, collaboration, and conditioning. We believe approaches to teaching and supervision that build on these philosophies of learning are valid and can be used appropriately with adult learners depending on their needs, the context, and the setting.

Criteria for Determining Supervisory Approaches

Related to these modes of teaching and learning are three orientations to supervision—*nondirective*, *collaborative*, and *directive*—described by Glickman, Gordon, and Ross-Gordon (2004). They recommend that supervisors determine the strategy to use with teachers by assessing their levels of development and expertise and their commitment to solving the problem at hand. This can be accomplished by observing teachers up close and by engaging in dialogue with them.

A nondirective supervisory orientation is most effective with expert teachers who accept full responsibility for solving the problem. Decisions are in teachers' hands as they have high levels of development, expertise, and commitment. They can examine a problem from multiple perspectives, generate solutions to it, and follow through on implementing a plan of action. The supervisor's role is to help teachers think through their actions by listening, paraphrasing, and asking clarifying questions. We discuss these and other communication skills in Chapter 10.

In a collaborative orientation, teachers are operating at moderate developmental levels. Supervisors and teachers share the responsibility for solving the problem they are facing. Both are equally committed to finding a solution and have similar levels of expertise. In comparison with the nondirective role, the supervisor takes a more active stance, engaging in a give-and-take, joint problem-solving discussion with the teacher. Both supervisors and teachers make decisions and may generate solutions. They operate on a level of parity.

In a directive orientation, the decision making shifts to the supervisor as the teacher is at a low level of development or is not very interested in solving the problem. Glickman et al. (2004) make a distinction between *directive control* and *directive informational strategies.*

Directive-control supervisory behaviors are used when supervisors are committed to resolving an issue and carrying out the resolution and teachers are not so inclined or may not understand its importance. The decision making rests with the supervisor, who determines solutions and sets expectations and timelines.

Directive informational behaviors are used with teachers who want to do well, but who do not have the skills, experience, or knowledge of an issue. They may feel confused and may even be unable to identify the problem. Supervisors take responsibility by identifying alternative solutions to a problem, and laying out the necessary structure and support for the teachers to succeed. For example, teaching techniques are modeled, and ongoing feedback and follow-up are provided. Directive informational supervision is a first step toward building teacher confidence and a baseline of competence in order that more self-directed problem solving can take place at a later point.

We have found that supervisors are often more comfortable using a collaborative approach; however, skill in directive and nondirective supervisory behaviors is needed as well, as staff members require different interventions at various stages in their development.

A major goal of staff supervision is to assist teachers in increasing the control, authority, and responsibility they have for their own teaching and professional development. As we described in Chapter 4, with caring and patient facilitating by supervisors, staff can gain confidence in themselves as constructors of knowledge.

Learning to "read" or assess supervisees to determine how to best work with them is a sophisticated skill. The professional literature on the developmental characteristics of adults offers supervisors useful information in determining appropriate strategies and in learning about themselves.

DEVELOPMENTAL DOMAINS

During the 1970s and 1980s in particular, researchers turned to theories of adult development to gain insight into teacher development, to be more responsive to teachers' needs, and to effectively support their professional growth.

Cognitive-Developmental Stage Theories

Cognitive-developmental stage theories, such as those of Piaget (1961), Kohlberg (1984), Loevinger (1976), Hunt (1971), and Perry (1969), were studied to predict an individual's level of functioning. These theories assume that humans process experience through cognitive structures called stages. The sequence of stages is hierarchical and becomes increasingly more complex. Movement from lower to higher stages is not automatic but is based on interaction with facilitating environments (Thies-Sprinthall, 1980). The assumption is that individuals who function at higher stages are more conceptual, reflective, and independent (Bents & Howey, 1981).

The research that examined the relationship between stage theories and teacher development and effectiveness led to the notion of matching the stage characteristics of the individual with intervention strategies to assist that individual. Some researchers also experimented with ways to help individuals move to higher stages of development and explored the implications of matches and mismatches of cognitive-developmental stages between supervisors and staff members.

Hunt (1971), for example, described the conceptual development of individuals in terms of a continuum from a low conceptual level characterized by concrete thinking to a high conceptual level where thinking is abstract. He proposed matching the degree of structure in the environment to the learner's need for it, based on the person's conceptual level.

Bents and Howey (1981) studied the implications of conceptual systems theory for staff development and suggested that staff developers should plan training in tune with the developmental characteristics of staff. They suggested that teachers who are lower conceptual learners benefit from staff development that is very organized and practical and specific to their teaching situations and class-rooms, while teachers at high levels would be expected to organize more of their own staff development and work in teams with colleagues.

Oja (1981) and Glassberg (1980) found that teachers who are at higher levels of cognitive, moral, and ego development function more effectively in a number of ways. They appear to be better able to think more abstractly about a problem and to generate more solutions to it than teachers at lower levels. They are also better able to see differences in the children they teach. As a consequence, they utilize the learner's frame of reference and adjust their teaching styles and methods to meet the needs of individual children.

An important finding was that the developmental stages of student teachers were raised when they were involved in role-playing, dilemma discussions, active listening, videotaping, individual conferences, and empathic responding exercises, illustrating the point that developmental levels are not fixed. Thus supervisors, staff developers, and teacher educators who provide opportunities for staff to be reflective about their practice can help them become more autonomous in their decision making and problem-solving.

Researchers have also examined the implications of this cognitive-developmental perspective in terms of the pairing of supervisors with supervisees. Grimmett (1983) studied the conceptual functioning and communication behavior of four supervisors and their supervisees during conferences. He found that supervisors who functioned more abstractly showed "flex" in their communication behavior. They were able to "read" their supervisees' needs and the situational constraints. Supervisors who functioned more concretely seemed unable to do this. The term *flex* suggests the supervisor's ability to vary or adapt his or her approach from a range of alternative behaviors. During a conference, for example, a supervisor might change from being directive to being collaborative to meet the personal, cultural, professional, or situational needs of a supervisee.

Grimmett (1983) also noted an increase in the conceptual functioning of teachers who worked with supervisors who were more abstract and conceptual, and a reduction in the conceptual levels of those teachers who were working with supervisors who functioned at more concrete levels. A study of student teachers and their supervisors by Lois Thies-Sprinthall (1980) had similar findings.

In a qualitative study of graduate students learning to be supervisors and their partner teachers, Arredondo (1998) examined the effects of support and challenge dialogues between them, based on an assessment of the cognitive complexity of the participating teachers. During conference dialogues, less support and more challenge was provided to teachers who evidenced high levels of cognitive complexity, while more support and less challenge was given to teachers who evidenced low cognitive complexity. Although results are not generalizable, participant pairs showed evidence of developing complexity and reflectivity in their thinking.

Since the cognitive-developmental stage theories noted above were constructed, however, investigators have become more sensitive to those whose experiences have been excluded from the literature because of gender, race, culture, or social class. The pioneering work of Gilligan (1982), for example, has broadened our understanding of human development to include women's lives. She found that women placed priority on the understanding of responsibility and on connection and caring, traits that labeled them deficient in an earlier conception of moral development based on men's beliefs (Kohlberg, 1984).

Keeping in mind our goal of promoting development in individuals and expanding opportunities for learning, cognitive-developmental theories, taken into perspective, can provide helpful information for supervisory practice.

Stages of Professional Development

The phases and stages of teachers' professional development and their needs and concerns at various points in their career paths are another source of information for supervisors, staff developers, and mentors as they strive to provide supportive and stimulating professional environments for teacher growth.

Francis Fuller (1969), who examined teacher concerns across time during the preservice experience, was a pioneer in this way of thinking about teacher growth and its implications for teacher preparation. Fuller and Oliver Bown (1975) described the stages of learning to teach in terms of the individual's concerns rather than the content that is being taught. Caruso (2000) also studied the preservice experience and identified six phases of cooperating teacher and student teacher development during the practicum.

Although there are many conceptualizations of teachers' career phases, those of Katz (1977) and Vander Ven (1988) are particularly relevant to early childhood educators. Katz (1977) identified four stages of preschool teacher development and the training needs for each stage. Stage 1, *Survival*, usually lasts through the first year of teaching, when the individual experiences self-doubt and feelings of insecurity. Katz recommends that teachers in this stage receive direct on-site support and technical assistance. During Stage 2, *Consolidation*, a teacher consolidates the gains made during the first stage and begins to focus on specific tasks and skills. Supervisors can support training needs during the first several years of teaching by providing on-site assistance, access to specialists, and advice from colleagues and consultants. By the third or fourth year, the preschool teacher begins to tire and to feel a need for *Renewal*, Stage 3. By attending conferences, joining professional associations, and analyzing their teaching, teachers can meet their needs at this stage. Finally, Stage 4, *Maturity*, which extends beyond the fifth year, is the time when the teacher benefits most from attending conferences, participating in institutes and degree programs, and writing for journals.

Vander Ven (1988) examined levels of professionalism of early childhood practitioners a little differently. She described a series of five stages, their accompanying role-level functions, adult/career developmental stages, and the level of guidance needed at each one. Practitioners at Stage 1, *Novice*, function as nonprofessionals; they have the lowest legally permissible levels of education, as well as the lowest salaries. Needing a high level of direct supervision, they often view issues based on their own personal experience. Individuals in Stage 2, *Initial stage*, also need direct supervision, but they have had some training and are seriously considering a career in early childhood education. They are usually receptive to supervision. Professionals at Stage 3, *Informed*, have a strong commitment to the field, hold a bachelor's degree, and are more likely to use developmentally appropriate practices. They have a broader perspective, identify with parents and families, and are becoming more self-reliant. Professionals at Stage 4, *Complex*, and Stage 5, *Influential*, take on leadership roles, supervise others, and have high levels of self-direction and autonomy. Guided by their wisdom, age, and expertise, professionals at Stage 5 in particular are likely to have a significant impact on the early childhood field.

An assumption behind these theories of teacher growth is that preservice supervisory support should change as the needs, concerns, experience, and preparation levels of teachers vary throughout their careers.

Adult Development: Life Stages and Transitions

A third developmental domain that can be helpful to supervisors as they work with staff members is that of adult development. Staff members working in early childhood programs represent all adult age groups. There may be high school and college students, women beginning or returning to work as their children grow up, and senior citizens working part-time to earn extra income or to have something interesting to do. These adults are at varying points in their life cycles. As they develop and change, so do their personal and professional needs and priorities.

As early childhood educators, much of our thinking has focused on child development, but development does not end with childhood. The important work of life cycle theorists such as Erikson (1980, 1982), Gould (1978), Sheehy (1976, 1998), and Levinson (1978, 1996), which place adulthood within a context of a life course or journey, has implications for supervisors, mentors, and staff developers.

Erikson (1980) studied a life from infancy to old age in terms of a series of conflicts or main concerns representing the inner and external worlds. Of the eight phases in his theory, four apply to adulthood. Stage 5, *Adolescence*, addresses the process of identity formation. Stage 6, *Intimacy vs. Isolation*, takes place in young adulthood and deals with the search for partnership in friendship and love, and social patterns of cooperation and competition. In Stage 7, *Adulthood* (ages 40–65 or so), the central concern is *Generativity vs. Stagnation*—that is, one's relationship to the next generation or absorption with self. And finally, during the last stage, old age, the major focus is *Integrity vs. Despair and Disgust: Wisdom*, the process of coming to terms with one's life and life experiences as one strives to balance integrity and despair.

Gratz and Boultin (1996) propose that early childhood educators consider Erikson's (1980) scheme in looking at their own development and the early childhood profession itself. For example, establishing teams within a program so that teachers can share ideas and work together is a way of reducing isolation and building intimacy in Stage 6; planning professional development opportunities for others and participating in classroom research that furthers the field enables one to help the next generation in Stage 7; and viewing accomplishments with satisfaction and knowing that we have made a difference for many children and families are ways to consciously develop the ego integrity that Erikson describes in his final stage.

Gould (1978) became aware of a predictable series of preoccupations in life through his work in supervising resident psychiatrists. He identified a series of false assumptions and illusions that individuals hold at each life phase that are challenged as they gain more competence. This thoughtful confrontation, which requires changes in viewpoints, enables them to make a transition to the next phase. For example, during the period between the ages of 22 and 28, *I'm Nobody's Baby Now*—the age level of a majority of child care workers—one of the major assumptions is "There is only one right way to do things" (p. 88).

This assumption might play itself out in early childhood classrooms in several ways. For example, beliefs about what a teacher does or how a teacher should relate to children that are imprinted on our minds in childhood may interfere with the reality of working with children on a daily basis and may not represent good practice.

The view of a teacher as someone who must be perfectly loving toward all of the children all of the time is one that is often held by novice teachers and one that makes it difficult for them to set limits with children. The process of asserting their teacher authority can be painful as they often feel guilty when they are forced to do so. Yet they cannot move forward in the role until they reconceptualize this idea of teacher authority.

The assumption held by many that teaching is telling or directing may also present challenges for supervisors as they explore ways to positively support beginning teachers by helping them to experiment with other ways of teaching so that development in them and in children can occur. Helping practitioners, as a group, to share, explore, and challenge their own assumptions about their work can lead to clearer communication, greater competence, a better understanding of colleagueship (Levine, 1989), and the creation of shared values.

Arin-Krupp (1981) synthesized much of the research about adults at certain ages and stages and identified implications for staff development. She advocated that supervisors match support strategies to an individual's key concerns at each stage in life. Although Arin-Krupp explored this notion almost a generation ago, it is a concept that continues to have relevance today. However, during the intervening years, a demographic, social, and cultural revolution has taken place in the United States that makes it necessary to reexamine the adult life span in relation to career development and learning opportunities in the workplace.

A New Life Stage

One of the most startling developments is that Americans are living longer, with life expectancy at a record high of 77.6 years (National Center for Health Statistics, 2003). In testimony before the U.S. Senate, Takamura (1998) reported that by 2030, 1 in 5 Americans will be over the age of 65, as the baby boomers, born between 1946 and 1964, join the ranks of older Americans. Freedman (2006) suggests that as a result of increased longevity and independence, and improved health, economic status, and education, we can expect to see the emergence of a new life stage between midlife and true old age, which might last for up to 30 years. During this period, he believes that adults will want to take on new challenges, make significant contributions, and will continue to learn and grow. Many of these adults, he says, will elect to participate in national and community service programs.

Retirees are finding ways to reinvent themselves by furthering their education and taking on new endeavors that they find challenging (Bushnell, 2004). Companies are beginning to tap older workers to benefit from their expertise and experience by offering incentives such as graduate school tuition reimbursement, social clubs, life-planning seminars, and subsidized health insurance to encourage them to return on a part-time basis (Jackson, 2004). Of course early childhood programs do not have the resources of major corporations and have always encouraged older adults to volunteer their services, but given these demographics, should greater efforts be made to recruit older caregivers to build support for early childhood programs and create an intergenerational workforce? And what type of education, training, and support would be needed to take advantage of this opportunity on a larger scale? In public schools, where early childhood teachers are likely to have experienced longevity in a position, are there roles that teachers at or near retirement age can take that would keep them in the profession, yet allow them more recreational time as well?

A Longer Transition to Adulthood

At the other end of the continuum, young people in their 20s are taking more time to make the transition to adulthood. Young people are engaged in considerable postcollege job hopping before settling into a position in their late 20s (Trunk, 2005), which is partly due to a new labor market in which inexperienced workers are offered temporary positions rather than full-time staff positions. The U.S. Labor Department (1998) reports that before the age of 32, the average American has had 8.6 jobs. The workplace landscape is slightly different in the early childhood field than in the U.S. labor market as a whole, but low salaries and wages certainly make it difficult for young caregivers to be independent, with many living with their parents or in group households because of financial necessity. Certainly the turnover in the early childhood field suggests that caregivers may take on several jobs before settling down.

A Redefinition of Marriage and Family

According to the U.S. Census Bureau, wedding bells are ringing later for Americans compared to those of a generation ago (Fields, 2004). In 1970 the average age for a first marriage was 20.8 for women and 23.2 for men, while in 2003, women were age 25.3 and men 27.1 when they made that commitment. The same report indicates that one third of men and almost one quarter of women between the ages of 30–34 have never been married. Of the marriages that took place in 2000, 50% are expected to end in divorce (Wen, 2005). With the legalization of same-sex marriage in Massachusetts and civil unions of domestic partnerships under discussion in many states, the institution of marriage itself is in the process of redefinition.

Households in America have also become more complex in terms of the makeup of families and relationships within a household. Although in 2003 the great majority of households were maintained by families, 26% of households consisted of people living alone. Since 1970 there has been an increase in one-parent family households, while the average household and family size has declined (Fields, 2004). In 2000 there were 3.9 million intergenerational families, such as a householder living with children and grandchildren. In some cases, grandparents are assisting in caring for grandchildren; while in other cases, young adults, ages 35 or younger, are caring for sick parents or aging grandparents while starting marriages, careers, and families (Jackson, 2005). Staff members working in early childhood programs are likely to serve children who live in a great variety of household arrangements.

A More Diverse Workforce

The U.S. workforce has become more ethnically and racially diverse, with roughly 20% of employees consisting of people of color today, compared to 12% in 1977 (Bond, Galinsky, & Hill, 2004). The early childhood workforce is probably even more diverse than the U.S. workforce as a whole today; Whitebook et al. reported in 1989 that one third of the child care teaching staff were members of minorities. What role does race, culture, and ethnicity play in an individual's career development? How do stereotypical images of minorities held by members of the dominant group affect the career success of minorities? And in what ways do cultural values held by members of the majority and minority cultures influence workplace relationships and outcomes?

In a pilot study of African American women in higher education, Alfred (2001) explored some of these questions. She found that bicultural competence—

the ability to navigate various cultural worlds and maintain relationships within those worlds—was critical to their career development, along with being knowledgeable about the organizational and role expectations of the institution in which they were working. Also important to these women was finding a safe space—a home space such as family, neighborhood, or community—where they could take a breather or a retreat from life in the dominant culture to affirm each other and preserve their positive selves. Mentors, sensitive to the cultural needs of minority caregivers, can play a critical role in facilitating their development, and of course, diversity training offered to supervisors and staff can increase cultural awareness and understanding.

Changing Attitudes and Expectations About Work and Family

The events of September 11, 2001, coupled with the competitiveness of our global economy, turbulence and uncertainty in the labor force, and fast-paced life styles, have caused many people to reexamine their lives, especially the meaningfulness of their work (Imel, 2002). They want work that is in line with who they are and they also want to spend more time working at living (Boyatzis, McKee, & Goleman, 2002). Of course one of the reasons early caregivers remain in the profession despite the low pay and benefits is the satisfaction they receive from working with young children. Our experience with student teachers suggests that many come to the early childhood field as a vocation or calling.

The desire for more meaning from life and work may be at the root of a shift in worker attitudes. Researchers at the Families and Work Institute (2002) conducted a study that examined how today's workers differ from workers of other generations in terms of their work and family priorities. They studied four generations in 2002: Generation Y employees were under 23, and Generation X employees were 23–37. Baby Boomers were 38–57, and Matures were 58 or older. They found that Generation Y and X employees were more likely to be dual-centric or family-centric; that is, they placed the same priority on job and family or a higher priority on family, in comparison with Boomers who were more workcentric. Matures, nearing retirement, were dualcentric.

They also found that Generation X fathers spent more time on their family lives than Boomer fathers. They spent more time doing household chores than married men did 25 years ago, while Generation X women are spending less time on such chores. Their findings indicate that father's time with children has also increased dramatically, from 1.8 hours to 2.7 hours per day, a 50% increase in male participation, while mother's time with children is roughly the same as it was 25 years ago. Of course 67% of mothers are working outside the home today. Both partners, then, are juggling work and family responsibilities.

One of their most startling findings about employees was that among college-educated men and women of Generations Y and X, and Boomers, there has been a dramatic decrease in the percentage of those who want to take on jobs with more responsibility. These are employees who are working very hard, who are likely candidates for promotion, but who are experiencing job spillover into their personal and family lives and do not want the trade-offs they would have to make to advance. These data should be of concern to organizations and programs who need to fill their supervisory/managerial ranks in the future.

An employee's life stage, family and household arrangements and responsibilities, attitudes toward work, and cultural values can affect daily supervision and are issues to be considered in planning staff development and learning experiences In Table 5.1, we have revised Arin-Krupp's (1981) original work to incorporate many of the changes described above, including the fact that we are living longer. Erikson's (1982) concept of the life cycle serves as a framework for the table. Please note that Erikson did not assign ages to his life cycle stages; in Table 5.1, we make this approximation.

In thinking about their staff members and strategies to use with them, supervisors may find that in some cases one of the developmental domains described above may offer more information and greater relevance than the others, depending on the individual teacher and the issue at hand. Supervisor and teacher, each at his or her own phase of development, are two components of the supervisory dynamic. The third is the context in which they work.

THE CONTEXT

Not only is information derived from the various developmental domains important in determining supervisory strategies, but equally significant is the relationship established between the supervisor and the teacher, the particular concern at hand, and the organization of which they are a part. These salient contextual elements that influence supervisor-supervisee behavior can have a bearing on the approach that a supervisor might take with a particular supervisee and how a staff member might respond to a supervisor.

Relationship

The existing relationship between supervisors and supervisees affects supervision. Staff members who trust supervisors and who believe that supervisors care about them and their professional growth are more likely to be open to a range of supervisory behaviors. If teachers feel secure with supervisors, for example, there is less likelihood that they will be offended or threatened by criticism or information offered to them. Of course, relationships that are too close can create division among staff and make it harder for supervisors to be objective. A professional-

Table 5.1. Adult Life Cycle and Implications for Staff Development

Approximate Age and Stage	Key Concerns	Characteristics	Implications for Staff Development
Late teens and early 20s **Life cycle stage: Adolescence and young adulthood** *Fidelity* (trust) vs. *Repudiation* (of childhood identification) (Erikson, 1982)	*Identity vs. Identity Confusion* Struggle for identity: Who am I? Changing self-image. Breaking away from parents and transferring need for parental guidance to mentors and leaders. Growing sense of competence. (Erikson, 1982)	Physically in prime. Very active socially. Time is endless. Considers viability of teaching. (Arin-Krupp, 1981)	1. Provide clear expectations. 2. Provide opportunities for independence, but recognize the need for dependence. 3. Be sensitive to the ups and downs of intimate relationships. 4. Foster exploration of the ramifications of teaching. (Arin-Krupp, 1981) 5. During student teaching, provide opportunities for interns to work in groups and to observe each other teaching or caretaking. 6. During student teaching, provide support and feedback. (Caruso, 2002)
The 20s to early 30s **Life cycle stage: Young adulthood and adulthood** *Intimacy vs. Isolation* Committing oneself to affiliations with others, which requires sacrifice and compromise Love: mature devotion Fear of remaining separate and "unrecognized" (Erikson, 1982)	*Flexibility and Stability* Maintaining a balance between the two. Searching for a partner. (Arin-Krupp, 1981) First marriage or partnership in middle-late 20s for some; others remain single. Parenting may begin for some. More unmarried partner households. (Fields, 2003) Both males and females focus on education and careers. Wanting to demonstrate competence on the job.	Physical and mental abilities still in prime. Idealistic and optimistic. (Arin-Krupp, 1981)	1. Provide mentor for new teachers. 2. Work with staff to plan and implement long-range induction program for new staff. 3. Clearly define parameters of the job. 4. Offer on-site and specific training. 5. Provide training in areas such as: classroom management, working with parents, teaching children with special needs, specific instructional strategies, and observing and assessing children. 6. Induct novices into the culture of the program or school. 7. Work with nearby colleges and universities, professional associations, and public agencies to provide on-site college-level courses for those who are ready. 8. Provide social activities for staff. 9. Encourage poor teachers to consider other career options.

The 30s
Life cycle stage: Adulthood
Generativity vs. Stagnation
Generativity (procreativity, productivity, and creativity: generation of new beings, new products, new ideas and caring for these)
Stagnation (periods of inactivity in generative matters)

(Erikson, 1982)

Stability-Advancement
Wants to feel a sense of accomplishment.

(Arin-Krupp, 1981)

Both men and women concerned about balancing work and family responsibilities.
One partner may take time off for child rearing.

(Arin-Krupp, 1981)

Job advancement may be a goal for some; others may be more dual- or family-centric and not want to make necessary trade-offs.

(Families and Work Institute, 2002)

De-Illusionment
Remove unrealistic aspects of life/work dream and modify it; become one's own person.

(Arin-Krupp,1981)

Social life revolves around partnerships and family or around close friends.

(Arin-Krupp, 1981)

More men and women choosing to postpone marriage.

(Fields, 2003)

1. Discuss relationship between career and family.
2. Know teachers and continue to build trust and respect.
3. Offer staff development that meets teacher's individual needs based on program goals.
4. Offer a variety of planned, long-range staff development and learning options, such as portfolio development, study groups, college-level coursework, and group supervision.
5. Develop ways to allow for job flexibility.
6. Offer support for those temporarily exiting the profession.
7. Encourage staff to become involved in professional associations.
8. Encourage staff to pursue graduate education.
9. Encourage staff to obtain advanced certification, such as NBTS.
10. Offer administrator/supervisor internships.
11. Be sensitive to cultural issues.
12. Provide teacher leadership roles and opportunities, such as head teacher, advisor, or coordinator, for those who are ready.

The 40s
Life cycle stage: Adulthood
Generativity vs. Stagnation
Continued productivity and caring
Periods of unproductivity

(Erikson, 1982)

De-Illusionment
To change careers or not?
Marriage—each partner respects autonomy of the other.
Stability-Satisfaction
To live out life within established structure.

(Arin-Krupp, 1981)

Continues to try to balance work and family responsibilities.
Elder care for parents/relatives may be a concern.
Becoming a model in the next generation's eyes.

Strength and endurance have peaked.
Mental activities still in place.
Friends are important.
Signs of aging.

(Arin-Krupp, 1981)

43% of marriages break up within first 15 years.

(NCHS, 2001)

1. Know teachers; individualize to meet teachers' needs.
2. Jointly plan teacher development to facilitate growth.
3. Value insights of experienced staff.
4. Respect differences, skills, and knowledge base among teachers.
5. Encourage teachers to accept leadership roles within teaching, such as mentor, grade-level coordinator, researcher, curriculum developer, head teacher, student teaching supervisor.
6. Assist teachers in understanding rationale for new curricula.
7. Provide thoughtful, thorough, long-range professional development and learning options for small groups of teachers and individual teachers.
8. Offer training and support for those reentering the profession.

(*continued*)

Table 5.1. *(cont.)*

Approximate Age and Stage	Key Concerns	Characteristics	Implications for Staff Development
The 50s **Life cycle stage: Adulthood** *Generativity vs. Stagnation* Continued productivity and caring Periods of unproductivity (Erikson, 1982)	*Integrity* Acceptance of life lived to best of ability. Becoming more mellow. Feeling creative, productive, and self-satisfied. (Arin-Krupp, 1981)	Health and physical changes. Partner is valued as companion. Emphasis on joy and sorrow. Wants to enjoy fruits of labor. Begins to think about retirement. (Arin-Krupp, 1981) Has broad view of profession, well-defined philosophy.	1. Include teachers in decision making. 2. Let complaints be aired. 3. Encourage older teachers to share. 4. Encourage teachers to accept mentoring roles. 5. Continue to listen and to be supportive. 6. Provide opportunities for self-directed development and learning. 7. Listen to what staff has to say, and act on it. 8. Encourage teachers to lead staff development initiatives: programs, workshops, courses, study groups. 9. Encourage teachers to carry out research that advances the field.
The 60s **Life cycle stage: Adulthood, beginning old age** *Integrity vs. Despair* *Maturity* (Erikson, 1982)	*Integrity* Mellowness and wisdom. Beginning to accept self as part of elder generation. (Arin-Krupp, 1981) *Generativity* Sharing wisdom. Reinventing self, creating new roles in retirement. (Freedman, 2006)	Mental ability may diminish, but still effective. Health issues may develop. Begins to see that time is finite. Enjoys leisure pursuits. (Arin-Krupp, 1981) May downsize lifestyle.	1. Prepare teachers for retirement. 2. Find and capitalize on unique contributions that these teachers can make. 3. Develop flex-time options. 4. Provide individualized professional development and learning. 5. Explore ways that teachers can pass on vast knowledge and expertise. 6. Offer teacher education roles to these teachers. 7. Help teachers recognize accomplishments.

The 70s **Life cycle stage: Old age** *Integrity vs. Despair* More active anticipation of dying A sense of life's summary *Wisdom* Reconnecting with the first stage of life, children and youth (Erikson, 1982)	*Generativity* Passing on accumulated wisdom. Seeks ways to contribute to community. Wants to be mentally active.	Health and aging issues. Time finite; taking advantage of each day. Enjoys fruits of earlier labor, but still seeks work, creative, or learning opportunities. Enjoys old friends, family, grandchildren. May be more patient and wise. Decline in mental abilities, but employs compensation strategies. Death is inevitable; may make arrangements. Free to be outspoken.	1. Offer part-time volunteer opportunities with training and support. 2. Incorporate knowledge/life experiences that seniors possess into curriculum. 3. Develop/support intergenerational community-wide programs and activities that bring children, teachers, and seniors together.
The 80s **Life cycle stage: Old age** *Integrity vs. Despair* More active anticipation of dying A sense of life's summary *Wisdom* Dying with dignity Reconnecting with the first stage of life, children and youth (Erikson, 1982)	*Independence/Dependence* Strives to remain independent as long as possible. Combats loneliness and boredom: needs connections to family and others.	Health and mobility issues. Mental abilities continue to decline. Likes established routines. May finalize estate arrangements.	1. Explore ways to link children and community services to seniors to assist them in maintaining independence, interpersonal connection, and contact with other generations. 2. Teach children to care.

personal balance in the relationship between supervisors and supervisees is most desirable.

The Problem

The nature of the problem being addressed also influences the approach to take. In working with a provider who arrives late and leaves early every day, for example, or a caregiver who talks roughly to children, or a teacher who simply does not have the skills to organize a small-group experience with children, a supervisor may have to be direct. On the other hand, if a teacher is involved in an emotionally laden issue with a particular child and cannot gain a clear perspective of the problem, the supervisor may have to reassure and comfort the teacher yet make an executive decision that may be disliked by that teacher.

In dealing with interpersonal conflicts among staff members or with intercultural issues, in planning for children who have special needs, or in exploring ways to improve the effectiveness of a program, collaborative strategies may be most appropriate. A supervisor may use listening, clarifying, encouraging, and other indirect behaviors with a teacher who is disheartened when a lesson that was thought to be exciting falls flat or with a young, inexperienced staff member who is involved in a family crisis that interferes with performance. The specific problem, issue, or concern at hand is always a significant variable in planning for supervision.

Workplace Characteristics

In her analysis of the school as a workplace, Johnson (1990) has identified a constellation of workplace variables that influence workers in all settings. We believe that these variables affect the supervisory dynamic and that an analysis of them with staff can serve as an important development and planning tool. The variables fall into seven categories: economic, political, physical, organizational, cultural, psychological, and sociological.

Economic factors include salary, benefits, job security, incentives, and rewards. We know that early childhood educators leave the profession because of low wages and minimal benefits (Whitebook, Phillips, & Howes, 1993) even though they love their jobs. Staff turnover greatly affects the supervisor's role, particularly with respect to recruitment and training, and it interrupts the flow of the supervisory process.

Equity and the opportunity to participate in governance issues are *political* considerations. In parent-run programs, for example, a supervisor's behavior may be governed by others who have influence over a program's policy and operation. Or a center-based director in a large system may receive pressure from an executive director with different values about people and programs. The agency might not allow adequate planning time for supervisor and staff to work together, forcing the supervisor to give up a process approach with staff in favor of issuing orders. Staff participation in decision making is an important factor in building a professional community within a program.

Physical issues are also important. Lack of adequate space for a program may create problems and pressures, as classrooms may be congested and there may not be facilities for private conferences or for staff to relax. The environment should be safe for adults as well as for children.

Staff workload and autonomy are aspects of a setting's *organizational* structure, along with such factors as opportunities for staff to collaborate, the manner in which they are supervised and evaluated, how authority is delegated and vested, and how other professionals such as social workers and psychiatrists are integrated into a program.

Each organization also has its own *culture* (Schein, 1985), which may be strong or weak, or supportive or nonsupportive of staff. Deal and Kennedy (1982) have described organizational culture in terms of its values, heroes and heroines, rites and rituals, and cultural networks. What is a program's philosophy? Are the center's values public and shared? Heroes and heroines personify an organization's values. They may be figures from the past such as Dewey or Piaget or Froebel or present-day individuals such as a program's founder or director. Rites, rituals, and ceremonies celebrate a program's culture. Gossips, whisperers, and storytellers are characters within a cultural network who transmit and interpret information and can reinforce a program's values and norms. A critical role of supervisors is to understand the culture and to work with staff to build and maintain a positive school culture.

Psychological variables such as job stress, meaningfulness of work, and opportunities for learning and growth are other significant workplace features. And finally, *sociological* features, which include the characteristics of peers and of children and families served, job status, and clarity of roles, are factors that can have an impact on job satisfaction and the supervisory process.

Workplace Flexibility

The changing attitudes and expectations about work and family and shifting priorities in the adult life cycle described earlier in this chapter suggest a critical need for greater flexibility in the workplace. There may be some creative ways to offer staff in day care and preschools flex-time to enable them to work fewer hours a day or fewer days a week, which might coincide with part-day and part-week enrollment options for children. Some schools build in job flexibility through the sharing of full-time positions. The notion of making the workplace more adaptable to today's employees and thinking about ways to allow individuals to enter, exit, and reenter the workplace over a lifespan is worth considering, despite some of the constraints peculiar to early care and education.

REFLECTIVE PRACTICE

A final aspect of the supervisory dynamic essential for development is reflective practice. The issues and problems that supervisors encounter on a daily basis are often unpredictable and complicated. Problematic situations may arise that require immediate decisions, yet a supervisor may have little previous experience in solving the specific problem faced. In these cases, supervisors may spontaneously draw on their inner resources and improvise as they make intelligent and important decisions. Schön (1987) calls the competence that practitioners display in these situations *professional artistry*, and terms its essential components *reflection-in-action* and *reflection-on-action*.

Reflection-in-action is the process of thinking about something while doing it. Teachers often experience this phenomenon while in the midst of teaching when they make on-the-spot adjustments such as reexplaining concepts in different ways or shifting from one activity to another when children become restless. Conferring with staff members is a form of supervisory artistry that requires reflection in which supervisors analyze the conference while it is taking place and make decisions as they work their way through it, striving to resolve the issue at hand. In these cases, a supervisor becomes a researcher in the practice of supervision, often experimenting and inventing new solutions. Both teachers and supervisors may engage in this reflective process as they "read" each other and plan responses to each other while conferring together.

A second type of reflective practice is *reflection-on-action*, which is reflection on reflection-in-action, a process Schön (1987) describes as a dialogue between thinking and doing that results in more skillful practice. Certainly this is a very sophisticated skill that has the potential to increase a supervisor's self-awareness and effectiveness and to deepen an understanding of one's work in supervision.

CONCLUSION

We believe that supervision is a reciprocal process by which the supervisor and the teacher influence each other's behavior. Both individuals function within a context that offers constraints and advantages and has a bearing on each person, the interactions, and supervisory outcomes.

We have reviewed three developmental domains—cognitive development, professional development, and adult development—that offer cues for facilitating the growth of staff members and for understanding ourselves. Contextual characteristics of organizations have also been described as they have a bearing on supervision. Lastly, we have emphasized the importance of reflection as a means of improving supervisory practice.

EXERCISES

1. Think about your family and schooling experiences and your assumptions about your supervisees. Describe how these factors may influence your supervision.
2. Do you have a preferred supervisory style? If so, describe it. When does it seem effective, and when has it not worked as well?
3. Analyze your setting in terms of some of the contextual elements mentioned in this chapter. In what ways do they help or hinder you with your supervision?
4. Using Table 5.1, make a list of the staff members in your program and place them at an approximate life cycle stage. Using the column at the far right as a reference, identify some of the ways that you are supporting them and some of the professional learning opportunities that are available to them.

CHAPTER 6

SUPERVISOR DEVELOPMENT

A S SUPERVISORS GAIN EXPERIENCE in their roles, they undergo a series of changes in how they view themselves and their jobs. Their feelings and concerns about supervision change over time.

We have identified three general phases that supervisors experience as they grow in their roles: beginning, extending, and maturing. Characteristic patterns of thinking and behaving tend to emerge during each of these phases as supervisors acquire new realizations concerning the supervisory role and the people with whom they are working. The significant characteristics of each phase are summarized in Table 6.1.

Since our first edition, supervisors have indicated to us that there is a prephase characterized by imagining what it would be like to be in a supervisory position and preparing for the role by enrolling in graduate course work or by moving up the career ladder in intermediate steps. Thinking about a job change and its implications, garnering support from friends and family, and taking some small steps in a new direction are all part of the process of separating from one position and anticipating and accepting the challenge that a new one can provide. And, of course, toward career's end, individuals may think about "passing the torch" on to others and may begin to limit their work in the field.

PHASE 1: BEGINNING

Beginning supervisors, like most novices, tend to have personal concerns: Will I be able to carry out the responsibilities of my position? What is my role? What is going to happen to me? Will I be able to meet the expectations that others have of me? These are some of the questions they ask themselves.

Beginners develop a number of coping strategies to survive the early months on the job. One such strategy is to play the role of supervisor by imitating role models from past experience such as parents, teachers, managers, directors, grandmothers, nuns, or deans. These role models have left indelible imprints as to how

Table 6.1. Supervisory Development

PHASE 1: BEGINNING	PHASE 2: EXTENDING	PHASE 3: MATURING
Concerned with self	"If only I . . ."	Knows self and can evaluate self openly
Anxious	Accepts leadership with ambivalence	Sense of being in charge
Critical of self	Can discuss problems and concerns more objectively	Greater sensitivity toward and understanding of supervisees
Seeks support from many sources		
Rewards are self-centered		
Copes in several ways	Concerns are centered on others	Recognizes expertise of supervisees
Plays the role of supervisor	Better understanding of others and of program	More realistic about job and what can be done
Avoids responsibility		
Orients self to role	More comfortable with authority	Concerned with ideas/issues
Uses trial and error	High expectations for self	Has well-defined philosophical frame of reference
In process of conceptualizing the role	More confident, more relaxed	Stimulated by outside contacts; gets rewards from solving problems
Uncomfortable with authority		
Develops new realizations about self		Continues to be critical, but sees self as learner

individuals in authority positions should behave, and it is only natural to imitate these familiar behaviors. Yet there is risk to coping by imitation, since the learned authority behavior may be inappropriate for early childhood programs, although it does give supervisors the feeling that they have "taken charge" and are "in control." This increases a supervisor's confidence, but only until problems develop. Solving problems requires meaningful deliberation and interaction with staff or board members based on an in-depth exploration of issues. Playing supervisor does little to resolve problems.

A second survival strategy that novices use is to avoid the responsibilities of the role by appearing not to have adequate time to devote to supervision because they are preoccupied with other urgent administrative issues. These supervisors continually find themselves preoccupied with other business and somehow never take on their supervisory responsibilities. Some may believe that supervision is not their forte, a rationale for devoting all their time and energy to administrative duties where they do have competence. Avoidance behaviors enable supervisors to pretend they are doing a good job and their programs are running smoothly. In the meantime, problems snowball.

A third way beginners cope is to reserve a period of time to assess and orient themselves to their new setting if circumstances allow. They do this by observing and gradually getting to know people, programs, and routines. One new director explained how she was going about this task:

> Right now I am sort of filling the role of somebody that had been with the center for, I guess, 6 years who is very well loved and, in some ways, a mother figure for a lot of the staff. I have been listening to a lot of the kinds of interactions that went on with this person in terms of staff meetings and that kind of thing. I have been sorting out for myself what I would like to do without rocking the boat too soon. So, I'm following a lot of the things that were set up by that person.

Information gathered during this initial period can be valuable in making important decisions later.

New supervisors also learn through trial and error, even more so when they do not have an experienced teacher or other support system to point them in the right direction. They often try different approaches to solving problems in search of one that works.

Learning to Handle Authority and Confrontation

It is not at all uncommon for new supervisors to feel uncomfortable about directly confronting a staff member about a particular problem. Beginners are often concerned about being too bossy or offensive. They are not sure they can deal with problems in a sensitive and constructive manner. These feelings are understandable, as early childhood supervisors have frequently moved into their new roles from teaching and are still learning to shift from nurturing children to working with adults.

Although supervisors may have worked out their authority relationships with children in their previous roles as teachers or parents, working with adults is quite different. The diversity of caregivers in terms of cultural background, experience, age, and maturity levels can present serious challenges to the authority of an unsure supervisor. Coming to terms with authority is part of the process of defining and formulating a conception of the supervisory role. It is often painful and worrisome, as this director describes:

> I think basically confronting and being able to say I am not happy with this or I don't like it is very hard, even though that is not exactly the way I would say it. I am trying to sort through in my own mind how to confront some situations, and I haven't done particularly well.

The new supervisor is faced with authority dilemmas daily in dealing with staff, parents, and curricular issues.

Conceptualizing the Role of Supervisor

Sifting, sorting, assessing, and testing are typical behaviors beginners use as they learn what a supervisor is and what a supervisor does. A conceptualization of the supervisory role emerges slowly, first in a narrow and ambiguous sense, and later with greater clarity and scope. Inexperienced supervisors, for example, tend to view their supervisees in general terms rather than as complicated individuals with special needs. They describe staff in terms of numbers and categories—"I have one head teacher and three aides"—rather than in terms of personal characteristics, strengths, and weaknesses, as experienced supervisors do. They simply don't know their staff members well enough to differentiate among them or to make discrete assessments of them.

New supervisors must also develop a total picture of the programs in which they are working. During the first months on the job, they have to learn about personal relationships among staff members, the political implications of decisions they may make, the special needs and problems of the community being served, the expectations of outside funding agencies or institutions that supply temporary staff, and other factors that will affect their success on the job.

Seeking Professional and Emotional Support

Beginning supervisors function in their own world, concerned and preoccupied with self. Most are aware of their own weaknesses and are interested in becoming more skilled. Self-critical beginners willingly identify deficiencies and are open to experimentation. They want to improve their supervisory behavior.

First-year supervisors need and seek professional and emotional support from many sources, including administrators, parents, board members, and staff members, as well as friends and relatives. As one beginning supervisor put it:

> I guess I need support. I need support from the staff. I need feedback from people in terms of what's happening from my end of things and how it is coming across to other people. I need open communication. I guess that is why I keep trying to work at building relationships because I feel it is really important that teachers be fairly open with me. And I need to learn a lot. I feel a little overscheduled sometimes about the role that I do play, and I guess I need to develop my own skills.

A number of supervisors we interviewed gained assistance from other directors who were part of a local group that met on a monthly basis. Such nourishment from others helps beginners acquire the confidence they need.

Rewards for novices tend to center around self, since they are less other-person oriented than more experienced supervisors. Compliments from parents or from people in superior positions, such as chief administrators or board members, are especially appreciated. Solving difficult problems and accomplishing important tasks bring feelings of satisfaction to beginners.

Supervisors in this phase, as well as in the ones to follow, are continually learning about themselves. They are forced to reflect on their personal style, philosophy, and goals as they confront such challenges as implementing change; supporting, training, and evaluating other people; coordinating many activities within one program; raising funds; and conveying a center's philosophy and activities to the outside world. After 4 months on the job, a new supervisor talks about what she has learned about herself:

> I guess what I think about is that there are a lot of things that I can handle simply by jumping in and doing them. I don't panic. I'm not afraid to do things, although I still have my nervous moments. I know what I feel like when I am nervous, but I still follow through. I can try new things and accomplish them. In terms of myself, I guess that I have learned that I am somewhat approachable and that is nice. I have relearned that I am a real workaholic in some ways. I have a hard time cutting down my hours. I guess that my feelings about being able to confront others is something I have wanted to develop.

PHASE 2: EXTENDING

Supervisors in this phase are no longer novices, yet they have not yet reached professional maturity. They are consolidating gains made as beginners, extending their knowledge and competence, strengthening their leadership, raising their expectations, and reaching out to staff.

Wishing for a magic potion or a wand that could make every part of a program perfect is the quintessential fantasy of supervisors in this second phase. As one day care director put it:

> If only I had more time! If only we had more money! Wouldn't it be wonderful if I could send some of my staff to NAEYC? I wish we had greater racial and economic diversity represented in our enrollment. I wish I had somebody who was observing me and telling me what I'm doing wrong and what I'm doing right. . . . And I'm not at all satisfied with my performance or my role or anything. I think that I wish I had some magic . . . some magic potion.

Having survived the first year and gained greater confidence and assurance in coping with daily crises, supervisors in this phase are concerned with perfection. Now able to look beyond personal wants, the supervisor thinks about the needs of others, the prevailing conditions under which the staff operates, and the positive and negative aspects of the learning environment created for the children.

Reflecting an innocence and naiveté, supervisors in this phase tend to believe that if they work hard and do their best, all of a program's problems and weaknesses will be corrected. Transitional supervisors set lofty goals, determined to make their programs exemplary ones, with visions of walking off stage with the "Early Childhood Emmy" flashing through their minds.

In contrast with beginners, who do not feel like supervisors and may even reject the notion of being boss, transitional supervisors accept the leadership role but are still ambivalent about it. As one day care director explained:

> I feel strongly that supervision is a big job, and there are a lot of people to supervise. I do feel like a supervisor in the sense that I know people are looking for supervision, and I try to do it. In the sense of feeling that I am really supervising every single person as it should be done, absolutely not. I know that there is no time. I don't have enough time to spend in classrooms really looking at what everybody is doing.

Another Phase 2 supervisor was still unsure as to how to enact authority appropriately:

> My problem is, how do you get somebody to see that she needs improvement in a particular area? Just because it is my problem doesn't mean it is going to be theirs. How do you get them to be motivated to change? How do you get them to ask, "How do you do that?" How do you tell them that

you are not 100% satisfied with their work without sounding like you're extremely unsatisfied?

Unable to meet their own expectations of perfection, supervisors in this phase are often faced with frustration. They constantly fall short of mastering the art of supervision, yet continue to try to do better. One director commented, "There is this story that no matter how much you do, it is always less than what you want to be doing." In some respects, these feelings are prerequisite to realizing that all of one's goals cannot be achieved. They are part of a process of acquiring a truer picture of what a supervisor can accomplish and what is beyond his or her control. Reassessment and reconceptualization of the role of supervisor occur over time as supervisors engage in trial and error and meet with success and failure.

Phase 2 supervisors who are extending their leadership can begin to discuss problems and conflicts more objectively. They are better able to separate themselves from their roles, to stand back and look at problems analytically, rather than ignoring them or feeling overwhelmed as beginning supervisors do.

Concerns, then, move away from self and are centered to a far greater extent around other individuals and specific issues. Supervisors in this extending phase are more conscious of the need to provide reinforcement and support to staff members. They begin to see themselves as mentors who can guide staff members toward new realizations and self-improvement. They strive to provide an atmosphere of trust and openness to enable staff to identify and engage in group problem-solving experiences. They recognize the need to develop good group-facilitation skills in order to foster positive interpersonal relationships among staff members.

With more experience, Phase 2 supervisors begin to make distinctions among staff members, to see them as unique individuals with special needs and concerns. They begin to realize that some supervisees need specific direction while others respond well to casual suggestions or praise. They provide different kinds of training for volunteers, part-time staff, and experienced full-time staff. This ability to vary one's approach to working with others, to individualize supervision, is more characteristic of supervisors toward the latter part of this second phase.

Gaining a greater understanding of a program, its people, and its parts is also characteristic of Phase 2 supervisors. This new awareness of a program's complexity is linked to the development of a less idealistic and more realistic sense of what a supervisor can and cannot do or change.

Supervisors in this phase often feel isolated. They discover that there really isn't anyone on the job at their level in whom to confide. They look for sources of support among associates in similar fields and other supervisors in similar positions. Reliance on new professional contacts for support lessens the burden on family and friends on whom beginning supervisors usually depend for nurturance.

Although there continues to be some self-centeredness in what Phase 2 supervisors find rewarding, they derive greater satisfaction when they receive praise from individuals they supervise rather than from those who supervise them, and when they see others making progress. As one supervisor stated: "I love it when people get excited about teaching children, when people can learn to relax and enjoy teaching." Seeing the center run smoothly, observing supervisees improve their ability to work with children, or motivating a caregiver can be especially rewarding.

Supervisors who are extending their leadership also feel more relaxed, less panicky, less overwhelmed, and in greater control. It is at this time that they make enormous gains in professional development. They move from being anxious, self-centered beginners to individuals who grapple with issues, strive to support others, and feel a sense of accomplishment. Although still occasionally subject to feelings of ambivalence, guilt, or frustration, supervisors in this phase develop greater confidence and the security that comes from success and familiarity with the job, the program, and its people.

The experiences supervisors have during this middle phase affect whether they remain in a particular setting or even in the profession. It is during this transitional period that many supervisors make a commitment to the field or decide to look elsewhere to fulfill their career aspirations.

PHASE 3: MATURING

Phase 3 supervisors possess the characteristics of mature professionals: self-knowledge, self-confidence, in-depth understanding of the problems and issues associated with their work, and the skills necessary to do an effective job. Maturing supervisors bring rich and disparate life experiences to their roles and can look back and understand how those experiences have made them who they are and how they contribute to present-day success.

Seasoned supervisors know and evaluate themselves. A college laboratory school director discusses her strengths and weaknesses openly:

> I keep reminding myself that I need to listen to people very carefully. I think that this is essential. It has been an improvement in my supervisory style to be a better listener; it is a positive development in my personality.
> I have become conscious of the way I must come across to people, and I am cautious because these are young people. I think a supervisee is in a very vulnerable position very often, so I have to be sensitive to that and cautious about being too overwhelming or too opinionated or coming on too strong. . . . I think that I see my work all the time as a process of growth for me.

The supervisor who made the above statement shares some of her anxieties about being too overwhelming or too directive with caregivers, a common concern of her colleagues who are in earlier stages. A difference, however, between individuals in this mature stage and those who are less experienced is the ability to make accurate assessments of behavior: to acknowledge their weaknesses and to be conscious of them as they strive to change, to compensate, or to live with them. Maturing supervisors have a sense of being in charge of their lives, of making conscious decisions, and of being accountable for their actions.

One of the most striking characteristics of experienced supervisors is their sensitivity to supervisees as unique individuals and their ability to individualize supervisory strategies. Mature supervisors view being able to assess each supervisee and plan appropriate interventions as a special challenge, as exemplified by this supervisor who talks about the teachers in her program:

> In terms of personality they are all different and I enjoy the differences. I think that because of their differences, they bring various agendas to supervision sessions. I do feel that supervisors can fall into all kinds of traps with supervisees—among them being overnurturing or undernurturing, being too critical, being too demanding. A supervisor has to be careful not to fall into that kind of trap. I think that we need to look at people's personalities. I think that our supervisees have different needs which evoke different kinds of responses.

In the following comments an experienced supervisor shows great insight and understanding of her staff members, and values and appreciates the special qualities each of them has:

> The three head teachers in this school are three different kinds of personalities and lead very different kinds of classrooms. For example, the head teacher upstairs works with the younger crew. I think that she is one of the most successful nondirective teachers I have ever come across. She is a rather young woman. This was her first job. She was trained here; she did a year's internship here, and she became a head teacher after that. She has a unique way of communicating with children. One never hears her voice in the classroom. And yet she is always talking with them or is at their side listening and communicating in other ways. Her presence is very much felt. The children are very busy doing their own thing. It is wonderful to see. That is a very special kind of personality and a very special set of characteristics.
> Downstairs we have a teacher who has had a lot of experience in a lot of settings with special-needs children and so on. She is mature, experienced, and a very directive person. She understands children and her values are right, and I trust her [im]plicitly. There is a vast difference in her approach. She does the right things for children. She is very good.

> In the afternoon, we have another teacher . . . who is very chatty, very warm, very connected with everybody. She is very interested in doing special projects with children. She has a special kind of energy that is just perfect for children who are tired in the afternoon. She works from 11:00 A.M. to 5:00, yet she doesn't get tired.

Supervisors who are professionally mature recognize and respect the strengths of their staff members. They are willing to share their authority, demonstrating a trust in their supervisees. They encourage their staff members to share their knowledge and skill with each other, recognizing that their diverse strengths provide mutual support for all and bring a richness to the program. Sharing authority is not intimidating to the mature supervisor.

Unlike beginning supervisors, who may not be aware of the problems around them, or moderately experienced supervisors, who acknowledge problems but are unsure of how to deal with them, experienced supervisors recognize and comprehend the depth and range of existing problems. They understand how much needs to be done and see problem solving as an ongoing task. Supervisors in this phase are less frustrated because they understand that, even if certain goals cannot be achieved, at least they can be addressed.

Seasoned supervisors tend to be less emotionally burdened by the problems they encounter. They have gained greater perspective and have acquired skill in managing time, coordinating and keeping track of tasks, motivating staff members to change, and building morale within a program. They are still concerned with resolving interpersonal issues among staff members, and they still need the emotional support of others, but they are no longer as overwhelmed by the demands placed on them. They don't feel as helpless or as powerless as colleagues who are in the earlier phases.

Maturing supervisors tend to be concerned with ideas, with groups, with relationships, and with broad issues. They possess a well-defined philosophical frame of reference and a commitment to standards of education for children. They are perceptive, sensitive, discreet, and tuned in to staff members. They seize opportunities for leadership:

> What I do is observe a lot, see a lot, and then confront a lot. From time to time, I remember calling a meeting of last year's staff to redefine our ideas for curriculum before we started again this year.
> I thought that was the best way of saying, "Look, gang! This is the way I would like it to be here," without telling any one person that . . . and they had a lot of opportunity to discuss this. I don't really have to have it my way. There is room enough for other people's ideas. Every once in a while, I feel as though I have to pull things in and pull things together. I think this school has style. I like us all to be sure we know what it is that

we are doing and why we are doing it. These are very important times
when we talk about children and our ideas about curriculum.

Like their less experienced colleagues, seasoned supervisors enjoy a "pat on
the back for a job well done." The rewards they receive from the job now tend to
be other-person, program, and professionally oriented rather than centered around
self. They receive stimulation from work in their own centers and in the educational community at large, interacting with other professionals through local and
national professional organizations, boards, and committees. They achieve satisfaction from the gradual resolution of difficult problems, from developing and
improving their programs, and from new responsibilities. Supporting staff members as they strive to accomplish their goals provides maturing supervisors with
additional satisfaction.

Supervisors at this stage are wise and skilled. They view themselves as individuals who are still growing, still learning, recognizing the need for renewal,
reeducation, and challenge. They believe they can play a vital role in making this
a better world for children and families.

REFLECTING ON PRACTICE

Supervisor growth during the beginning, extending, and maturing phases is ongoing but frequently uneven. They move back and forth from one phase to another during their careers, and even mature, educated, and talented supervisors
may demonstrate some characteristics of beginners when they work in new roles,
in unfamiliar settings, or with people they don't know. Some supervisors may never
move beyond the first or second phase.

Reflecting on practice is an avenue toward becoming a more effective supervisor and advancing from one phase to another. Keeping a supervisory log to
document events or a supervisory diary are ways to stimulate reflection. Diary
entries could also be posted on a common Web site for supervisors as part of a
virtual support group.

Learning journals in which supervisors describe and follow issues over time,
indicating new understandings and realizations, are another tool for reflection, as
are supervisory portfolios. Various artifacts representing the supervisory process,
such as memos to staff, observational records, samples of professional development experiences for staff and supervisors, can be placed in a portfolio as part of
a supervisor's professional development or assessment plan. Writing stories in
the form of case studies about their work with staff, which are shared and discussed with other supervisors, can also lead to learning and growth. Portfolios
and storytelling are discussed more fully in Chapter 16.

Lastly, simple self-assessment, such as informally reviewing and rating oneself on published criteria such as NAEYC's program administrator competencies

(see below) or selecting one or two competency areas as goals to emphasize for the year, can provide a sense of accomplishment and direction.

CONCLUSION

Supervisors undergo a process of growth and development over time. They face similar problems and frustrations in each phase, but their ability to handle problems changes as they move toward maturity (refer to Table 6.1). The context in which they work, the nature of problems they encounter, personal characteristics, previous experience, and job training and preparation are factors that can influence the path of development from early to later phases. We believe that these phases, coupled with their place in the adult life cycle (described in Table 5.1) and cognitive-developmental stage, affect a supervisor's work with staff members who are also growing and changing personally and professionally.

The presence of support for supervisors is critical to their development, yet it is often lacking. This means that individuals may have to take the initiative to seek out and build a support system for themselves. Support may take the form of a local network of directors or educational coordinators. Finding a mentor, shadowing others to observe how they carry out their roles, visiting nearby programs, taking courses and workshops, and joining and becoming active in professional organizations are all ways to build knowledge and competence and to meet people in similar positions who can be called on for help and suggestions when needed. Incorporating deliberate ways to reflect about practice is also important to the growth of supervisors.

The notion of supervisors experiencing phases of development while on the job is sometimes surprising to teachers who may think of someone in a supervisory role as a "finished product." Becoming aware of the phases of development of supervisors may create greater understanding and empathy on the part of teachers and reassurance among those already holding supervisory positions.

PROGRAM ACCREDITATION

The core competencies for early childhood program administration from *NAEYC Early Childhood Program Standards and Accreditation Criteria: The Mark of Quality in Early Childhood Education* (NAEYC, 2005; adapted by NAEYC with permission from the Illinois Director Credential) fall into two broad categories: management knowledge and skills and early childhood knowledge and skills. These are not discrete categories: They overlap conceptually and practically, and some competencies go beyond supervision and support of staff. We list the major headings under each category here. Please see the above text for definitions of each competency area.

Management Knowledge and Skills

Administrators need a solid foundation in the principles of organizational management, including how to establish systems for smooth program functioning and managing staff to carry out the mission of the program. Core competencies include the following:

1. Personal and Professional Self-Awareness
2. Legal and Fiscal Management
3. Staff Management and Human Relations
4. Educational Programming
5. Program Operations and Facilities Management
6. Family Support
7. Marketing and Public Relations
8. Leadership and Advocacy
9. Oral and Written Communication
10. Technology

Early Childhood Knowledge and Skills

Administrators need a strong foundation in the fundamentals of child development and early childhood education in order to guide the instructional practices of teachers and support staff. Core competencies include the following:

1. Historical and Philosophical Foundations
2. Child Growth and Development
3. Child Observation and Assessment
4. Curriculum and Instructional Methods
5. Children with Special Needs
6. Family and Community Relationships
7. Health, Safety, and Nutrition
8. Individual and Group Guidance
9. Learning Environments
10. Professionalism

EXERCISES

1. Which phase would you place yourself in and why?
2. Describe the ways in which your present phase of supervisory development affects your job effectiveness.
3. What kinds of support do supervisors in each phase need?
4. Keep a log, reflective diary, or learning journal.

5. Select one competency area from the NAEYC list and develop a portfolio over a yearlong period with entries to illustrate that competency.
6. Working with colleagues in your area or through your local AEYC, establish an electronic supervisory support network.
7. If you are thinking about moving into a supervisory position, interview someone already in the role and learn about their phases of development and steps they have taken to climb the career ladder.

CHAPTER 7

SUPERVISEE DEVELOPMENT

IN INTERVIEWS ABOUT THEIR WORK, caregivers of different ages, in contrasting roles, and at various stages of development described key areas for professional growth, which resemble in some ways those that supervisors go through as they become more familiar with and expert in their jobs. The competencies we describe below do not represent the full range of skills and abilities needed to work effectively in early childhood programs, but they can serve as guides for informal mutual assessment of staff members and as a basis for planning for continued improvement.

LEARNING TO COMMUNICATE EFFECTIVELY

In order to teach and care for young children, staff members learn to communicate with a variety of people for different purposes as part of their daily experience. As team members responsible for a group of children, teachers learn to plan together, to share duties, and to cooperate with each other to support the children they serve. They participate in the supervisory process with head teachers and/or directors. They interact with outside consultants such as doctors, social workers, psychologists, and community workers who provide support to children and their families. Being an effective communicator is critically important to forming relationships with colleagues. Working productively with other staff members requires mutual exchange, which can take place only in an atmosphere of openness and respect, where people are honest with each other.

Sometimes caregivers become board members and teacher educators, roles that require good listening and effective speaking skills. One of their most important and difficult jobs is working with parents, helping them increase their understanding of young children. The caregivers we interviewed who appeared to be the happiest and most successful in their roles were those who had become effective communicators.

BECOMING A SELF-CONFIDENT TEACHER

Some teachers enter the profession with little experience or knowledge of the field of early childhood education. In fact, quite a few of those we interviewed became involved in child care because their own children or younger siblings were enrolled in day care or Head Start. They often began their careers as volunteers, some eventually returning to school to complete requirements for a high school diploma. For those who dropped out of high school to marry and have children, the position of aide or assistant teacher may have been their first job in the profession, although they gradually moved up the ranks to become a teacher or head teacher.

Teaching young children, which requires an understanding of child development and an ability to communicate with other professionals, can be threatening to persons with previously unsuccessful experience in school settings or to those who are holding a regular job for the first time. Beginners require time to become comfortable in the work setting. It is common for them to feel timid when leading children or when talking to strangers, as this caregiver describes:

> When I first came here, I was very shy as far as talking to parents. I was very shy at starting out like leading songs in front of a big group, sitting on floors, and really getting to play with the kids. Now, I don't think anything about going up to a parent and saying, "You know, your kid had a great day!" or "You know, he didn't have such a good day." I don't feel funny about leading songs in a great big group; I don't feel funny about getting down on the floor and pretending to be an animal with the kids, where, at first, I was a little shy about it.

As they become more confident, caregivers tend to be less dependent on supervisors. They no longer have to be told what to do and how to do it. In supervisory roles themselves, they make their own judgments about whether to step in if a teacher is having a difficult time with a child. They act without needing a director's assessment and opinion. A teacher shares her thoughts about responsibility:

> When you're a trainee, you have someone who is, more or less, directing you and telling you what to do. You don't have as much responsibility as you do as a teacher. As a trainee, all you have to say is, "Well, I have a problem with this. Will you help me? I'm not sure how to do this!" and someone will say, "Well, do it this way." You have a teacher to kind of fall back on. But when you're the teacher, you are the one who's doing the supervising and who has the responsibility for the children in the classroom. The health and safety of the children is all your responsibility. Everything falls back on you.

Training and staff development can have an exciting effect on the self-confidence of caregivers who began at different developmental levels. One teacher describes the profound changes that participation in an associate's degree program had on her confidence:

I think, too, that my education had a lot to do with making me feel more confident and being able to relate to people on different levels of a profession. This past year, I had a meeting at Children's Hospital about a child I had in my room who had a special problem. I had to meet with the social service director, the educational director, two doctors, a psychologist, and a dietician. They wanted to hear my opinion. "What!" I thought. Six or seven years ago, I probably would have died, "Oh, my God!" But I knew what I was talking about. I felt comfortable because I knew what I was talking about.

UNDERSTANDING CHILDREN

Working with children on a daily basis over time advances a caregiver's knowledge and understanding of child development. Even though many supervisees are parents before they become early childhood professionals, they often lack such basic information about child growth and development as when most children should be speaking or walking or using alternate feet to climb stairs. As a result of their experience in early childhood programs, two caregivers help us realize the metamorphosis that some undergo:

I now look at children differently. I looked at them before as more of a parent than as a teacher because I am a parent. I would be saying, "Oh, you don't want to do that because you're going to get yourself all dirty." Whereas now, I let them go ahead and do it. We can always take their clothes off and wash them. I was looking at children from a parent's eye rather than with a teacher's eye.

All I can think of is there was a time in my life when I know I didn't know that a baby doesn't go to sleep when they're tired. You know, my conception was that they just fell asleep. The fact that you have to put them to bed was pretty obvious, I guess, but I didn't have basic knowledge of how infants should be treated.

Caregivers report that their understanding of young children deepens as they learn to observe children and be more in tune with their needs. As beginners they might have overlooked the clumsy, withdrawn, or abused child, but as experienced teachers with new understanding, they are more sensitive and can note and address important problems. Caring for children who may be unloved, undernourished, or delayed in their language development increases a child care worker's ability to look at the whole child and to recognize the interconnectedness of a child's emotional, social, cognitive, and physical development.

UNDERSTANDING ONESELF

The very nature of work with young children—observing children, interacting with parents and other professionals, teaching adults and children, and participating in in-service education activities—challenges staff members to change their own attitudes and behaviors and to reflect about their own growth and development. As one infant caregiver puts it,

> I look at infants, and I am constantly learning about myself; just how people become and how they are. It all starts when you're born and then, I think about how I was treated in a certain way . . . and how I turned out the way I did. You see how infants are so honest and uninhibited and unable to cover up anything about themselves. I mean, it's all written on their faces. You know, the older you get, the more and more you learn how to protect yourself, to cover up.

Some supervisees completely change their own attitudes toward learning. They come to view themselves as learners, embracing and valuing education. This new perception of self can represent a transformation from an earlier time characterized by school failure or dropout. A caregiver's motivation to enroll in workshops and courses, some leading to a General Educational Development (GED) certificate and even a college degree, is an indication of this new outlook. Involvement in such activities, at a stage in life when one has obligations as spouse and parent, can create family disruptions, stress, and conflict. But staff members often see these opportunities to achieve new meaning in life, to enhance their self-concept and self-respect, as outweighing the inconveniences and sacrifices they might endure.

Strength derived from supervisory support can help supervisees to understand themselves better as they cope with crises confronting the children with whom they work. An assistant teacher talks about contending with child abuse:

> When I first came here, I just did not want to talk about or even think about child abuse. I mean I could not accept it. I didn't want to deal with it. I felt that there was just no way that I could deal with it myself. . . . As time went on, we had a lot of workshops, a protective service course, and I

really got to understand where child abuse might begin, things to look for, and ways of working with children and families. I had a lot of support.

As they gain more experience on the job, supervisees are better able to deal with the developmental tasks that are part of the life cycle. Supervising others, as well as having support from a supervisor, provides caregivers with experience and nurturance that, as one worker describes it, stimulates them to "think about how I would like to be, where I am, and what I need to do to improve. It also makes me think about what's going on with me that I'm not performing the way I'd like to."

RESPECTING OTHERS

Developing a deeper understanding of oneself also promotes greater understanding of and respect for others. Working with children, families, and professionals enables caregivers to meet people they might ordinarily not have had the opportunity to know.

For those who come from backgrounds where relations outside the immediate neighborhood or community are limited or who have associated mainly with White, middle-class individuals, exposure to people from other cultures and people who speak other languages can be especially meaningful, as this coteacher points out:

> I've learned to respect other people's ways. We have a lot of Hispanic
> people here. I was brought up in another part of town where there were
> not many Hispanics, so I did not understand the culture. By working here,
> I understand. I have really broadened my thinking about other people's
> cultures: They might be different, but they're not strange, they are okay.
> I've learned about all different types of holidays because we are a multicul-
> tural school. We celebrate many holidays, including Three Kings Day and
> an African American holiday which I had never heard of. I've learned a lot
> of things about other people's cultures. You can respect them.

Supervisees learning to appreciate the cultural and ethnic differences of others will often need help and training. Staff development experiences that provide information and allow discussion of stereotypes and feelings can be of great value in helping staff gain this understanding.

Staff members show that they value other human beings in their daily work by the empathic and understanding ways that they communicate with parents, by the approaches they take to resolve differences with colleagues or supervisors, and by helping peers in times of need.

DERIVING SATISFACTION AND STIMULATION
FROM PROFESSIONAL GROWTH

Like supervisors, staff members with less experience and limited expectations about their roles tend to be satisfied with rewards that are personal and immediate. Foster grandparents or high school volunteers, for example, are likely to receive adequate gratification from a child's spontaneous hug or kiss. They derive satisfaction from loving and taking care of children and from getting to know their families. Displays of affection brighten any caregiver's day of course, but as an individual grows and develops professionally, other rewards come into play.

More experienced caregivers, for example, gain satisfaction from observing children for diagnosis of problems or to obtain greater understanding of their lives. More abstract rewards for experienced caregivers are the challenges of the job; the planning, development, and implementation of new programs; teamwork with colleagues; and participating in professional groups and associations.

One of the most remarkable aspects of the growth process of teachers is the way in which their roles change over time when they are fortunate enough to work in nurturing environments. Centers that lack organization and flexibility, where supervisors ignore staff development in favor of administrative duties, are environments that foster burnout rather than excitement, creativity, and growth. In programs where individuals are valued, it is not uncommon for supervisees to begin their careers as volunteer workers or floating substitutes and to take on new roles with major obligations as they gain experience. They may broaden their roles by training and supervising other adults, by greater involvement with families and communities, and by assuming such administrative duties as recruiting aides, helping with supplies, formulating agendas for team meetings, planning menus and preparing food, organizing social functions, and doing general paperwork. In centers where caregiver interests are considered, staff members create new roles and responsibilities for themselves based on their personal interests, which may vary from playground or classroom design to child advocacy work.

Children, of course, always come first, but professional growth opportunities for staff increase their competence and enable and motivate them to explore new dimensions of their jobs. Supervisees who feel challenged, stimulated, and enriched by their daily work may be willing to remain in their jobs over longer periods of time, despite the low pay and occasional frustration.

FORMULATING A PHILOSOPHY OF LEARNING

With experience, teachers tend to develop strong points of view about how children learn best. Early years in the education profession are usually characterized by tentativeness and ambivalence regarding teaching the right or the best way. Over time, these feelings of uncertainty are usually replaced with well-developed views of what comprises good education and child care.

As beginners, staff members are concerned with survival: learning new routines, meeting supervisor's expectations, and coping with hard-to-manage children. Everyday challenges prevent the neophyte from thinking about deeper issues pertaining to educational philosophy. Lack of experience and education, combined in some cases with little knowledge or expectation of their roles, can also slow the pace of development of a set of values and beliefs about what is best for young children. With experience and training, however, supervisees begin to formulate their views of how things should be done. Disagreements with supervisors or conflicting opinions with colleagues about how certain children should be handled or how a play area should be designed can be viewed as a positive sign of professional maturation. This comment made by a child care provider reflects the type of growth we are describing:

> Three years ago, I had much less confidence in how I felt about my work. You know, I was the one who would watch everybody else, and often I worked with teachers whom I disagreed with. I wasn't sure if I was right. I knew that I didn't agree with them, but I had no idea if my ideas were better. I just knew they were mine. Now, I can definitely walk into a situation and observe and see if the program is good or not.

VALUING GOOD SUPERVISION

Staff members also grow and change in their expectations about the type of supervision they want to receive. Expectations differ depending on supervisees' age and experience, the positions they hold, whether they are full- or part-time, and whether they are volunteers or part of the regular staff. The standards that supervisors set for them also affect their views of the supervisory process.

Part-time volunteers, for example, who help out several mornings a week with routine tasks and who provide various children with individual attention, expect little from a supervisor. They do not expect to be trained, observed, or evaluated. They often view themselves as ancillary help who are not an important part of the program. They may not anticipate that their roles will expand or change in any way. Supervisors who do not perceive volunteers to be an integral part of a center's operation may provide them with some initial direction and then leave them alone unless they create problems. This is hardly a desirable state of affairs.

The picture is quite different for regular, full-time, paid staff, particularly those who are experienced and who have gained confidence as professionals in the field. They have high expectations for supervisors and can be critical when adequate supervision is not provided. Our interviews with caregivers reveal that they hold definite opinions about the qualities they want their supervisors to have.

Honesty is one quality that was mentioned repeatedly. A caregiver who works with infants and toddlers sums up her feelings about supervisors this way:

> First of all, a supervisor should be someone who can be honest. Someone who can tell you what they think. Someone who can criticize you and praise you productively in ways that you can learn and understand and get whatever reinforcement you're supposed to get from them. Somebody who is sensitive to your needs and to the job. Somebody who believes in what you're doing, not somebody who thinks that babies would be better left at home with their parents. Somebody who knows what they're doing and knows the field.

Many supervisees emphasized the value of a supervisor who is willing to spend time with them, to listen to their thoughts, feelings, and concerns. They also wanted to be supervised by someone knowledgeable in the field. As one teacher noted:

> Somebody who can really talk about things, you know, very personal things about families, kids, and yourself. Somebody who can really, really see before a problem hits and be able to talk about it. Someone who can say, "Is something wrong?" To be able to come out and ask you this. Somebody who really has a lot of training, who can really understand because we are dealing with a lot of people who have very little in common. Supervisors need to understand how to help out families and how to help us out.

Supervisees appreciate receiving criticism that is direct and constructive. As one caregiver put it, "To give constructive criticism that would help you, not make you kind of back down. Also, to let you be creative. To make you feel that your creative ideas flow a little, too! And to be there when you need help." She also commented on the importance of feedback: "Giving feedback and following through on actual goals and work responsibilities rather than being palsy-walsy; being practical and to the point."

Staff members believe, too, that they should be able to give their supervisors constructive criticism. As one caregiver stated: "Just because their title is supervisor doesn't mean they're perfect. They shouldn't act defensive when they are criticized when it's good criticism."

Supervisees want supervisors who seek their input when making important decisions, who engage them in group problem-solving activities, and who are good role models. Such ideal supervisory qualities are not easily found in one person. A major point, however, is that staff members, especially those in advanced stages of their professional development, have high expectations for supervisors.

SEEING THE BIG PICTURE

Supervisees often begin their careers with a limited understanding of themselves, of the children and adults with whom they come in daily contact, and of the programs in which they are employed. Like supervisors, they progress through stages of concern: from self to task and others, and then to impact. Experience and maturity enable supervisees to see themselves and their work not only within the context of their programs and communities but within society at large.

With maturity, they gain understanding of the complexity of the problems facing children and families; of their social, political, and economic contexts; and of the relatedness of people and programs and the dynamic forces affecting them. This new awareness enables caregivers to be more realistic about their work and to set priorities for the future. By knowing who they are and what they want to do, they gain a sense of comfort and power.

CONCLUSION

We hope the growth shown by caregivers in our interviews offers encouragement to supervisors. Staff progress points to the value of education and supervisory support. Professional maturation does not come about automatically, quickly, or in a natural progression, but all staff members have the capacity to improve. In Parts III and IV, we will describe the specific strategies supervisors can use to help staff reach their potential.

PROGRAM ACCREDITATION

NAEYC Early Childhood Program Standards and Accreditation Criteria: The Mark of Quality in Early Childhood Education (NAEYC, 2005) includes numerous criteria related to staff under Standards 1–9, too many to list here. However, we include the topical headings of Standard 3: Teaching and suggest that supervisors consult the above text for detailed criteria:

3.A. Designing Enriched Learning Environments
3.B. Creating Communities for Learning
3.C. Supervising Children
3.D. Using Time, Grouping, and Routines to Achieve Learning Goals

3.E. Responding to Children's Interests and Needs

3.F. Making Learning Meaningful for All Children

3.G. Using Instruction to Deepen Children's Understanding and Build Their Skills and Knowledge (pp. 28–33)

EXERCISES

1. On 5" × 7" cards, write a brief informal description of each staff member in your program and write down 1–3 action steps that you can take to help them develop further.
2. Suggest to new staff that they keep a log or diary to record significant events and/or new insights and understandings related to growth in their role.
3. Ask staff members to identify 2 or 3 criteria from the CDA competencies (Council for Professional Recognition, n.d.), NAEYC teaching criteria (NAEYC, 2005), or the early childhood standards of the National Board of Professional Teaching Standards (NBPTS, 2004) and to develop a plan for demonstrating those criteria during the coming school year.

THE DEVELOPMENTAL DYNAMIC AT WORK: A CASE STUDY IN SUPERVISION

IN CHAPTER 5 WE DISCUSSED three components of the developmental dynamic: supervisor, supervisee, and context. We also pointed to the necessity of assessing a staff member's developmental level and the problem being addressed to determine the most appropriate supervisory strategy. In Chapters 6 and 7, we elaborated on some of the developmental characteristics of supervisors and staff members. The purpose of this chapter is to illustrate the elements of the developmental dynamic at work.

BACKGROUND

The Supervisor

Rebecca is a graduate of a liberal arts college where she majored in politics and government. After graduation, she spent a year as a trainee in a large department store chain but left since she did not like the work. She is single, 29 years old, and lives on the outskirts of a major city on the East Coast.

Rebecca received her master's degree in early childhood education after teaching in a Head Start program for 3 years. For the past 3 years, she has been the director of a medium-sized day care center. As a third-year supervisor, Rebecca feels pretty comfortable in her role. She has a strong theoretical base in child development. The experience she had working in Head Start has been enormously helpful to her. Rebecca is reasonably confident in her ability as director of this program but occasionally gets thrown off guard when conflicts arise.

The Supervisee

Mrs. Warren is a 66-year-old widow who lives with her daughter and two grand-children. She belongs to a senior citizen's organization that has provided her with part-time employment in this children's center. The job enables Mrs. Warren to earn spending money and to feel that she is doing constructive activity in retire-ment. She has been on the job for 3 months. She is in excellent health, depend-able, and always at work early. Mrs. Warren enjoys her work, especially the unqualified love and affection she receives from most of the children.

The Context

Located in a small city, the East Side Child Development Center is a nonprofit cen-ter funded through the state department of social services. Most of the children are from low-income families, and about 15% are "protective" children, placed in the center because of abuse or neglect. The center has two groups of 3-year-olds, two of 4s, and a kindergarten. Each classroom has a teacher and an aide, and at least one senior citizen aide from a state-funded program. There are also several practicum students from the local community college. Rebecca has the help of a head teacher who is released half-time to work on curriculum and staff development.

Rebecca has strived to establish a collaborative atmosphere in her program where people work together. She places great trust and confidence in her staff members, but she does find it difficult to confront them about problems, as she does not want to be disrespectful to them or tarnish the humanistic climate she has worked so hard to establish.

The Problem

Mrs. Warren is great with kids, except in areas of discipline. When she does take disciplinary action, she often shouts and sometimes overdoes the punishment. For example, when a little boy was flipping a plant around on a wire hanger, she went across the room and shouted loudly at him to stop and made him sit in a corner. After 5 minutes, the head teacher told the child to return to his play. Mrs. Warren felt that her authority had been undermined. The one time that Rebecca raised the issue of disciplining children with Mrs. Warren, Rebecca was flabbergasted when Mrs. Warren admonished her for letting the children get away with certain things.

ASSESSING THE SUPERVISEE

At this point in her life, Mrs. Warren has developed strongly held views of child rearing. Whether she is open to learning and to modifying her ideas and values is a question Rebecca plans to explore. Mrs. Warren has been in this position for only 3 months, however, and there is much that she could learn about group care for young children.

Mrs. Warren does not see herself as an important part of the center. She keeps pretty much to herself. She carries out assigned duties, as a beginner, but she does not have a total picture of the operation and mission of the program.

Rebecca has noted Mrs. Warren's enjoyment of her work and that she is effective most of the time; on the other hand, her apparent lack of flexibility is an area of concern to Rebecca.

Based on observations over time, Rebecca views Mrs. Warren as being at the lower end of the continuum in terms of level of abstract thinking and in the middle to upper range in terms of commitment to her job. Taking this information into account with what she knows about Mrs. Warren's status as a beginner in the program, and what she has summarized about her strengths and her needs and goals during retirement, Rebecca has determined that her initial supervisory approach will primarily be directive, with the intention of moving into a collaborative mode when possible.

ASSESSING THE SUPERVISOR

Two years ago, Rebecca probably would have ignored this problem. Although she is anxious about her upcoming conference with Mrs. Warren, she is determined to go through with it, since she knows she cannot permit staff members to use such punitive measures with children.

Although she is certain she will feel uncomfortable in being directive with a proud woman who is old enough to be her mother, Rebecca has been gaining confidence in herself as a supervisor. She knows which behaviors are developmentally appropriate for children, and she is very clear about the nature of the environment she wants to create for them. Because of her graduate work and previous teaching experience, Rebecca is aware of resources she can use to train her staff, and she has definite ideas as to what the content of the training sessions should be and how to conduct them. Rebecca is determined to make her program a model one, and she devotes a great deal of time and energy to her work.

THE SUPERVISORY PLAN

Rebecca has formulated a plan for working with Mrs. Warren. She may use all of the possible strategies she has identified or may choose from among them. These include the following:

1. Going out of her way to make Mrs. Warren feel like a special person and recognizing the good work she has been doing.

2. Working out a structured daily schedule for Mrs. Warren that emphasizes routines and clarifies her role in working with 5-year-olds.
3. Holding an immediate conference with Mrs. Warren to deal with the issue of shouting at children. She expects to be very directive in dealing with this issue.
4. Taking time to observe Mrs. Warren in the classroom.
5. Holding individual conferences with Mrs. Warren on a regular basis. Recognizing that Mrs. Warren is a mature adult who has a high degree of self-respect and self-esteem, Rebecca believes that through these conferences, Mrs. Warren will feel respected, even though she and Rebecca may disagree on when and how children should be reprimanded.

    During these conferences, Rebecca hopes to learn more about Mrs. Warren's previous work and family experiences. She also plans to discuss the issue of disciplining children by eliciting from Mrs. Warren descriptions of her past experiences in raising children and connecting those to the conditions, needs, and behaviors of children in the program.

    By providing feedback to her from observations and by raising questions to clarify situations, Rebecca expects Mrs. Warren to begin to reflect on her behavior in disciplining children.
6. Providing monthly training sessions for Mrs. Warren and the other two senior assistants to deal with child care techniques and to provide them with opportunities to share their thoughts with each other and with Rebecca. These sessions will include demonstrating and role-playing behaviors, which will illustrate how to respond to children when they misbehave. Child growth and development issues will be discussed. In this way, Mrs. Warren will be able to test new behavior in safe situations and test her thinking with peers.
7. Inviting Mrs. Warren to staff meetings with the full-time staff so that she will feel part of the program and learn from other staff.

CONCLUSION

In formulating her supervisory plan, Rebecca has considered Mrs. Warren's stage of professional and personal development and the specific issue at hand—how and when to discipline children in light of their own growth and development. Rebecca has also made some judgments about Mrs. Warren's commitment to the job and her ability to analyze problems and generate solutions to them.

Rebecca and Mrs. Warren are at different points in their lives and careers. The knowledge, experience, competencies, and goals that each has, of course, will affect the outcome of this case. By taking into consideration personal, professional, and contextual factors relating to Mrs. Warren and to this particular problem, Rebecca has been able to develop a plan that is both realistic and growth oriented. She has mapped out a variety of avenues for supervision, so that she can confront the problem while also providing support. She will then be able to move toward a collaborative style, and perhaps eventually to a nondirective mode, while maintaining the humanistic climate that she values.

A good resource for additional work with cases is *On the Case: Approaches to Language and Literacy Research* (Dyson & Genishi, 2005). If you are interested in writing cases or teaching with cases, you may wish to consider *Teaching and the Case Method* (Christensen & Hanson, 1987).

EXERCISES

1. What aspects of the "developmental dynamic" described in Chapter 5 are illustrated in this situation?
2. Develop your own case study based on a problem that you have encountered with a staff member. Use the information from the chapters in this part to make a plan for supporting your supervisee.
3. Ask staff members to write a minicase or vignette of one or two paragraphs describing a critical incident in their work with children. Duplicate these and use them as a basis for a meaningful professional development program by having staff read and discuss them.

PART III

A FRAMEWORK FOR SUPERVISION

CHAPTER 9

CLINICAL SUPERVISION

C LINICAL SUPERVISION WAS DEVELOPED in the 1960s at Harvard University by Morris Cogan (1973) and Robert Goldhammer (1969). Originally, it was designed as a collaborative, interactive process among teachers, interns, curriculum specialists, and professors who worked in Harvard's Master of Arts in Teaching program (Goldhammer, 1966). Its purpose was to assist graduate student interns in improving their teaching of children who were attending summer school in a nearby district. During the years since its original inception, the clinical supervision model was adopted by many school districts; however, its focus was changed. It primarily became a one-to-one encounter between administrator and teacher whose main goal was the evaluation of a teacher's performance.

In recent years, however, there has been a return to clinical supervision as it was originally intended—with a focus on the ongoing professional development of staff members. This change reflects a convergence of several trends in education: the establishment of new mentor programs, the recognition of the important role that peers can play in the supervisory process, a greater understanding of the significance of teachers taking charge of their own learning, and the realization that supervision concentrating solely on evaluation is limited in its ability to assist staff members in improving the ways in which they carry out their jobs. Now colleagues in the roles of mentors or partners are participating in the clinical supervisory process, working in groups or on a one-to-one basis (see Chapter 15 for some examples).

Teachers unfamiliar with this model or already accustomed to supervision as evaluation may need assistance in understanding their role as a full partner with the director, head teacher, or mentor in the clinical supervisory process. Clinical supervision has the potential to strengthen the relationship between supervisor and teacher, as an ongoing dialogue about their work with children promotes an openness and fosters change.

Both individual and group clinical supervision can take place within a program that has a multifaceted approach to supporting staff. Some teachers benefit from one-on-one supervision with a director, mentor, or head teacher some of the time; however, pairs of teachers on their own or groups of teachers with or without their supervisor can learn to work together and take responsibility for their own growth and development.

THE FIVE STAGES OF CLINICAL SUPERVISION

Clinical supervision is carried out through a series of stages that are repeated to form an ongoing cycle. The five stages are the preobservation conference, the observation, the analysis and strategy, the supervision conference, and the postconference analysis (Cogan, 1973). The behavioral content of these stages varies depending on the purpose that supervisors and/or staff members establish.

Stage 1: Preobservation Conference

During preobservation conferences, participants have an opportunity to begin to establish positive working relationships with each other, laying the groundwork for the development of mutual trust and respect throughout each stage of the supervisory cycle.

Initial conferences are occasions to diffuse anxiety and to explain the cycle of clinical supervision and the roles of each participant in this new relationship. Preobservation conferences, in general, offer opportunities to discuss serious concerns, to review the purposes and procedures of an upcoming lesson with children, to make plans for an observation, to agree on its focus, and to establish a time for the postobservation conference.

Stage 2: Observation

Supervisors or peers may observe teachers and/or children at work during formal lessons or informal periods. The specific purpose of an observation is usually agreed on during the preobservation conference, during which the type of observation to be made and the tools for observing are determined. The observation is the link between the plans made during Stage 1 and actual practice. It affords supervisors or peers an opportunity to see the situation in which the teacher's questions and concerns originated and to determine whether answers can be found (Cogan, 1973).

Stage 3: Analysis and Strategy

As teachers often prefer to talk with their supervisors right away, it is tempting to provide immediate feedback at the conclusion of an observation. However, taking the time to analyze observational data and to think about the conference that is to follow increases the success and power of the clinical supervisory cycle. During the analysis and planning stage, supervisors or peer teachers "reconstruct" observed events, note the context in which they occurred, identify patterns of behavior and critical incidents that developed. Observed events are analyzed in terms of the concerns raised during the preobservation conference, and strategies are formulated for use in the postobservation conference. The teachers who were observed also need time to reflect about their teaching and to plan for the follow-up conference.

Stage 4: Supervision Conference

Cogan (1973) states that "the conference is a shared exploration: a search for the meaning of instruction, for choices among alternative diagnoses, and alternative strategies for improvement" (p. 197).

The conference is a time for teachers to reflect on the lesson and to share their analyses and for the observer(s) to provide feedback to the teacher about the observation. Both parties can jointly formulate strategies for dealing with problems and can raise issues of concern. During the conference, observers can also offer specific help if appropriate, explore the rewarding and satisfying aspects of a staff member's performance, and plan for the next observation. Each conference varies in purpose, in content, and in the nature of supervisor-supervisee or peer interaction, depending on the individuals and circumstances involved and the balance of power and control between them.

Stage 5: Postconference Analysis

The postconference analysis is a means of self-improvement for supervisors and staff members. It is a time when participants assess the nature of their communication during the conference, the effectiveness of strategies used, the role that each individual played, and the extent to which progress was made on the issues discussed.

GROUP CLINICAL SUPERVISION

While a director, coordinator, head teacher, or mentor may carry out this five-stage cycle with individuals, opportunities for staff to engage in group or collaborative clinical supervision maximize a supervisor's use of time and place supervisors in the role of facilitator, which can be very rewarding.

In her classic study of workplace conditions for school success, Little (1982) found that continuous professional development—that is, "learning on the job"—is most likely and thoroughly achieved in those schools that provide opportunities for teachers to discuss their classroom practice, to observe and critique each other's teaching, and to work together in preparing curriculum and improving instruction. Group clinical supervision can foster these conditions.

Group clinical supervision also has the potential to create a culture of community and colleagueship among staff members. Cogan (1973) viewed clinical supervision as professional company for the teacher. This notion of "keeping the teacher company" conveys a positive image of supervision. Groups of staff members working together with a supervisor can have the effect of reducing isolation and bolstering self-confidence and morale because of the company and support provided.

We view group clinical supervision as a process whereby teachers, other professional support staff, and supervisors engage each other in planning, observing, and assessing instruction. Each program will have to develop its own format for group clinical supervision; however, we do make some suggestions for a structure in Chapters 10 and 11.

CONCLUSION

Clinical supervision offers early childhood supervisors a framework for working with staff members. It is a planned and systematic procedure for fostering the development of caregivers. It is one approach that early childhood supervisors can use to support individuals who are undertaking different personal and professional tasks and who have varied preparation and experience levels. For a more detailed description of clinical supervision, we suggest that you read the texts already cited in this chapter, as well as *Approaches to Clinical Supervision: Alternatives for Improving Instruction* (Pajak, 2000).

In the two chapters that follow we will discuss aspects of clinical supervision in more detail. In Chapter 10 we describe the purposes of the supervisory conference, communication skills that supervisors need in order to conduct successful conferences, and the key ingredients in any supervisory conference. The material in Chapter 10 is directly connected to Stages 1, 3, and 5 of clinical supervision. And in Chapter 11, we describe some approaches to observing staff—Stage 2—and give specific suggestions for constructing observation instruments. We also describe a type of group supervision called Lesson Study in Chapter 15.

CHAPTER 10

THE SUPERVISORY CONFERENCE

T HE CONFERENCE IS THE HEART of clinical supervision. It enables supervisors and supervisees to come together to jointly solve the significant problems of caregiving and teaching. In addition to ensuring ongoing and systematic communication between supervisor and supervisee, supervisory conferences are held to:

- Discuss, interpret, and evaluate issues pertaining to teaching/caregiving
- Develop long- and short-range plans with staff members
- Discuss issues regarding specific children and/or families
- Enable supervisors and supervisees to raise concerns and to resolve problems
- Transmit and discuss basic information about program policies and procedures
- Plan for an observation or to discuss staff performance after an observation
- Show interest in teachers' work
- Convey a planned disciplinary action
- Present and discuss a formal evaluation
- Enable the supervisor to obtain advice and information

Regardless of the reason for meeting with teachers, a goal of the conference is to help staff members think about, think through, analyze, and make decisions about their work with young children. Through the conference dialogue, which includes asking questions and offering information, supervisors can assist teachers in the decision-making processes involved in planning for teaching, reflecting on their practice, and applying what they learned.

Although a supervisor may have informal conversations with a supervisee during the course of a day, these meetings are not good substitutes for scheduled conferences where issues can be explored in depth and in thoughtful ways. When supervisors make a commitment to confer with staff members on a regular basis, and not just for evaluation purposes, caregivers believe that supervisors value them and their work.

THE CONTEXT

The success of the supervisory conference is largely determined by the nature of the existing relationship between supervisor and staff member and the professional culture in which they are working. The climate, context, and mood of a conference are affected by previous contacts that the two individuals have had and by the assumptions, beliefs, expectations, and perceptions that they have about themselves, each other, and each other's roles.

Power and Control

As supervisors are in official positions of authority and power, they set the tone for the supervisory conference. What kind of powers do early childhood supervisors have, and how can they use them judiciously?

Individuals in supervisory positions possess knowledge and expertise about young children and strategies for facilitating their cognitive, social, and emotional development. These can be shared to strengthen a caregiver's capacity to interact with young children and to cope with problems. Supervisors have access to material resources and to a network of human resources that can make the caregiver's role easier to carry out. They have control of the ways in which caregivers spend time within a program, which permits them to limit the demands placed on a staff member. They can directly influence how peers and those in higher positions think about particular staff members. Most important, they can use their power to encourage supervisees to become more independent.

Supervisees also have power. They have expertise, in some cases more than their supervisors. They have contractual agreements, especially in public school settings, that guarantee them certain rights and privileges and that protect them from abuse. They can influence the opinions and attitudes of their peers. And they have the power to refuse help.

Either party can control a conference. The person doing most of the talking may be dominating and controlling the conference if he or she allows the listener few opportunities to ask questions or to make a point. On the other hand, supervisors who consciously refrain from talk to permit supervisees to express their thoughts and feelings are still in control and are helping without dominating.

Establishing the conference agenda is another form of power. If all or most of the issues discussed are supervisor initiated, then the supervisee may not have had an opportunity to set priorities and may not have thought about those issues prior to the meeting. Such "ceremonial" conferences lead to feelings in staff members of being cut off from expressing immediate concerns so they often choose instead to end the ritual as soon as possible.

The pace and timing of conference dialogue are other indicators of who is controlling the conference. One party or the other may rush through or abort discussion of a certain issue. Refusal by the supervisee, or the supervisor for that matter, to elaborate on a problem and to express true thoughts about it is a way of exercising power.

Developmental Levels

The stage of development of a staff member is a factor for the supervisor to consider in determining the nature of help to provide during a conference. Staff members who have difficulty analyzing problems and thinking of solutions may be assisted by supervisors who probe and ask clarifying questions that focus and gradually lead supervisees toward solutions. In other cases, supervisors can be enablers by holding back, listening to teachers think through problems without offering information. By informally assessing the developmental characteristics of staff members described in Chapter 5, supervisors can make better decisions about which strategies to use with which individuals.

Communication Skills

We believe that much of the success of a conference depends on the clarity of communication that takes place between supervisors and staff members. The characteristics of people who facilitate the growth of others, as Carl Rogers (1962) has described, have special relevance within the context of helping:

> The helping person is more likely to make the relationship a growth promoting one when he communicates a desire to understand the other person's meanings and feelings. This attitude of wanting to understand is expressed in a variety of ways. When he talks, the helping person is less inclined to give instruction and advice, thus creating a climate which fosters independence. He avoids criticism and withholds evaluative judgments of the other person's ideas, thoughts, feelings, and behavior. He listens more often than he talks and when he speaks he strives to understand what the other person is communicating in thoughts and feeling. The comments of the helping person are aimed at assisting the other individual to clarify his own meanings and attitudes. Such behavior on the part of the helping person communicates the all important desire to understand, which in turn breeds the trust and confidence which are so essential to growth and development. (p. 417)

By conscious use of specific communication skills, supervisors can increase the possibility that they will attain shared meanings and understandings with supervisees. Listening, questioning, and offering information are three of these communication behaviors. Paying attention to nonverbal messages is also a consideration when conferring with staff.

Nonverbal Communication

There is much truth to the old adage that "It's not what you say, but how you say it." Darn (2005) reminds us that approximately 90% of our communication is nonverbal and that it generally has three purposes: defining relationships, managing identity, and conveying attitudes and feelings (not ideas). There is a great variety of types of nonverbal communication, which Darn classified into the following 13 categories: kinesics (body language), proxemics (space), haptics (touch), oculesics (eye contact), chronemics (time), olfactics (smell), vocalics (voice tone, volume, speed), sound symbols (grunting, mumbling), silence, adornment (clothing, jewelry, hairstyle), posture, locomotion (walking, running), and expression (frowns, grimaces, smiles). Many of these categories can be useful for analyzing supervisor/teacher conferences, even informally. *The Nonverbal Dictionary of Gestures, Signs and Body Language Cues* (Givens, 2005) is a wonderful resource for learning more about interpreting this aspect of our communication.

Being an effective listener and a skilled observer of nonverbal cues takes practice. Supervisors can start by consciously watching facial expressions, eye contact, and body posture and gestures for meaning. Being aware of one's own nonverbal signals and the messages they are conveying is also an important first step as well as recognizing that different cultural groups have different interpretations of nonverbal expressions.

Active Listening

Active, attentive listening is one of the most critical supervisory conference skills in facilitating open and effective communication without dominating. Like teachers, supervisors often believe that they are not helping another unless they are telling, advising, and offering suggestions. The tendency by supervisors to talk a great deal during conferences can have the effect of making them feel good but can also cut off serious communication and, despite good intentions, can prevent helping.

In active listening, we show respect for the person and interest in what that person is saying. Eye contact and body language are ways that we convey interest. Checking our understanding of what that person really means is important before we respond. This can be done by asking the speaker to repeat what was said. Oftentimes, a person clarifies a statement when it is repeated. Asking the speaker to clarify a term used and to elaborate is also helpful:

- What do you mean when you say, "Alex misbehaves"? Could you give some examples?

Another technique is to paraphrase our understanding of what the speaker said by transposing it and putting it into our own words and asking for verification:

- So you are suggesting that Ann has excellent interpersonal skills with adults and would make a wonderful mentor teacher? Am I correct?
- I hear you saying that you are frustrated by Jamie's behavior. Am I right?

The good listener works on several levels to understand both the person—what he or she is feeling, wanting, or hoping—and the message.

Silence

If we come from a culture in which talk is expected most of the time, we are sometimes uncomfortable with silence. Supervisors striving to be good listeners, however, need not fear moments of silence. In certain situations, silence is golden (Johnson, 1979):

> *Silence almost never offends.* While almost anything someone says can be seen as offensive under some circumstances, silence is gloriously neutral. It calls for no rebuttals, defenses, or new evidence.
> *Silence is a verbal cathartic.* Most people are unable to tolerate silence for long. If two people are in a room together and one is silent, the other will feel a compulsion to say something, if only to fill the silence. If you want someone to speak, keep quiet, and before many seconds have elapsed he will.
> *Silence is nonjudgmental.* Most people are careful of what they say because they expect to be judged. When a subordinate tells you he hates his job and would rather [not] . . . work another day, and you respond with silence, he will be greatly relieved at your failure to make a judgment. If you aren't more careful with your silence, he may even wind up thinking you're a nice guy. (pp. 75–76)

Asking Questions

Questioning is critical to accomplishing conference goals and in training supervisees to think through and analyze their behavior. Supervisors ask questions for different reasons, so the form of questions should change based on their purpose. For example, soliciting information from a supervisee usually requires *simple questions* to bring out facts or to clarify a problem so that both supervisor and supervisee have a common basis to build on for discussion:

- Can you tell me something about how you and your aide plan together?
- Why don't you describe your daily schedule so I have a clearer picture of how free play fits into the whole program?

Supervisors also ask questions to help teachers understand children's behavior, the causes of behavior, and the relationship of observed behaviors to previous behaviors. *Probing questions* invite the caregiver to think about the teaching act and to articulate reasons for behavior:

- Mario was throwing paper and hitting other children during cleanup. I've noticed that he has done this before. Do you have any thoughts as to why he tends to act out during these times?

- Tell me your strategy for working with Yolanda. She has improved so much. Why do you think she is responding?
- What would you like the children to gain from the lesson you plan to do on the calendar?

Questions that solicit consideration of *alternative decisions*, and *predictions* of what might happen with each alternative, help the caregiver make plans for future teaching:

- Can you think of some ways to change the arrangement of the dramatic-play area that would encourage the children to put the clothes away when they are through?
- What do you think they're likely to do if there are cartons for the clothes versus having them on hangers?

Questions that *ask for opinions*, whereby supervisees evaluate something that has taken place; questions that encourage supervisees to *express their feelings* about a particular situation; and questions that ask supervisees to *clarify* by repeating a statement or by providing an example or illustration also contribute to clear communication:

- That was the first time that you used the "Wiggly Fingers" song with the children. In your opinion, was it effective? Why? Why not?
- The children really got into finger painting. You seemed a little overwhelmed. Did the mess bother you?
- When you say, "It's always so wild," are you saying that they are too excited about going out or that they aren't sure what they're supposed to do?

Offering Praise

Regular conferences, whether to discuss particular problems or for other purposes, are a perfect opportunity for the supervisor to offer praise. Praise must be authentic, however, before its true value as a positive reinforcer and climate builder can be realized. Most teachers understand themselves well enough to know when praise is deserved. They can easily distinguish between superficial "stroking" and sincere encouragement, appreciation, and praise.

Praise is more effective when it is specific, as it enables supervisees to know which behaviors supervisors are pleased about. Reinforcing staff with praise when they demonstrate desired behaviors encourages them as they struggle to develop skills or to overcome problems. Pointing out these behaviors and avoiding the use of "good" is a more effective way of praising:

- When the children were pushing each other and you quietly walked over and gently placed them in line, they quieted right down.

Supervisors are often preoccupied with staff members who have problems and sometimes overlook and take for granted those caregivers who meet their expectations. These individuals need support as much as the others. Offering special encouragement or recognition when a staff member believes that he or she has just overcome a hurdle or made a significant accomplishment can also have lasting benefits.

Offering Information

Supervisors frequently offer information to supervisees during conferences. As leaders with knowledge and experience, supervisors are expected to share their expertise with staff members at appropriate times.

One of the most difficult supervisory habits to overcome, however, is offering too much information too often. This tendency probably arises out of a supervisory perception of "information giving" as helping, coupled with a need and desire to help.

A different conception of helping is to hold back information in favor of listening or questioning. This is a valid means of providing the supervisee with "thinking space" to arrive at his or her own solutions to problems. The trick, of course, is to make the right decision about when to offer information and when not to, keeping in mind the goal of enabling staff to be effective in their work and to assume responsibility for their own improvement.

There are many instances when giving supervisees specific information is appropriate. Staff members may need new ideas and suggestions. They may want to be connected to human and material resources to provide for an enriched program. They might benefit from particular illustrations of individual or group behaviors as a way of understanding themselves or the children with whom they are working. But this information is best brought forth after they have had time to try to discover it for themselves and when they are ready to hear it.

Another consideration in offering information is how to disclose data. Supervisors often confer with supervisees after a classroom observation, during which they collected data about teacher and child behavior and/or the learning environment. Showing this information to staff members in a nonevaluative manner can become a basis for mutual discussion. Supervisees then have an opportunity to select which issues to explore and to determine whether their behavior is congruent with their values and goals.

Listening, questioning, praising, and offering information are communication behaviors that need practice to become natural parts of the supervisory dialogue.

Intercultural Communication

Harris and Moran (2000) describe *intercultural communication* as a process of sharing perceptual fields. A person's distinctive *perceptual field* consists of familial, educational, religious, and social backgrounds, and enables each person to process information uniquely. Two individuals can thus receive the same message, but interpret and filter it differently. Each person processes those segments that are consistent with his or her own cultural background and reality. When the originator of the message is from one cultural group and the receiver from another, the interaction is intercultural communication.

When supervisors confer with staff members who have cultural backgrounds and perceptual fields different from their own, it is important that their communication be culturally sensitive. Realistically, it is not possible to be intimately knowledgeable of the language and the cultural patterns of every culture represented among families and staff members within a program, but it is possible to be aware of those cultural variables that have a bearing on communicating with understanding, and to learn about a culture that is represented by a majority of staff members and children in a program and even to study their language if it is different. There are several specific cultural factors that can affect communication and supervision.

Time Sense

Mainstream North American culture places importance on being prompt for appointments, meetings, classes, and work. Some groups, however, have a different sense of time. Supervisors sometimes strive to get things accomplished in a short amount of time because there is so much to do. This situation can create pressure to rush through supervisory conferences, causing internal conflicts in supervisors and dissatisfaction in supervisees, particularly if supervisees come from cultural backgrounds that place a great value on human relationships. Supervisors and staff members who come from cultures where individuals have a "long view" of time and/or prefer to allow more time for activities involving human interaction may be offended by hastened communication.

Space

Some North Americans, depending on cultural background, feel that their personal space is invaded if the distance between themselves and others when engaged in conversation is too close. They like a comfort zone. Others come from cultures that prefer closer speaking distances and are used to body contact when greeting each other and during conversations. Individuals who are comfortable with contact may view those who aren't as unfriendly; those who prefer closeness may be perceived as being forward, loud, or aggressive by persons accustomed to distance.

Verbal and Nonverbal Communication

Metaphors, stories, or examples used in conversations to explain an idea or a concept may be culture-bound and can impede understanding between individuals. When conferring with staff who speak a native language different from theirs, supervisors need to be aware of the complexity of language used. Bowers and Flinders (1991) suggest that it is best to employ a common vocabulary, avoiding words with multiple meanings. Further, how something is said is as important as what is said; loudness and softness, pitch, and rhythm have various cultural connotations. Loudness in one culture, for example, may set an accusatory tone, while in another it is simply a common way of speaking.

The pace of conversation is also culture-bound. Whereas some individuals may be comfortable with fast-paced dialogue, others may come from cultures where conversation is slower, where more time is taken for questions and reflection, where pauses are longer, and where partners have greater opportunities to respond.

As supervisors and supervisees "read" each other during conferences, they often pay attention to nonverbal cues in order to make decisions about when to speak, what to say next, and what content direction the conference should take. As pointed out earlier, facial expressions, body posture, gestures, and eye contact convey meaning; these messages can vary from culture to culture.

Values

Cultural attitudes, assumptions, beliefs, and values held by supervisors and staff members influence decision making and behavior in the workplace and are likely to be at the heart of many discussions between them, particularly when they do not have the same background. For example, a supervisor may believe that change is needed in the program, a staff member's primary obligation should be to his or her work, and each staff member should express his or her opinion freely. A staff member, on the other hand, may value tradition, continuity, and stability and thus resist change; may place family responsibilities and the pursuit of relationships first; and may defer to the supervisor as the person in authority and therefore say very little, raise few questions, and be reluctant to express opinions in supervisory conferences. It's easy to see how these assumptions on both sides could cause confusion or miscommunication.

Concepts of Authority

Concepts of authority are formed in one's early family and schooling experiences. In some cultures, children are raised in very protected family environments where dependence is encouraged as well as strict obedience to the authority figure, who is often the male head of family. Women are not expected to take on authority roles, and girls in particular are taught not to question authority. In schools, giving a teacher a correct answer may be valued over independence of thought. Also, individuals from cultures where the political climate is autocratic expect those in school supervisory positions to be authoritarian and may view nondirective supervisory behavior as a form of weakness.

Values; concepts of time, space, and authority; and aspects of verbal and nonverbal language are factors that have a bearing on intercultural communication. By observing, asking questions, and careful listening in pre- and postteaching conferences, supervisors and teachers can come to know each other's assumptions and presuppositions about teaching and value systems that affect their decisions in the workplace and relationships with children, colleagues, and supervisors (Bowers & Flinders, 1991). Sensitive intercultural communication among adults in the early childhood settings can contribute to positive experiences for children.

STRUCTURING THE CONFERENCE

Each type of conference has a different focus and purpose, which can alter its structure. Different approaches might be required, for example, to resolve a particular problem, to plan an upcoming observation, to discuss a completed observation, or simply to maintain good communication. A conference requested by a staff member to discuss serious concerns might be open-ended in nature, while a postobservation meeting might be formal and highly structured. There are, however, common elements to all conferences, regardless of the topic being discussed: preparing, climate building, purpose setting, guiding, closing, and analyzing.

Preparing for the Conference

Careful thought about an upcoming conference offers greater assurance that it will be productive and successful. The extent of preparation necessary varies depending on the purpose of the conference and the sensitivity and seriousness of topics being discussed.

Location is an important consideration. Finding a suitable and private place to talk is most desirable, although it can be a problem for supervisors who work in more than one site or in a small or crowded center.

Arranging for a block of uninterrupted time, free from telephone calls and other disruptions that disturb the flow of communication, can also help both parties relax and think more clearly. Having adequate time, yet setting a time limit, is also helpful.

As a supervisor, in preparing for a conference, you might want to ask yourself the following questions:

- What do I want to accomplish in this meeting?
- Are there specific understandings to develop with the caregiver?
- If the conference is one of a series that has focused on a staff member's behavior in certain situations, what do I want that individual to know or to learn in this meeting about his or her behavior?

You may also wish to plan conference questions or statements ahead of time to use as needed, especially when anticipating difficult conferences concerning interpersonal or evaluative issues. If it is a postobservation conference, it is helpful to study the data collected at the time of the observation to refresh your memory. If it is an evaluation conference, it may be useful to review notes kept over time and to examine the materials in the staff member's portfolio. Rereading the program's evaluation policy statement, having at hand pertinent materials such as evaluation forms or the center's handbook, and thinking about how they might be used during the conference are also steps that can be taken to increase supervisory confidence, and to facilitate and add depth to the meeting.

You may find it helpful to identify a conference agenda beforehand and to prioritize issues that should be discussed. Flexibility is important, however, since an agenda may have to be abandoned to deal with a supervisee's immediate concerns. A conference should be focused so as to address one or two main issues in depth, instead of superficially covering a range of issues, which can serve to raise the anxiety level of a supervisee.

Teachers should also be encouraged to prepare for the conference by thinking about their goals and by laying out a tentative agenda ahead of time. The purpose of the conference and developmental levels of the teacher and supervisor will determine the extent of each party's participation and the agenda that unfolds.

Creating a Climate

The supervisor who is competent, helpful, and in control of the situation creates a positive conference climate. Actions that convey honesty and professionalism and that focus on performance contribute to the image of supervisor as a qualified and supportive individual.

Conferences can be threatening to staff members, since topics that are discussed often have to do with their performance. If a delicate issue is to be raised, the supervisor might also be anxious about the meeting. Anxieties are lessened when the supervisor, as leader, takes the initiative to set a working tone for the meeting.

The physical arrangement of the conference space—placement of furniture, noise level, ventilation, and so forth—adds to or takes away from the tone the supervisor wishes to achieve. A supervisor who sits behind a desk establishes a formal atmosphere, one in which the supervisee is clearly in a subordinate role to an authority figure. There may be times when a supervisor will need to reinforce and execute his or her authority through a formal setting, but in most cases conference environments that help staff members feel at ease, raise concerns, and ask for suggestions and advice are preferable. An informal arrangement, which puts supervisor and supervisee face-to-face on the same level without artificial physical barriers, is much more conducive to these goals.

Friendly comments, a cup of coffee, or a humorous story can break the ice, diffuse anxiety in either individual, and lay the foundation for a productive meeting. On the other hand, if both parties are braced for a tense encounter, it may be best to get to the issue directly. The decision of when to address the key concern often has to be made on the spot.

Setting the Purpose

When the purpose of a conference is clear and agreed on ahead of time, there is no need for you and your supervisee to guess the reason for meeting. You can focus on the agenda much more quickly. You might wish to set aside a few minutes at the beginning of the session to clarify its purpose and to enable the caregiver to suggest issues to be explored. Once an agenda is mutually agreed on, items can be prioritized.

For example, the following issues might be discussed in a postobservation conference after a single classroom visit:

Making cleanup go smoothly
Settling the children into nap time
Handling a disruptive child
Extending children's thinking during free play

Although the overall conference purpose would be to analyze the activities observed, each specific issue could become the central theme of one or several conferences so it is important to narrow the agenda. The staff member may raise issues independently and decide that getting help in working with the disruptive child is most critical at this time. Concurring, the supervisor will encourage the staff member to share that concern. If the teacher failed to raise this important matter, the supervisor would have to do so.

Unexpected issues, which cannot be planned for, also arise during conferences. Artful supervisors learn when to pick up on a thought, when to screen it out, and when to pull back from one issue or push ahead to another.

As mentioned earlier, the developmental characteristics of the staff member and the nature of the issue(s) to be discussed will in large part determine the extent to which the supervisor or the supervisee takes the lead in setting the agenda and the structure for the conference.

Guiding the Conference

The body of the conference is the part during which the issues selected are elaborated on, explored, and discussed. During this phase, the conferees describe the behavior of teacher and children, share and analyze data from an observation, raise problems, note progress, and exchange basic information. The supervisor has an opportunity to reinforce a staff member and to put into practice the skills of asking good questions, listening attentively, and offering appropriate information. By describing and asking questions, supervisors can assist teachers in the reflective process.

Describing means to provide the supervisee with an account, a portrait of what was observed, without making judgments about it; for example, having chosen "working with a disruptive child" as a focus, here is a nonjudgmental description by a supervisor:

> I noticed that Mark was poking Sharon and Gail during circle time. When it was over, he went into the block area and knocked over Josh's tower and kicked the blocks with his feet. He then took the cards that Josh was using to label his buildings and ran to the far corner of the room with them. You were getting ready for the cooking lesson when Mark was disturbing Josh in the block-building area.

Once the behavior has been described, the supervisor can begin to assist the supervisee in interpreting and evaluating it by questioning and listening:

> Why do you think Mark was so disruptive today? He started to misbehave during circle time. How did you respond to him then? How else might you have handled the situation? What could you do to be more aware of what is taking place in various parts of the room?

When the conversation goes off on a tangent, a supervisor will find it necessary to bring it back into focus. If a staff member has difficulty thinking through an issue or arriving at possible solutions, then the supervisor may have to offer more information and ask fewer questions.

A way to signal the end of one discussion and the start of another is to summarize what has been said and change the subject by moving to another that needs to be talked about.

Planning Next Steps

In planning the next steps, supervisor and/or supervisee identify and develop problem-solving strategies, which usually involve changes in teaching behavior. Once new behaviors or possible strategies have been explored, supervisor and supervisee agree on which of these should be implemented, when, and how. The supervisee may say:

> Before I start circle time activities tomorrow, I plan to describe to the children how I expect them to behave. If Mark continues to misbehave, I will tell him in a very firm voice to stop, instead of ignoring him as I did today. I also will make certain that I am sitting next to him before we begin. I'm also going to set up the cooking area before school so I can move about the room during the transition from circle time to activity period.

The supervisor may respond:

> Those are excellent ideas. As you suggested, I'll come in tomorrow at the beginning of circle time. I'll especially watch Mark, and I'll pay special attention to the transition from circle time to activity period. Let's get together tomorrow afternoon to talk about the effects of these changes and share more ideas.

Or if a caregiver is unable to offer a solution, the supervisor might say:

> Tomorrow, I will serve as a role model for you during circle time. I would like you to observe my teaching and management techniques and pay particular attention to the ways in which I work with Mark. Write your observations down. We can discuss these when we meet tomorrow afternoon.

A supervisor might also recommend that a caregiver participate in a particular professional development activity before they meet again to work on this problem together. Supervisors are not expected to have all the answers and can refer a teacher to outside sources for new ideas. Keep in mind that new skills may take several months to acquire and that a staff member will need ongoing support and feedback, as well as new knowledge through appropriate staff development.

An agreed-on and limited set of steps that both the supervisee and supervisor will take before the next conference gives both individuals a sense of accomplishment and direction. Writing down this action plan, with a proposed timeline, can add clarity and serve as a reference for both parties.

Closing the Conference

During the closing phase, the supervisor summarizes what has taken place during the conference period, reviews initial goals in terms of conference outcomes, and restates agreed-on future plans and timelines. If progress has been made, both parties sense achievement. The closing is also a good time to ask caregivers to offer feedback about the conference itself. This is not a time to be defensive, but rather to be a good listener. Asking the supervisee to share thoughts and feelings about the conference builds trust and open communication.

After an evaluation conference, you may find it beneficial to write a brief summary of what has taken place. A signed copy of the summary can be forwarded to the supervisee for his or her signature. If the supervisee disagrees with the summary and both of you cannot agree on revisions, then the supervisee can have the option of submitting a written summary of his or her own. This procedure is especially important when a serious problem is being addressed.

Preparing, building the climate, setting the purpose, guiding, planning next steps, and closing are six phases that give a conference structure and flexibility, regardless of its purpose and the number of individuals participating. It is important to note that throughout the conference, a supervisor closely observes and listens to the supervisee, engaging in on-the-spot decision making about which communication skills to use and at which point; when to be direct, collaborative, or indirect; how to keep the conference in focus; and when to bring it to a close. A final, postconference stage is analyzing the conference.

Analyzing the Conference

One way for you to improve your performance is by consciously and systematically thinking about and questioning your own supervisory behaviors. This is an aspect of the conference that is often overlooked. Such self-analysis takes time, but the result makes the process worthwhile.

We recommend making audiotapes of at least a few conferences for the purpose of analysis. When told of the purpose, caregivers are usually receptive, since they recognize that their supervisor is striving to become a more effective leader. Supervisors usually find this experience quite revealing. Videotaping a conference allows one to later analyze both verbal and nonverbal behavior, but individuals sometimes become overly conscious of the camera, and making arrangements for videotaping can be overwhelming.

When reviewing the audiotape of a conference, it is best to listen to the entire recording first to refresh your memory and to get a holistic view of the meeting. Then, when playing the tape again, listen for specific purposes:

- In what ways and to what extent did you achieve your goals for the conference?
- In what ways were you successful in practicing the specific communication skills that you had set as a priority?
- In what ways did the supervisee respond to the conference climate and to your communication behavior?

- What are your goals for yourself for your next supervisory conference with this individual?

Scrutinizing your supervisory behavior during conferences fosters your own growth and development and advances the notion in staff members that all adults, including supervisors, are learners.

THREE-WAY CONFERENCES

Although most conferences include just a supervisor and a staff member, there is need on occasion to have a third party participate. Student teachers, job trainees, or Child Development Associate (CDA) candidates are often supervised by a representative of an outside program, who works in cooperation with the coordinator or head teacher. Although the caregiver may spend more time in the field setting and receive most supervision there, he or she must meet the requirements of both organizations and the expectations of both supervisors.

As the two programs and their representatives interface, it is critical that the staff member being supervised and both supervisors meet on a regular basis. Without ongoing communication among the three individuals, splits can develop whereby two develop mutual trust and common goals to the exclusion of the third. There is, therefore, the potential for misunderstanding and conflicting expectations.

Three-way conferences are also useful with individuals within a program. They can be especially effective in handling conflicts among staff members, in resolving contractual issues, and in dealing with parental concerns.

Conferences about grievances usually have clear and well-defined step-by-step procedures that directors must follow. Conferences about serious interstaff conflicts are particularly troublesome and should be carefully planned as well.

Heathfield (2006) believes that mediating conflicts among staff comes with the territory of being in a supervisory position and that supervisors should not make the mistake of avoiding conflicts, hoping that they will go away. She suggests that managers take the following multistep approach to resolving conflicts:

1. Meet with both parties together, letting both briefly summarize their point of view without interruption.
2. Ask each person to describe what steps he or she would like the other to take to resolve the problem.
3. As a supervisor, ask if there are aspects of the work situation that are contributing to the problem.
4. If further exploration is needed, ask each individual what the other person can do more of, or less of.

5. Have all participants discuss and commit to make whatever changes are necessary to resolve the issue including a commitment to notice that the other person has made a change and to respect each other.
6. Let both parties know that you will not take sides and that you expect and have faith in their ability to work together as adults to resolve their differences.

Summarizing agreed-upon solutions and how they will be carried out and evaluated is an important final step as well as setting up a time for a follow-up conference to review progress made. Using effective listening skills, paraphrasing, and asking clarifying questions, as well as praising, during this process will help bring it to resolution. Effective early childhood leaders develop and practice conflict-resolution skills and teach staff that conflict is expected and normal and can be an impetus for personal and professional growth (Rodd, 1998).

While it is often difficult to find and arrange a time when all three individuals can meet, the three-way conference has several advantages. It builds relationships among individuals through a collaborative process where each individual has input. The presence of a third person can take pressure off the other two and that person can bring new insights into the conversation. Each person involved has an opportunity to hear and to understand the other's point of view about a child, the teaching role, or a problem. Usually, during a three-way face-to-face conference, individuals use more careful descriptive language, which promotes greater respect and understanding. Three-way conferences that deal with conflict have the overall effect of reducing stress and anxiety among those participating.

GROUP CONFERENCES

A supervisor may wish to bring small groups of staff members together using the five-stage cycle of clinical supervision described in Chapter 9. Groups may include teachers and assistant teachers of varying or of similar levels of experience and expertise who may or may not be on the same teaching team and/or any other relevant staff members such as curriculum specialists. Groups can be formed to explore a new curriculum theme or simply to become familiar with or to refine particular teaching strategies. Two of the stages in clinical supervision, the pre- and postobservation conferences, provide an opportunity for group planning and reflection and for building mutual support among staff members.

The supervisor's role in group conferences is that of facilitator. As teachers often have little experience in mutual planning, analyzing teaching, and giving feedback to others, the supervisor as leader creates an appropriate structure and format for group supervision, laying the groundwork by establishing a time and space for meetings and guiding the group until staff members are prepared, comfortable, and able to carry out group supervision on their own, with teachers eventually becoming group facilitators, perhaps on a rotating basis. Facilitating group conferences includes the steps described earlier in this chapter for all conferences: preparing, climate building, purpose setting, guiding, closing, and analyzing.

If, as a supervisor, you decide to initiate group conferencing, we suggest you begin with a pilot group of volunteers who are enthusiastic teachers and who are likely to work well together. In this way, you have an opportunity to explore the role of group facilitator and to observe and listen to teachers engaged in the process before attempting group supervision with your entire staff.

Describing the purpose of clinical supervision and the five-stage cycle is an essential first step. You should set a positive tone and place an emphasis on collegiality and staff development, while making clear that the purpose of group clinical supervision is not staff evaluation. In addition, you should help staff to become aware of effective communication skills and to be conscious of using them during group sessions.

Preobservation Conference

One way you could begin group clinical supervision is to ask a teacher to present an idea for a lesson to the group and ask the group to plan the lesson together. Giving group members an opportunity to ask the teacher questions about the children who will participate and the teacher's goals is an effective way to start.

You can provide group structure by offering participants some questions for discussion that can help to focus the dialogue. Below are some sample questions developed for use in a preservice teacher preparation program (Caruso & Graham, 1994):

- What do the children need to know and/or to be able to do prior to this learning experience in order for them to succeed?
- What are your main objectives?
- What are the skills and concepts (cognitive, social, emotional, physical) that you wish children to acquire?
- What are some strategies and materials that you could use to accomplish your goal?
- What kinds of problems might occur during this experience?
- How might you achieve curricular integration through this experience?
- What are some different ways to assess children's growth as a result of this experience? (p. 1)

Preobservation group conferences enable the teacher to think through the learning experience he or she is focusing on whether it is dramatic play, block building, or morning meeting. Dialogue with colleagues can help clarify its purpose, to anticipate problems, and to obtain ideas and suggestions for teaching strategies. Other group members, particularly those with less experience, are also likely to benefit from the discussion. At its conclusion, the teacher reflects on the conference and creates his or her own lesson plan using the input provided.

During the conference, as supervisor, you should not dominate the discussion but should manage the communication flow, encouraging the participation of all group members. Being sensitive to the developmental levels of staff members and "reflecting-in-action" (Schön, 1987) can help you make decisions about the nature and extent of your participation.

You may conclude the preobservation conference by asking the group to analyze the conference. You can contribute by helping them summarize the discussion, pointing out effective communication that took place, and outlining next steps.

The Observation

The teachers who helped develop the plan during the preconference should have the opportunity to observe their colleague teach the lesson or facilitate the experience. The observation might take place by watching a videotape if teachers in the group cannot be released from their duties to observe it firsthand. The staff member who is teaching/facilitating may also be more comfortable with videotaping. One teacher from the group could assume the taping responsibility.

Analysis and Strategy

The teacher needs time to review the videotape, to reflect on his or her experience, and to prepare for the postobservation conference. Teachers may find it helpful to bring the tape home where they have ample time to watch it and can be joined by friends and family for an additional critique. The teacher may note critical incidents, patterns in behavior, particular children, and so forth. The teacher decides which highlights of the tape to show to the group and prepares an analysis.

Postobservation Conference

Once the teacher and observers have had time to reflect, a postobservation conference with the planning group can serve to build the teacher's self-esteem and to help others learn some effective teaching strategies.

As facilitator, you might open the conference by restating the importance of listening, questioning, and other communication skills as the observers respond to the video, and by emphasizing the supportive nature of the process and of being sensitive to the teacher whose lesson is being discussed. Reviewing the content of the preobservation conference is also a helpful way to refresh the memories of group members and sharpen the group's focus.

The teacher who was taped takes a leadership role in the meeting by quickly sharing the final lesson plan he or she developed and by showing segments of the videotape to the group. Because one goal of the postobservation conference is to help the teacher become more skilled at self-assessment and reflection, the teacher should open the discussion by sharing his or her analysis first, followed by questions and comments by group members.

We suggest that group members be given the responsibility of offering feedback about specific aspects of the lesson. This helps to keep the discussion focused. An observation guide can provide members with a structure for conference discussion. Sample observation instruments appear in Chapter 11.

In our experience, these postconferences are lively and positive, as group members have excellent insights and observations to share. Again, your role as supervisor is to facilitate communication by sharing thoughts, asking questions, and intervening to maintain the flow and the focus when necessary. The extent of your involvement will depend on the development levels of members of the group.

Postconference Analysis

At the conclusion of the conference, you may assist the group in reflecting about the conference by analyzing the effectiveness of their communication and the feedback given, and in summarizing the conference. Plans are also made for the next preobservation conference, the beginning of another cycle in group clinical supervision.

CONCLUSION

A conference, whether two-way, three-way, or group, provides a director the opportunity to practice the art of supervision. Planning, problem solving, and evaluating can take place in conferences, and teachers can express themselves and get recognition and praise. Conferences are central to maintaining continued communication between supervisors and staff and to ensuring that caregiving and teaching are of high quality.

For additional reading on communication and interpersonal skills and on conflict resolution, you may wish to refer to *Leadership in Early Childhood: The Pathway to Professionalism* (Rodd, 1998).

EXERCISES

As part of a staff training session in supervision, participate in small role-playing groups to consider the problem situations described below. Individuals take the roles of supervisor and caregiver. An observer whose primary function is to offer feedback to the supervisor should also be included. At the conclusion of an agreed-on time segment of role-playing, individuals switch roles so that everyone has an opportunity to practice supervisory behavior. The observer might create a category system for analyzing conference behavior to examine a particular type of comınunication skill such as questioning technique. Each role-playing sequence need not be long, and at the end the observer should report the results of the analysis to the supervisor. Practicing supervisors might write and discuss a hypothetical plan for resolving each dilemma.

Two-Way Conferences

1. George is concerned that his kids aren't playing well together, particularly with Keith. Keith is an aggressive and active 4-year-old. His parents have been separated for several months and are planning to finalize their divorce very soon. Keith does not see his father and has lots of babysitters. He is at school from 9:00 a.m. to 5:30 p.m. Role-play this conference with George.
2. Yolanda has come to you with a concern. She is very frustrated as the children are sloppy with their food during snack time. She complains, "The kids don't stay seated like they're supposed to, and milk gets spilled all over the place!" She explains that some of the children finish their snacks early and get bored and others never have a chance to finish. The kids who finish early get up to throw their containers away and bump into others, and the children who don't finish get up and go to their activities leaving their partly filled milk cartons on the floor to get kicked over. Role-play this conference.
3. Diedre is an assistant teacher in your Head Start classroom. She is from a middle-class family and has a college degree. She has a hard time accepting and appreciating the lower-income children and families who are at the center. When her activities do not go well, she becomes angry and usually blames it on the children, "who don't know anything," "never learned manners," or "don't even speak the language." While she appears to be sweet with the children, you sense that there are a lot of feelings of anger and frustration underneath. Diedre is quite argumentative, and your suggestions have often been met with strong opposition. She feels that she is doing an excellent job, and your criticisms are usually dismissed because "you didn't really see what was happening." The tension is mounting. You have decided that it is time to talk with her about the situation.

Three-Way Conferences

1. You are a head teacher in a child care center in a large corporation. All the parents are employed by the corporation and tend to be quite conservative. Your assistant teacher, Cassandra, is very imaginative and has a unique and rather flamboyant style. She often wears sequined purple sneakers, brightly colored tights, and short skirts; at other times, it is flowing Indian skirts and a headband (à la 1960s). Her activities with the children are age appropriate and creative but represent a different lifestyle from those of the parents (e.g., body painting, Yoga, Tai Chi, vegetarian cooking). She is wonderful with the

children, and you feel that she offers a good balance to the daily businesslike atmosphere of the site. One day Diane, a parent, calls to say that she is distressed about the "crazy things" her child is learning and feels that Cassandra should dress and behave in a "more appropriate manner." You think that both people would benefit from hearing the other's point of view. Role-play that meeting.

2. You are a director of a child care center with a culturally diverse group of families and staff. You have recently hired an assistant teacher, Elena, who came from Russia last year. She is in her 40s and has the equivalent of a master's degree in education. Her head teacher is an American woman in her late 20s who has a bachelor's degree in education. Elena has had more years of teaching experience than Diane, her head teacher, but most of it was with older children. Elena is finding it difficult to take direction from a person with less education and experience, but at the same time she is not finding it easy working with 3-year-olds. Diane, on the other hand, finds Elena to be somewhat intimidating and is having a hard time establishing a good working relationship with her. Both have come to speak with you about their frustrations in trying to work together. You have decided that it is time to have a three-way meeting. Role-play that meeting.

CHAPTER 11

OBSERVATION AND ANALYSIS

O BSERVATION PROVIDES THE CONTEXT for conferring with supervisees in the clinical supervision cycle. When supervisors and supervisees talk about what is happening in the classroom, their discussion is based not on speculation, but on what each has experienced directly, through either participation or observation. Through supervisory observations and follow-up conferences, staff members can receive accurate information and feedback on what they are doing, enabling them to compare it to what they think they are doing and what they would like to be doing.

When observation is used within the cycle of clinical supervision, it can become part of a joint inquiry into what is happening in the classroom, an important process for adult learners. Within this context observation can:

- Provide a mirror for staff members' actions so they can have objective feedback on what they are doing
- Serve as a vehicle for working together with teachers to help them develop, improve, and maintain their skills in working with children
- Provide information that supervisors and supervisees can use together to diagnose and solve teaching problems
- Help teachers understand how the classroom/learning environment affects children's growth and development, and enable them to act on this information
- Aid teachers in assessing the effectiveness of their program for children and of changes they have made in it
- Provide data for evaluation based on shared criteria and standards (Acheson & Gall, 1997)

At its most basic level, observation is a way of gathering and recording data, yet it clearly involves more than entering a classroom, watching what is happening, and recording what is seen. The very complexity of the teaching-learning process makes effective observation difficult. The many interacting forces—teaching staff, children, the physical environment, the time of day, the activity—must be sorted out in some way. Observers have opinions and feelings about what is going on, and their prejudgments must be accounted for in planning accurate and reliable recording of information. The many layers and subtleties of social meanings, contexts, and feelings present in the classroom must be revealed but not confused with the "facts." Finally, the information collected must be conveyed to the persons observed in ways they can understand, accept, and use. Thus supervisors who are helping teachers become active participants in their own learning might describe observation more as a way of inquiring than as a way of gathering data.

OBSERVATION WITHIN THE CLINICAL
SUPERVISION CYCLE

Most supervisors find it advantageous to use a variety of ways of observing. In a study of the methods used by 300 supervisors during observation and analysis, Noreen Garman (1982) found that they actually used five "modes" at various stages in the cycle of supervision. At each stage there were different assumptions and, therefore, different methods of observation and analysis. "Each has a different, yet vital, purpose in a comprehensive plan for supervision" (p. 50).

The first mode, *discovery*, is an open-ended search to discover the reality of the classroom and to begin thinking about what questions should be explored further. Various systems of observation could be used at this stage. At this point the data from these observations are usually analyzed by identifying the teacher's stated intent and comparing it with what has been observed.

In the second mode, *verification*, more objective and structured systems of observation are used. This is an important step, as it is used to verify the degree to which features or problems identified in the discovery stage do indeed exist.

In the *explanation* phase, both open-ended and structured methods (see discussion below) are often used. At this time the supervisor and supervisee begin the analysis process, together trying to come to terms with their individual and—most important—perhaps differing perceptions of reality.

Interpretation is the search for meaning, the attempt "to get at what really matters" (Garman, 1982, p. 51). The supervisor's knowledge, experience, and insights are used to help the supervisee find the deeper significance beneath the surface of literal descriptions and explanations.

It is in the *evaluation* stage that the supervisor and supervisee examine values and make judgments about specific aspects of the teacher's behavior. The criteria for these judgments are the specific information gathered and the goals of the supervisor and supervisee. These become the basis for setting priorities.

In clinical supervision, which is the basis for ongoing professional development, the supervisor or peer coach serves the teacher, keeping the teacher professional company in the classroom (Cogan, 1973). This means that the purpose of the observation, the role of the observer, and the type of data to be collected are agreed upon by supervisor or peer coach and teacher in the preobservation conference.

The descriptions of approaches and methods that follow are presented in the context of an individual supervisor-supervisee relationship. However, most are appropriate for use by teachers and assistants as well, either individually or with a group of peers, with or without a supervisor. (See introduction to group usage in Chapters 9 and 10, and further discussion in Chapter 15.)

APPROACHES TO OBSERVATION

Observation can be approached in several ways: (1) informally, as a casual visitor to a classroom; (2) as a participant observer, having both involvement in the classroom and a systematic way of recording observations; and (3) formally, completely detaching oneself from the activities in the classroom and recording them in a systematic way.

Informal Observation

Because of the informality and open structure of most early childhood classrooms, adults who are not regular members of the classroom staff can usually move in and out without disrupting the children or the program. Children tend to ignore visitors or to welcome them as new sources of help, amusement, or interesting information. When a supervisor sits down with children during free play or pitches in with cleanup, teachers' apprehensions are often lessened. In fact, many teachers welcome informal visits from supervisors because they think that the supervisor will have a clearer picture of what their classrooms are really like and will be better able to empathize with their problems.

Many directors and educational coordinators make casual visits to classrooms because they like to be with children in order to break the routine of their office work or, more deliberately, to get the flavor of day-to-day center activity. From such visits, they can obtain a general sense of the tone of the room, a teacher's style, the ways staff work together, and the organization of the learning environment. This kind of information can add depth and dimension to a supervisor's knowledge and understanding of classroom life. It must not, however, be counted on as the major source of information for evaluation purposes.

Because informal observations are usually unfocused and are recorded, if at all, after the fact, what is likely to emerge is only a general impression of the room and the teachers or a record of events or factors that stand out or are unusual in some way. If such visits are made to all rooms on a relatively regular basis, however, they decrease (but do not eliminate) the need for formal observation and round out the supervisor's picture of life in the center.

Participant Observation

Participant observation is a method in which the inquirer has considerable involvement in the setting being studied. Anthropologists use this form of observation to "get inside" a culture so that they will be able to see the world as the members of the culture see it.

True participant observation goes beyond informal observation. Supervisors in this role must be very conscious of their perceptions, because they really play two roles: (1) an observer who is responsible to the program as a whole and (2) a genuine participant in the classroom, who thus "has a stake in the group's activities and the outcome of that activity" (Guba & Lincoln, 1981, pp. 189–190).

Supervisors with teaching responsibilities who use observation as a supervisory tool are by definition participant observers of staff in their own rooms. When nonteaching supervisors use this method, however, they must take part in classroom activities and spend enough time in a classroom to immerse themselves in what is going on. Only then can they see the classroom through the eyes of the teachers and children and determine strategies for assistance from these viewpoints. This can be an especially valuable method for supervisors who work with staff or children whose cultural backgrounds differ from their own, or with teachers or programs whose early childhood goals or methods are very different from theirs. Teachers, too, can become participant observers. Some may be interested in learning to do action research to study their own classrooms (see Chapter 15). Their journals and child observations can also be used as a basis for supervisory conferences or seminars.

Formal Observation

Formal observation differs from participant observation in that the supervisor remains aloof from the situation, observing as objectively as possible. Formal observations are recorded on the spot, and the observer does not take part in the classroom activity. A variety of recording systems, as described in the next section, can be used to observe in a formal way. These include open-ended systems, such as narrative descriptions of what is occurring, and systems that limit what is recorded to a set number of behaviors or events that the observer checks off or tallies. Because the observer is not taking part in the classroom activity and presumably has no stake in it, these records should be the most accurate of any of the three approaches.

We want to emphasize again that as part of the clinical supervision cycle, the data to be collected during a formal observation are agreed upon by supervisor and teacher. After the observation, sharing the data assists supervisor and teacher in their analyses and plans for the postobservation conference.

Formal observations are often conducted outside of the clinical supervisory cycle for evaluation purposes. In these cases, both parties will benefit from written documentation that can serve as a basis for planning next steps in the change process.

METHODS OF OBSERVATION

The methods used in observing are usually divided into two categories: closed (also called *quantitative*) and open (also called *qualitative* or *naturalistic*). To some extent, each is based on a different assumption and point of view about the role of the observer. For supervisors, however, using both types contributes breadth and depth to their assistance to teachers.

Closed Systems

These systems grow out of the "scientific" view of supervision, stressing the use of methodology that limits the inferences that observers are required to make (thus "closed"). Methods of this type can be very useful when there is a need to focus on only certain elements out of all that is going on in a classroom. The observer tallies or codes behaviors as they occur, or checks off characteristics of the setting. When analyzing this data afterward, the supervisor can see, for example, how many times a teacher responded verbally to children or was unresponsive, or other similar information. The context, the exact words, and nonverbal nuances are not revealed, but the frequency of certain behaviors and, with some systems, the duration and sequence of events do emerge.

A limitation of these methods is that they can obscure individuality. The use of predetermined categories into which all teachers are expected to fit may make it difficult to take stylistic or cultural differences into account. Further, they do not lend themselves well to interpreting the meaning of behavior.

Procedures

The following procedures and instruments are those most commonly used for observing in classrooms. Each has its own advantages and limitations.

The simplest method is a *checklist*, a list of characteristics or behaviors that are simply checked off if they are present. See Figure 11.1 for an example.

Similar to checklists is a method called a *sign system*. It differs only in that the observer tallies *every time* an activity or behavior occurs, either continuously or at time intervals.

A method that can be used when a supervisor and supervisee are interested in obtaining more information about a limited area of classroom life (for example,

Figure 11.1. Checklist

Teacher or aide available to talk to parent	
Teacher or aide greets each child	✓
Teachers encourage independence in taking off/hanging up coats	✓

verbal interaction) is referred to as a *category system*. Within this limited area, categories of behavior or events are listed ("praises," "responds using child's words," "asks direct questions"). Again, the observer tallies events as they occur or at specified intervals, sometimes using a coding system. The goal is to see which of these actions take place and what their balance is within a segment of the day. An "other" category may be used to make sure that everything that happens is accounted for. (Examples of the use of sign and category systems are given in the case study later in this chapter.)

Rating scales have sometimes been used as observation instruments. However, they have limitations because the observer must make on-the-spot decisions about the degree to which a teacher shows a particular characteristic (e.g., creative vs. rigid). These procedures are much better used to summarize information obtained from several observations and from other sources. Rating scales are discussed in Chapter 16, in the context of evaluation.

It sometimes makes sense to use a published teacher observation tool. The Child-Caregiver Observation System (C-COS-R) (Boller & Sprachman, 2001) looks at one-to-one interaction between caregivers and children and affective qualities of the interaction. The Child Development Associate (CDA) assessment system (Council for Professional Recognition, n.d.) is very comprehensive. It includes an observation instrument, competency standards, and parent opinion questionnaires. The *Early Childhood Environmental Rating Scale* (Harms, Clifford, & Cryer, 2005) is also wide-ranging, addressing areas such as room arrangement for play, staff-child interactions, and staff interaction and cooperation. Such published systems, however, may not focus on the specific behaviors that are of concern to a supervisor and caregiver at a particular time, so they may not be practical in day-to-day supervision. It often makes the greatest sense for observers to construct their own instruments.

Guidelines for Using Closed Systems

Consider the following points when creating or selecting observational instruments:

1. Decide on a focus. Think in terms of people, behaviors, context, and setting, and narrow the observation to the interaction of two of these.

2. Determine whether there is a need to record everything that takes place (category system) or only certain behaviors or events (checklist or sign system).
3. Decide whether merely noting that something is present is sufficient (checklist) or whether you would gain from having information on the frequency or sequence of events (sign or category).
4. Make sure that behaviors do not overlap. For example, "asks question" and "makes statement" are clearly different behaviors. "Asks question" and "talks to child" are not, since asking a question is a kind of talking.
5. Define each category precisely. Two people should be expected to agree that the behavior in question fits the category (one of the problems when using rating scales). Very broad categories ("warm behavior") make agreement more difficult. Very narrow ones ("points," "motions with open hand") usually do not provide much meaningful information unless they represent specific behaviors a caregiver is trying to develop or eliminate.
6. Keep the instrument simple. Since behavior is complex and occurs rapidly, it is better to make two or three different instruments than to cram too much into one.

Open Systems

In recent years, there has been a growing interest in open or naturalistic inquiry among both practitioners and researchers. At its most basic, this means writing down in continuous fashion everything that happens while observing in a classroom. Early childhood educators have used similar methods for observing children (Cohen, Stern, & Balaban, 1997), although perhaps not in systematic ways.

Narrative

Open systems, which make use of the ethnographic techniques developed for use in field studies, are based on the assumption that different people see events from different perspectives. The narrative helps them focus on "multiple realities that, like layers of an onion, nest within or complement one another" (Guba & Lincoln, 1981, p. 57). The observer tries to see the world from these differing points of view and understand their relationships. Whereas observers using closed systems try to screen out human judgment from the process, naturalistic observers seek to sharpen and refine their judgment skills in order to become "more personally and environmentally sensitive" to what is unique in the situation and its meaning to the participants (p. 129).

The use of narratives can help teachers to become reflective, to construct their own knowledge about children and teaching, as discussed in Chapter 4. Elizabeth Jones (1993) and her colleagues have found this method especially helpful with adults with limited educational backgrounds, who have not had experience with constructive criticism. Narratives help teachers to "come to see themselves as *people who know*—thereby, people capable of making appropriate choices for themselves and for children" (p. xiii, emphasis in original). We have found this especially useful in CDA training.

Elliot Eisner (1982), in an approach he calls *connoisseurship*, stresses the importance of recognizing each person's characteristic style, which should be developed and strengthened rather than molded into a particular "good teacher" model. This is especially important with supervisees whose interactions with children are influenced by a culture different from that of the supervisor. Eisner encourages supervisors to develop the ability to use rich language to convey their observations to supervisees.

Advocates of naturalistic methods point to their flexibility and to the detail that is made available to help observers discover what is happening below the surface. Teachers and supervisors are thus free to examine, interpret, and reexamine the descriptions in various ways as they make plans to improve performance. This process can enhance joint inquiry, reflection, and dialogue, helping teachers to construct their own knowledge.

There are limitations, however. Because observers are free to record anything that occurs but cannot get everything, there is a possibility of bias in what they focus on and in how they convey and interpret events to staff members. In addition, care must be taken so that descriptions do not become confused with judgments and interpretations.

A way to ensure that these two types of information are kept separate is to use a two-column format:

Description	*Comments*
Four children in house corner.	
Justin enters. Others continue with dialogue.	
J. gets down on floor.	
Marie (teacher) walks over, sits down.	M. is casual; doesn't intrude.
M: I like the way you're playing. . . . Who's the daddy?	
Beth: I'm the dog.	Has M. misinterpreted their theme?
J: I'm the big dog.	

We strongly advocate a system like this; it helps observers stay alert to the difference between description and interpretation, while making it possible to include feelings, thoughts, inferences from nonverbal cues, and questions to be followed up in the postobservation conference.

Guidelines for Using Open Systems

1. Develop an understandable (to you) shorthand system so you can get on paper as much as possible of what is taking place.
2. As soon as possible after the observation, while your memory is fresh, fill in whole words and details that you were not able to write down during the observation itself. Edit the narrative where the language is imprecise or ambiguous.
3. As you become experienced in recording observations, try to use more descriptive language so that nuances can be conveyed more accurately. For example, instead of "T. goes over to Fred," use "strolls" or "strides with long deliberate steps" to convey the feeling tone of the child's actions. (Cohen et al., 1997, include wonderful examples of such language.)
4. When possible, get the exact words used by teachers or children. This helps teachers become sensitized to the impact of their words on others and become aware of their own verbal style. Describing or paraphrasing can change or make ambiguous the meaning of what was said. "Tells children to stop throwing sand" could have been "Stop that!" or "It's not nice to throw sand" or "Sand stays in the sandbox," each of which conveys a different message to the children.
5. Separate inferences and conclusions from the descriptive data. Avoid judgmental labeling such as "She was inflexible about that rule." Describe the behavior ("Immediately put child in chair") and perhaps add an interpretive comment ("Seemed to feel the rule must be upheld at all cost"). Recheck at the editing stage to ensure the objectivity of the narrative.
6. Note the time periodically in the margin to assist interpretation. If you become distracted or tired and lose some data, time checks alert the reader. Time checks also help portray the stream of events more accurately.
7. Finally, analyze the narratives for patterns of behavior or specific areas to be discussed in the postobservation conference or to be verified during subsequent observations. If the observation is made at the discovery stage of the clinical supervision cycle and with an open-ended agenda, you may have noted areas of concern or special interest during the observation itself for follow-up. If a specific focus was agreed on during the preobservation conference, analysis should be made on the basis of that concern. A copy of the narrative should be shared with the supervisee to foster cooperative analysis.

Combined Systems

Supervisors have wide latitude in developing observation forms for specific purposes or situations, using any combination of closed and open systems. The specific needs or interests of the caregiver, the characteristics of the situation, and the supervisor's and caregiver's creativity are the only limitations beyond following the guidelines for construction of reliable observation instruments.

A system that combines tallying and description can be a very useful teaching tool. For example, a listing of behaviors that support a child's self-concept could include space for the exact language used by the teacher or a description of the specific incident (see Figure 11.2). Because both the specific behavior and the outcome are described, caregivers are able to see exactly what they do and how this behavior affects children. In the case illustrated, only positive behaviors are listed, allowing the supervisor to reinforce what is desirable, rather than emphasizing that which is not. This technique is especially useful with staff members who have had little experience with field supervision or training, and for whom positive feedback and confidence building are especially important.

Another method is to use a narrative but limit the focus to a few categories of behavior. In the example in Figure 11.3, used by a CDA trainer, some of the descriptors for the CDA Functional Area "Communication" have been listed (Council, n.d.). This system provides a way for supervisors to observe and record only behaviors relevant to that area. Additional detail provides backup and feedback to the candidate.

Observations do not always have to be recorded in written form. Videotaping and audiotaping also have valuable places in supervisory observation, making available a permanent, credible record of what actually took place. The record is not limited by the observer's attentiveness, ability to write fast enough, or unconscious biases. In videotaping, nonverbal as well as verbal nuances are captured, revealing the "feel" of classroom interaction. The material can be reviewed and analyzed in a variety of ways.

A major benefit of using such equipment is that caregivers are able to assess their own behavior, becoming less dependent on the supervisor, thus increasing the mutuality of the supervisory process. Since both supervisor and supervisee have the same information to work from—whether the teacher reviews the tapes alone, as is often desirable, or with a colleague, a group of colleagues, or a supervisor—real problem solving can result. At the same time, hearing or seeing oneself directly is so powerful and even anxiety producing that caregivers should not

Figure 11.2. Checklist with Comments

| Gets down to child's level | ✓ | Ch. tugs on T's shirt. T. squats down, asks Ch. to tell her what she wants. Ch. does. |
| Uses extended praise | ✓ | "You did a good job wiping up the spilled paint!" Ch. grins. Carefully puts sponge where it belongs. |

Figure 11.3. Focused Narrative

FUNCTIONAL AREA 6: COMMUNICATION

Name: **Chris G.**   Date: **3/5**

Listens attentively to children, tries to understand what they want to communicate, and helps them express themselves.

Tran pulls at Chris's jeans. C: Yes, Tran, what is it? T. points. C: You'll have to tell me, Tran. T: Mark.... C: Yes — Mark...? T: Mark playing with my truck.

Talks with children about special experiences and relationships in their families and home lives.

Sees Teresa looking at Guinea pig. Picks it up and gives it to T. to hold. T: It's soft — like my kitty. C: Oh, you have a kitty? T: Yes. His name is Tigre. He gets lost sometimes. (Continues story.)

be required to use these media. If you do use taping with your teachers, you should be especially sensitive in follow-up discussions as you try to assist the supervisee in identifying and analyzing what is significant and as you comment on or ask questions about the events that both of you have seen.

Group Observation

Most of these methods of observation can be used by teachers as well as supervisors as part of the group clinical supervision cycle described in Chapters 9 and 10. Very interesting insights can emerge when the information from individual observations is compared and analyzed. The data become "thicker" because each observer may record different aspects of what has been happening. The discussions that follow often bring broader or deeper meaning to the events than might be evident with a single observer.

Members of the group could be asked to observe different features of the learning experience they have planned to look at, based on the goals that have been set in the preobservation conference. Some, for example, might focus only on children; others on the teacher. Different kinds of instruments could also be used, some using checklists or category systems, and others narratives. Again, in the postobservation conference this information must be integrated, along with the views of the teacher who was observed, in order to make it meaningful.

SPECIAL CONCERNS FOR SUPERVISORS AS OBSERVERS

Observer Bias

At several points in our discussion of observation, we have emphasized the importance of discovering the meanings underlying the situations that you are observing. Any attempt to interpret meaning, of course, brings with it the possibility of misinterpretation, based on the limits of what you can perceive and on biases stemming from values and preconceptions. While these biases are natural and even legitimate at times, they must be brought to a conscious level, or they will limit your ability to make accurate and meaningful observations.

Clearly, two people can see the same thing and interpret it differently: the parent who sees "just playing," and the caregiver who sees what the children are learning when they play; the teacher who sees May baskets for the children to take home, and the supervisor who sees children who are bored or close to tears because the project is not developmentally appropriate; and the supervisor who is concerned because a Vietnamese caregiver does not use children's names, while the caregiver is actually functioning in a culturally appropriate way (Binh, 1975).

One source of bias, as we noted earlier, is the complexity of the observational field, which can cause observers consciously or unconsciously to attend to some features and ignore others. One way to overcome this is for you to take time before recording to look around a room and take into account all that is going on and all the kinds of things that could be observed. Another is to practice recording with a colleague, noting differences in what you record. Reviewing your own observations periodically can also reveal patterns you may not have been aware of.

Another source of bias is preconceived expectations about a person or situation. Previous experience with a teacher as a fractious participant in staff meetings, a report on an aide indicating that she is lazy, or the observer's strong feelings about the use of nonstandard English grammar can influence what a supervisor looks for and the interpretation of what is seen. Conversely, when observing a person known to have especially good qualities, a supervisor may take more time to try to understand a problem situation or overlook issues that may be significant. Using a variety of observation tools, both open and closed, makes it more likely that you will view and interpret situations accurately, since they can be seen from different perspectives.

Cultural Differences

Teaching styles often differ based on the cultural values of individuals or a community. A study of Amish classrooms (Cazden, 1979) indicated that teachers used a very directive, even controlling, style of teaching. Because the teachers were from the same background as the children in this closed community, children understood this style quite differently than would children (or adults) who were not attuned to the expectations built up through a similar home and community environment. This directive style made sense for them within the context of everyday routines and was supported by an underlying trust, accountability, and warmth that outside observers may not have perceived or understood. Cazden also describes two bilingual first-grade classrooms, where children and teachers were all of Hispanic background. Although their teaching styles (one open, one structured) differed, the teachers' styles of classroom control were quite similar. Both teachers used endearments and other behaviors characteristic of parents, such as kissing and holding children in their laps when working with them individually.

Supervisors unfamiliar with adult-child interaction patterns in either of these cultures might have judged the behavior of these teachers inappropriate. Conversely, the absence of such behaviors might seem problematic to an Amish or Hispanic supervisor.

Observers in classrooms in which there are cultural or social-class differences must be especially concerned with looking for clues to the meaning of events to children and to adults. In such situations, data from both structured and naturalistic observations of children and adults aid in interpretation. Discussions with supervisees about the meaning of events during the verification and explanation phases of supervision (Garman, 1982) are especially important when differences in cultural values are present. The discussions of cultural and linguistic issues in Chapters 10 and 12 provide additional information that can assist both supervisors and teachers when observing in classrooms.

Personal Considerations

When one member of a classroom team is being observed, particularly if that person is an aide, staff relations may become strained. If you visit a teacher often for written observations, other staff members may feel inhibited, perhaps suspecting that they are being judged. Furthermore, when classroom schedules are disrupted for supervisory conferences, even in a minor way, the change in normal routine can be unsettling and lead to hard feelings, especially when another caregiver has to take over in the staff member's absence.

You can avoid or alleviate much stress if you take time to make frequent contact with the teacher or other classroom staff members with an explanation of the purpose of the observations. Giving positive feedback from time to time to all classroom staff members and unobtrusively pitching in at busy times can temper many uneasy feelings. Staff members will often say that they do not mind these intrusions, but over a period of time, resentment can build if there are too frequent changes in patterns of responsibility or if communication is not maintained.

GENERAL GUIDELINES FOR OBSERVING

The following points relate to observing in classrooms in general. They can be helpful in establishing trust, making the act of observing a positive experience for you and your supervisees, and creating records both reliable and useful.

1. When beginning an observation, especially if it is in an unfamiliar room, try to immerse yourself in what is happening. Try to become part of the world of the teachers and children so that the interrelatedness of its various aspects can be understood. It can be helpful to "map" the setting, noting the number of children and adults, including those who are non-English-speaking or bilingual, or have special needs; physical features, equipment, or materials that might affect what takes place, with perhaps a simple sketch of the room arrangements; and any other information that might assist in interpreting events.
2. Try to find an inconspicuous place to sit while observing. This decreases the pressure on the caregiver and lessens the disruption of the class as a whole. Curious children feel honored when told that someone is writing about what they are doing.
3. Plan with an individual caregiver or with the classroom team when formal written observations are to be made. This is basic to making them part of a cooperative learning experience, rather than subjects of an examination. Dropping in for a written (as opposed to informal) observation without notice or planning is seldom effective or necessary, except when there are serious concerns that cannot be documented in any other way.
4. Make several short observations so that you can discover and verify patterns of behavior. This avoids the problem of drawing conclusions based on a single observation.
5. Build time for observing and conferencing into your weekly schedule. This makes it more likely that it will actually happen. Even 10% of a 35-hour week is 3½ hours—a substantial amount if regularly planned.

PUTTING OBSERVATION TO WORK: A CASE STUDY

For the purpose of the following illustration, put yourself in the role of supervisor working with a teacher, Maria, who has been with your program for about 2 years. You will note that, in addition to a variety of observation methods, all the steps described in Garman's (1982) study are present. As supervisor you use a discovery mode in the early stages of observing the teacher. You then verify your hypothesis, explain by sharing points of view, interpret the meaning of events and behaviors, and evaluate in relation to what you and the supervisee think ought to be occurring.

Not all supervisors will be able to take the amount of time or use all of the methods described in this example—at least not very often. As you read this section, we suggest that you focus particularly on two things: the process of working with a supervisee using observation, and the use of various observational methods in context.

Sequence of Observations

As a result of her evaluation at the end of last year, you and Maria have agreed that she needs to work on improving how she organizes and manages free play. You have made informal visits to Maria's room in the last few weeks, sitting in with children during the free-play period. Your general impression was that she is warm with children and has a wonderful sense of humor. You observed that she has some interesting group activities that children are free to take part in during this time. The period is not chaotic, but a number of the children do a good deal of aimless wandering and occasional roughhousing. Not all areas of the room are used.

In your initial meeting with Maria to plan how you will work together, she seems unsure about the purpose of the free-play period. She knows that children "learn through play," but has never been quite sure what this means or what her role as teacher is. Her main concern about free play is that certain children "don't make use of their time effectively." You suggest that by observing what is actually happening, you may be able to find ways to help her restructure the program so that these children become more involved.

You begin with a naturalistic observation. Your mapping of the room indicates that there are a limited number of learning centers. The block area seems small, the furniture in the house and block areas is mostly lined up on one wall, there is a large open area in the middle of the room, and there are no places for privacy. Four to six children at a time were finger painting at one table. The others were in and out of water play, in the house corner, or at the easel. There was again a good deal of wandering and tussling, especially in the open area in the middle of the room.

In analyzing your narrative description, you note that Maria and her assistant seemed to function in two ways. Either they were in a kind of "rescuing" role, constantly responding to what wasn't going right, finding things for wandering children to do, cleaning up a spill, or stopping roughhousing; or they were "waiting on" children, responding to a child's request by getting materials, putting names on papers, hanging up wet paintings, telling children to let others have a turn, and even drawing a cat for a child who said he didn't know how.

During your next conference, you shared this observation with Maria, who said she was pleased with the finger painting activity and that the children liked water play. In response to the description of aimless activity, she said that she had noticed that Roberto, Jared, and Vanessa often seemed to run out of things to do and acknowledged that the block area of the room was not used much. She had recently seen a film on blocks and was interested in working on this area. When you asked what she thought about the teacher's role in free play, she stated, "To make sure children have what they need, and to prevent and solve problems."

Although you are concerned about the overall picture of free play and Maria's limited perception of her role, you agree to work with her on the block area, using observation as a tool. It is something she is interested in, and by working in this limited area, you may be able to help her develop techniques that will help her with free play as a whole. It is also a logical place to involve the restless children.

Focus on the Children

You and Maria decide that your first focused observations will be used to verify what children do in the block corner and in the room as a whole during free play. There are several advantages to beginning with observations of children. First, it is often easier for teachers to look at children's behavior than at their own, especially if they have not been observed before. Second, observing children can serve as a means of verification and explanation of what actually is happening. Third, it puts the teaching role into perspective by looking at children first, focusing on learning rather than teaching.

The major disadvantage to an initial focus on children's behavior is that it may divert attention from the caregiver's behavior at a time when changes need to be made. Nevertheless, focusing on the children first can create a base from which to work with the caregiver because of the information that is revealed.

In order to develop a set of categories, you and Maria brainstorm about what could or should take place in the block corner, discussing what kinds of behaviors she would like to see there, what might go on that is inappropriate, and how categories can be defined with as little ambiguity as possible.

A list of many possible behaviors is eventually whittled down to a few. They are described and defined as together you construct a manageable observation tool. The discussion that leads to this point helps Maria—and you as supervisor—think more specifically about goals for children in the block area and in free play in general. You choose the following categories:

- *Building*. Interacting with blocks in any constructive way, or with accessories related to blocks; knocking buildings over if clearly acceptable to those involved

- *Other constructive play*. Using materials from another area; playing exclusively with accessories (trucks, people) without involving blocks
- *Watching*. Observing; passive behavior; not actively part of block play but present in the area
- *Nonconstructive play*. Interfering with others, nonconstructive block play, unrelated rough play in area
- *Other*. All other behavior (where possible, note specific behavior)

Using this form you can periodically record the number of children in each type of activity. The "other" listing ensures that you can capture all of what goes on. The form can be refined if in actual use you find that you must use the "other" category too often, or that a category is too limited or too broad.

Recording at approximately 3-minute intervals during a 15-minute observation should provide enough data to reveal patterns of activity within one free-play period (see Figure 11.4). By doing several of these over a period of days, you will get more meaningful information.

You also decide to construct an instrument to use in observing the free-play period as a whole, listing all the areas of the room. Here you record the number of children in each area. (When you use time intervals, it is sometimes possible to use two forms during the same observation period, alternating between the two.) Figure 11.5 shows the patterns of play on a different day from the block area observation above.

On examining the free-play observations, Maria discovers that they confirm the low use not only of blocks but also of manipulatives and books. At the

Figure 11.4. First Instrument

Block Area Room **Maria** Date **10/20**
Time begun **9:15** Time ended **9:30**

Behavior	9:15	18	21	24	27	30
Building					2	2
Other Constructive Play		1	1 *			
Watching						
Non-constructive Play						
Other						

Comments: * Lenny takes out a truck, wheels it around for a while, then "drives" it out to central area.

Figure 11.5. Second Instrument

Free Play	Room **Maria**	Date **10/21**
	No. of Children **14**	No. of Adults **2**
	Time begun **9:20**	Time ended **9:35**

Activity	Time 9:20	:23	:26	:29	:32	:35
Directed	5	5	4	2	3	3
Manipulatives	2			1		
Blocks		1	2			
Easel	2	2		2	1	1
House			3	3	3	2
Books					1	1
Water Play	5	4	3	2	3	4
Uninvolved		2	2	4	3	3

Comments: Children in finger paint area changed. Water + house had same core of children — same ones as yesterday.

same time, she is uncomfortable about the number of children who are "uninvolved." For Maria the use of this form has seemed more objective than your initial narrative.

Maria goes to the center library and looks through *The Block Book* (Hirsh, 1996) and the section on blocks in *The Creative Curriculum for Preschool* (Dodge, Colker, & Heroman, 2002) to discover new ideas about what children can learn from block play, to formulate clear goals for that area, and to identify ways to arrange the area for greater involvement. After discussing these ideas with her assistant, together they make plans to rearrange the entire room to make the block area larger. Since this affects the other areas as well, Maria and her assistant re-think the goals of all the underused areas in the room. Over the next several weeks, things begin to change and Maria is excited! She is now concerned, however, that although children use the block area more, they are not building as elaborately as she would like.

Focus on the Teacher

As you and Maria discuss ways to enhance the children's play, you bring up your original concern that she and her assistant seem to spend much of their time rescuing things and waiting on children. She agrees that although the children are functioning more independently and she has more time, she still does not spend much time sitting with children while they play. It had not previously occurred to her that she could actually plan for free play. You suggest that she read the chapter "Interacting with Children in the Block Corner" (Dodge, Colker, & Heroman, 2002). Based on the examples in that chapter, you and Maria develop categories for another observation (see Figure 11.6). This instrument uses a system that focuses only on specific behaviors (*sign system*), not all those that could occur.

As a result of this observation, you discover that Maria has relied heavily on direct questions and suggestions rather than on the indirect behaviors illustrated in the article. The change from asking convergent questions like "What color is it?" to "How could"-type questions or descriptive statements is not easy. Your postobservation discussion with Maria reveals that she isn't convinced that the children will learn as much if she uses indirect language. She needs a chance to come to terms with this idea, to practice new skills, and to find a balance that makes sense to her. You feel comfortable that she is now looking at free play in a different way and will continue to find ways to make it a positive experience for the

Figure 11.6. Third Instrument

Teacher's Verbal Encouragement: Block Play

Labels what child does	I	1
Asks "What if" questions	I I	2
Asks child to label	⊦⊦⊦ I	6
Makes direct suggestions	I I I	3

Definitions:

Labels: "You've used a *square* block." "The truck went right *through* the building instead of going *around*."

"What if" questions: "What would happen if you used a bigger one?" "Would it fall if you used a different block?"

Asks child to label: "What shape is this?" "Is this taller or shorter than your block?"

Direct suggestions: "It won't fall if you put bigger ones on the bottom." "This one would work better."

children. You leave her with the suggestion that she do some participant observation and journal writing about children's responses to her statements and questions, evaluating which kinds encourage more elaborate building, problem solving, and experimentation. She can call on you to observe her or the children again when she feels ready to do so.

This hypothetical sequence of observations illustrates some of the ways supervisors and supervisees can work together to improve teaching and learning. Many of these observations could have been made using a naturalistic mode, providing a more holistic, but less focused, view. Another alternative would be to have the caregiver do the observations of the children, which would allow him or her more direct knowledge of what is happening. This has the disadvantage, however, of removing his or her own influence from the dynamics of the situation.

Since there are a number of problems or situations that tend to recur with different teachers over the years, instruments that you have developed for one situation can be used with little alteration in a number of others. The free-play form (refer to Figure 11.5), for example, could also be used to examine teachers' activities during free play. By writing in staff members' initials at periodic intervals, a classroom team could have their own behavior mapped to help them plan strategies for cooperating more effectively.

CONCLUSION

Observation is a fundamental tool for staff growth and change, serving as the major source of the content of supervisory conferences. It enables supervisors to provide feedback on what actually goes on in classrooms, providing a credible basis for planning improvements in classroom practices. When supervisors are able to spend time in classrooms informally, while regularly scheduling time for more formal observations, trust is developed, making it less likely that they will need to observe only in crisis situations.

As both supervisors and supervisees become skilled inquirers about classroom life, they will find many advantages to planning together what is to be observed and discussed, analyzing the data and discussing how they will follow up.

EXERCISES

These exercises are most effective when done "live" in a classroom, but videotapes can also be used. Be sure to have a postobservation conference with the person observed.

1. Develop a list of categories that could be observed during circle time or small-group time. These could include teacher and/or child behaviors or environ-

mental factors. Develop a form from a few of these, try it out, and refine it with one staff member as part of a clinical supervisory cycle.

2. Develop a checklist or "sign" system, based on similar information, using either only behaviors you want to encourage or examples of both positive and negative behaviors. Try your system out and refine it.

3. Do a naturalistic observation using the two-column system—one for description, the other for comments. Role-play or carry out a conference with a supervisee to identify a specific focus for another observation.

4. If you are teaching, become a participant observer of your own classroom by setting aside a few minutes each day to focus on one dimension of classroom life. Use this technique to analyze your own program or as a way to assess strengths and needs of assistants or volunteers who work with you. (See Chapter 15 for more detail on action research.)

5. Participate in one of two groups who are to observe the same situation, focusing on the same concern, for example, a teacher's use of encouraging behaviors. One group should use a naturalistic system, and the other, a closed system. Compare the information, and discuss it in terms of the usefulness of each for ongoing staff development or evaluation.

6. Try out one of the published observation systems, such as *The Child-Caregiver Observation System* (*C-COS-R*) (Boller & Sprachman, 2001), *The CDA Assessment System* (Council, n.d.), or the *Early Childhood Environment Rating Scale* (Harms, Clifford, & Cryer, 2005).

7. Discuss how supervisors in different kinds of settings can find time to observe.

CHAPTER 12

Special Issues Affecting Early Childhood Supervision

S UPERVISORS IN EARLY CARE and education often encounter issues and situations that those working with teachers in schools for older children do not. They work with teachers who may or may not have degrees or formal education in the field. Compensation remains low. In some programs staff work year round and spend long hours with children in work that is sometimes tedious, with few opportunities for adult stimulation. If not attended to, these conditions can lead to stress, low morale, and staff turnover, which in turn affect the quality of life for children.

Other issues that may need special attention from early childhood supervisors are not very different from those for teachers who work with older children. As in most schools today, staff members often need help in their relationships with children who are from a variety of cultural and linguistic backgrounds, or whose families have many problems.

In this chapter we examine issues affecting staff morale and turnover, and the need for addressing cultural, racial, and linguistic diversity. We look at how each can affect early care and education programs, clarify some factors that underlie them, and establish a basis for managing them.

STAFF MORALE

It is not easy for caregivers to focus on meeting children's needs when their own are not being met. If they are unhappy with working conditions, are not getting along with other staff members, and/or feel powerless to affect job decisions, how can we expect them to be effective in their work with children?

Employee morale is a major issue for any supervisor, whether in business and industry or in the human services. When morale is high, people are motivated to do exciting, innovative, and growth-oriented work. When it is low, they do their work in a routine fashion at best. They often withdraw, complain, become cynical, or leave.

Low Status

Almost everyone who works with young children has at some time, in one way or another, been given the feeling that their job requires few skills or that it is one that any woman can "naturally" do. Child care staff, especially those in home settings, are characterized as "just baby sitters," and many teachers are seen as "merely" supervisors of children's play. Helping staff members to view themselves as professionals can be difficult when the knowledge and skills needed for their work are not recognized by the public or sometimes even by state licensing standards. Low pay, which reflects a lack of recognition of the difficulty of providing a quality program for children and the staff training required, further erodes caregivers' self-image and their desire to stay in the field.

Public school kindergarten teachers generally have higher status than teachers in day care or nursery schools, causing many people with degrees in early childhood education to seek jobs at this level. Even they, however, along with public school preschool teachers, are often not seen as "real" teachers by their colleagues, especially if they use approaches that support children's play and thus have classrooms that do not look like "real school" (Jones, 1994).

Exclusion from Decision Making

Control over day-to-day decisions, the flexibility connected with the job, and the opportunity to learn and grow are high on the list of satisfactions of teachers of young children. Bloom (1997) found, however, that more than three quarters of teachers responding to a national survey felt that they had less decision-making influence than they thought they should have. The greatest concern was their lack of involvement in interviewing and hiring new staff, a process that could encourage considerable self-reflection. Although most teachers believed that they had influence on planning and carrying out daily activities, many felt left out of determining program objectives and ordering supplies, areas that clearly have an impact on those day-to-day decisions.

The place of aides and assistants in this picture is of special concern. Early childhood educators often state with pride that all members of a classroom team are seen as "teachers." Job descriptions frequently reflect this view, since aides are able to fulfill many of the same roles as teachers. Although this is undoubtedly a source of real satisfaction to many assistants, it can also be a source of resentment. In spite of the fact that they carry equal responsibility for day-to-day classroom decisions and sometimes for curriculum planning, their pay and benefits are lower than those of teachers—sometimes considerably so. In addition, aides may be arbitrarily excluded from certain tasks and major decisions to which the teachers with whom they are working are a part. Since aides in multicultural settings are more likely to be people of color, while teachers in the same settings, especially where they are required to be certified, are predominantly white, these status differences gain added significance (Jones, 1994).

An important aspect of the findings of Bloom (1997) was that directors believe that they do give staff opportunities for involvement to a much greater degree than is perceived by teachers. These data suggest that supervisors need to work toward being open to hearing teachers' perceptions of lack of influence, and should review the opportunities that are available to all staff, especially aides, for participation in decisions in areas that affect them. Through regular staff meetings and classroom team meetings, supervisors and staff can clarify what is actually happening and discuss how things could be improved. This can, however, open leaders up to uncomfortable criticism. Perceptions, of course, do not necessarily represent "the truth" on either side; but perceptions have their own reality, and it is this that must be dealt with.

Examining and updating job descriptions periodically with staff input helps ensure that expectations of both aides and teachers are clearly delineated. Pay scales can also be reviewed and brought closer together where job expectations are substantially similar. Perhaps most important, however, is to provide career ladders to help lower-level staff move into higher positions and pay levels, so that the skills and knowledge obtained through in-service training, experience, and college courses are recognized.

Frustration, Tedium, and Exhaustion

Watching children grow, creating successful learning experiences, and being warmly responded to by children are the kinds of rewards that attract people to the field of early childhood education. But the very humanness of children, which makes them loving and joyful, can be difficult to manage in group settings. Even with the warmest, most skilled caregiving efforts, children don't always respond positively, and handling one or more aggressive children on a daily basis can be exhausting and can lead to anger and fear in staff members. Uncooperative parents who refuse to acknowledge a problem or permit an evaluation add to the frustration.

Homeless children, traumatized children, and children with developmental disorders and severe special needs present unique challenges to staff members. Working with children with such serious issues sometimes makes staff members feel inadequate and overwhelmed.

What Bloom (1995a) refers to as the "treadmill of activity" can also consume teachers' time and energy. Infant caregivers spend much time in routines such as changing and feeding, and all teachers can become bogged down when they feel they know every puzzle by heart, have said "Tell me about your painting" too many times, and have had their 40th cup of coffee in the house corner.

This can easily lead to their losing sight of the importance and meaningfulness of what they are doing.

Isolation

A great deal of the caregiver's time is spent immersed in the world of children and isolated from other adults. Their autonomy, which they value, may also lead to missed opportunities for collaboration and learning from one another. In family child care settings providers often have little contact with adults, and none with others doing the same job unless they are part of a support network or training program. In center- or school-based programs, although two or three adults usually work together, their focus is mainly on children and classroom concerns. Sometimes teachers solve this problem in their own way by engaging in personal talk when they should be interacting with children. It is easy to label this lazy or irresponsible behavior, but feelings of isolation may be involved.

Caregivers are really dealing with isolation on two fronts—personal and professional. Both are supervisory concerns. Times set aside for open discussion of daily problems in the context of professional sharing can help teachers deal with their feelings about themselves and the children. Supporting collaborative efforts in a variety of ways, such as through mentoring relationships, is also helpful. At the same time, purely social situations, from coffee breaks to staff parties, can provide opportunities for adult, non-work-centered interaction.

Stress and Burnout

At times factors such as those described above can come together leading to stress, sometimes resulting in what is often referred to as *burnout*.

Burnout occurs in many organizations where there is high person-to-person involvement. It can be either individual or organizational. It shows up in three ways: (1) emotional exhaustion, that is, being drained of energy and the ability to give to others; (2) depersonalization, characterized by negative attitudes toward oneself and work, cynicism, and a detached, callous attitude; and (3) a lack of a sense of achievement in the workplace (Boyd & Schneider, 1997).

Although a number of factors have been found to contribute to burnout in early childhood settings, Boyd and Schneider (1997) found that lack of involvement in decision making was the strongest predictor of both emotional exhaustion and depersonalization. They found, too, that lack of a feeling that the whole staff is working toward the same goals (*goal consensus*) was an important factor contributing to these aspects of burnout. Tension between parents and caregivers, lack of clear communication with supervisors, and few opportunities for advancement are other elements that may also contribute to stress.

Administrators and supervisors, especially when they have little funding or other support for providing the kind of program they think is necessary, are also vulnerable to these feelings. One might speculate as to whether developing a process for staff input, especially for identifying overall goals for a program, would strengthen supervisors' own emotional well-being, professional accomplishment, and sense of belonging.

Not all stress is of an emotional nature. Health and safety issues within the work environment affect the physical well-being of staff members. Lifting children and moving equipment, sitting on the floor without proper support, and frequent reaching for objects can cause pain and back injury. Being exposed to young children who are prone to colds and childhood diseases can cause illness among caregivers, making the practice of good health habits essential in child care environments. Health and safety education workshops can be an important component of ongoing professional development.

Stress does not arise exclusively from factors directly within the workplace, however. Trying to make ends meet and address family needs on the pitifully low salaries that caregivers receive, even if combined with a spouse's, can add additional strain and tension. When a caregiver is confronted with major problems at home—a spouse out of work, children in trouble at school, divorce—the daily task of caring for someone else's children can seem especially difficult. Family dynamics can also be negatively affected by positive job outcomes. For example, an aide's growing confidence and competence at work can sometimes change his or her relationship with a spouse, creating tensions that can, in turn, impact on that person's work.

Raising Morale and Creating Community

Individual and group morale can and will be low from time to time without leading inexorably to burnout. Supervisors who recognize that morale is a legitimate supervisory concern and are alert to burnout symptoms at their early stages can work out both long- and short-term strategies for dealing with it.

Regular and constructive staff meetings where colleagues are able to socialize informally, provide each other with support, receive advice and clarify goals, and exert some influence on the policies of the center help staff to feel that they are part of a group and making a difference. Margie Carter (1995) suggests the idea of staff meetings as "circle time." When this setting is "physically comfortable, emotionally safe, and full of active listening" (p. 53), it can, as it does with children, build a sense of belonging and accomplish many of the above goals. Providing time for teachers to evaluate themselves and learn about each teacher's strengths and special abilities, as well as creating opportunities for them to express and share these unique skills, are some other ways to reinforce the concept of community (Kloosterman, 2003).

Strain and Joseph (2004) point to the importance of engaged supervision as a means of helping staff feel less overwhelmed, stressed, or disrespected. They suggest that acknowledging the feelings of staff members, adopting and fostering a problem-solving attitude, and working collaboratively on a mission statement can lead staff toward gaining a greater sense of efficacy.

Ensuring that basic personnel policies are met is critical to maintaining staff morale. Providing simplified retirement plans and health and other fringe benefits that are often tax deductions for programs are other morale boosters (Battersby, 2005). Even simple, low-cost benefits like being able to make local telephone calls, serving refreshments at meetings, and giving small gifts like flowers or books can go a long way toward making staff feel valued.

Finally, opportunities for professional growth and development that build competence and confidence in staff, some of which are described later in this text, are critical to avoiding burnout among staff.

STAFF TURNOVER

It is a rare early childhood program that does not experience frequent changes in personnel from year to year. This turnover results both from changes in paid staff and from the movement of volunteers, students, and trainees in and out of programs. Supervisors are thus faced with the task of continually orienting and training new personnel and maintaining and building systems to support a cohesive staff while also trying to develop a quality program.

As we indicated in Chapter 3, members of the early care and education workforce continue to receive low wages and inadequate benefits, contributing to this cycle of instability in programs. Some directors, under stress created by staff turnover, also leave their positions, as do some staff members who are discouraged by the ongoing entry and exit of colleagues (Whitebook et al., 2001). This vicious circle of stress which creates turnover which in turn increases stress may have an effect on the overall mental health of staff members and, of course, on the well-being of the organization itself.

Staff Mental Health

How does the mental health of staff members affect their work performance, and does it affect turnover among personnel? More than one quarter of center-based directors, slightly over one fifth of teachers, and 16% percent of licensed family care providers met the criteria for depression in Whitebook and colleagues' (2004) study of the early care and education workforce of Alameda County, California. Few studies have been carried out, however, that examine the relationship of caregiver depression to job turnover.

Most staff in early care and education are women, and women tend to be more susceptible to depression as they juggle their various roles as employee, wife, mother, and daughter. Tennen (2004) reported the results of a recent survey by the National Mental Health Association, which indicated that if depression remains untreated, it can become an obstacle to professional success, causing some employees to call in sick, avoid coworkers, and develop physical disabilities associated with depression. The same study found that depression affects about 5 million women working outside the home. This problem is not limited to women, however; by 2020, depression is expected to be the second most common disease, accounting for 15% of the disease burden in the world (Goldberg & Steury, 2001).

The need for supervisors to be advocates for higher wages and benefits, which would reduce financial strain, was noted above, but how might supervisors address mental health issues? Since directors and others in supervisory roles are not clinical psychologists or physicians, the most sensible approach is to encourage staff to get help and to refer them to professionals who are competent to meet their personal needs. Often individuals do not know where to go for help, may lack the motivation to get help, and/or may feel helpless. Some research may be required on the part of supervisors to uncover available community mental health services for low-income wage earners. Forming collaboratives with community mental health providers is an investment in the emotional well-being of staff members and of children as well (Koplow, 2002).

There are ways that supervisors can directly address the social and emotional needs of staff and strive to develop their emotional competence. Helping staff find positive meaning in their work, recognize and manage their emotions, and feel a sense of connection with their colleagues are steps that can lead to caring, healing, and responsive early education environments.

In their book *Bringing Yourself to Work: A Guide to Successful Staff Development in After-School Programs*, Seligson and Stahl (2003) propose a model for change in after-school programs that has implications for other types of programs as well. Their model promotes becoming more self-aware, building relationships, and being a member of a group. They draw heavily on the work of Daniel Goleman (1995) and his best-selling book *Emotional Intelligence*. Goleman believes that people who know and manage their own feelings and who can interpret and deal effectively with other people's feelings are likely to be content and effective in their lives.

Seligson and Stahl (2003) offer practical suggestions as to how caregivers can become more aware of their emotions and understand why they feel the way they do. Writing in journals, analyzing their responses to problems by describing interactions in challenging situations, naming the feelings they are experiencing during these encounters, and pinpointing desired alternative responses are several ways for caregivers to be more in touch with their emotions. The authors also identify some of the main characteristics of people who have a gift for building healthy relationships. These are individuals who respect, care about, and empathize with others and who can sense mood shifts in other people. They are also self-aware, are honest with themselves and others, and believe that they can make a difference in the world. Assessing their own emotional intelligence and examining the dynamics of their work groups are major steps that staff can take to devclop their relational abilities, which will bring about positive change in their work environment.

There are a number of other ways (Koplow, 2002) that supervisors can help teachers retain their emotional well-being and balance at school. Retreats away from the school environment focusing on their mental health sends teachers a message that they are cared about and that the school recognizes the connection between teachers' and children's well-being. Monthly mental health support groups, individual therapy with members of the school's mental health staff, and encouraging teachers to explore different avenues for emotional expression outside the school are some additional steps to responding to teachers' needs. Relaxation therapies, such as yoga, meditation, and muscle relaxation, have been found to be effective in combating anxiety, stress, depression, and related physical symptoms (Fredrickson, 2000). Offering classes in yoga or meditation on-site as part of a staff development and support program is an inexpensive and useful strategy for addressing mental health issues.

Of course, one of the important roles in staff supervision is to give teachers feedback about their work. How we critique staff members affects their feelings and self-image and, in turn, has an impact on their motivation and commitment on the job. Psychologist and former corporate consultant Harry Levinson (1992/ 2005) describes an artful critique as one that leaves an employee with a sense of hope, that opens doors by providing valuable information as to how one might improve, rather than a feeling that one has been personally attacked.

Barbara Fredrickson's work (2000) on the power of positive emotions and how they counteract negative emotions and cultivate health and well-being has implications for those in supervisory and leadership positions. She has developed a "broaden and build model" of positive emotions. The basic idea behind this model is that positive emotions undo negative emotions and fuel resilience. Unlike negative emotions which narrow how an individual thinks about and responds to stressful situations, positive emotions broaden what she calls a "thought-action repertoire." In other words, positive emotions support coping strategies to respond to stressful events and restore flexible thinking to help us to be more receptive to different ideas and actions. Over time, positive emotions build and form a surplus "storehouse or bank" of positive sentiments that can be called upon to solve problems and support interpersonal relationships.

Fredrickson (2000) points to a study of caregivers in the health field and how they cope with stress done by Folkman, Moskowitz, Ozer, and Park (1997). It revealed that people counteract depression and find positive meaning in everyday life by feeling connected with others and cared about, being distracted from everyday cares, feeling a sense of pride and achievement, feeling hope and optimism, and receiving validation from others. Fredrickson believes that positive emotions reverberate throughout an organization and may produce optimal functioning among its members. Leaders can cultivate positive emotions by helping staff find positive meaning in ordinary events, by expressing appreciation for a job well-done, and by focusing on newfound strengths among staff (Fredrickson, 2001).

Little research has been carried out on the effects of depression among child care workers on children, colleagues, and the organizations themselves. More attention needs to be paid to mental health initiatives for the early care and education workforce. Studies about the role of emotions in our everyday lives may provide supervisors with some cues for promoting positive mental health and well-being among staff members. In addition to the sources cited above, other resources include *Leading With Emotion: Reaching Balance in Educational Decision-Making* (McDowelle & Buckner, 2002) and *Bouncing Back: How Your School Can Succeed in the Face of Adversity* (Patterson & Collins, 2002).

Creating Stability

In addition to promoting a positive social-emotional environment, supervisors can address many of the other factors contributing to staff turnover. First, a program should be analyzed to see what is causing people to leave. As Marcy Whitebook (1997) put it, "*Is* it low pay, or is it that there's only one bathroom?" and then suggests, "Staff are adults: ask them!"

Stability is enhanced among both permanent and temporary staff members when there is a system for orienting all new personnel, paid or volunteer (see Chapter 14). Support should also be provided for teachers when they take responsibility for supervising temporary staff or for mentoring new teachers. Recognition, along with training in communication and supervisory skills, develops teachers' confidence as well as their competence in carrying out these responsibilities. Extra compensation, if at all possible, increases the caregiver's status and sense of responsibility for this work.

Follow-up studies of centers that have received NAEYC accreditation indicate that turnover in these programs is considerably lower than in others, and that staff have a greater commitment to their jobs and pride in their programs (Bloom, 1995b). Both the accreditation self-evaluation process and the improved quality that results contribute to this.

Working relationships with programs or agencies from which volunteers and trainees come will be smoother if there are agreements about the roles and responsibilities of the parties involved. If standards and expectations for the selection of people who will work with children are established, temporary staff can be screened to ascertain whether they are truly interested in and have an aptitude for working with children. Alternative placements can then be arranged when appropriate. These and other policies are recommended by the Center for the Child Care Workforce for centers that employ welfare recipients fulfilling work requirements.

Written material describing the program's goals, philosophy, and daily schedule also aids in matching resources and needs. A contract between the agency and the center is recommended to clarify the commitment and expectations of each, whether or not money is involved. Such agreements have proven especially useful in Child Development Associate (CDA) training programs, even when the candidate is a regular member of the staff.

Increasingly, resources are becoming available to assist practitioners in developing skills for negotiating with boards and for advocating for better salaries and benefits. The Center for the Child Care Workforce (see Appendix), which has become a major national voice for the empowerment of early childhood staff, has now merged with the American Federation of Teachers Educational Foundation (CCW/AFTEF) to become an even more powerful voice in advocating for improved jobs for child care workers. It is expected that this collaboration will help in the effort to organize early care and education professionals and expand public policy and public awareness efforts.

Following the merger, the American Federation of Teachers launched a new campaign called First Class Teachers (http://www.firstclassteachers.org) to improve wages, benefits, and working conditions of the child care workforce, which includes a Web site that offers a range of resources such as advocacy tools and message boards, as well as educational loans and insurance for members. The work of the Worthy Wage Campaign, formed more than 10 years ago, has been successful in developing leaders and advocates working to improve child care job conditions and continues through the Worthy Wage Network.

The fruits of the labor of advocates from these groups and others include such policies and programs as the Washington State Early Childhood Education Career and Wage Ladder Pilot Project (Brown, 2002), which incorporates wage increments based on experience, responsibility, and relevant education. In comparing ladder centers in this project with a control group, researchers found that the ladder centers offered higher wages and more benefits and that their mean staff retention rate was 21% higher than that of the control group centers (Brown, 2002). Also, staff morale in the ladder centers was higher, and staff had attained significantly higher levels of education.

Another program is T.E.A.C.H. in North Carolina, which gives annual bonuses of up to $2,000 through its Child Care W.A.G.E.$ Project to teachers/ caregivers who have reached certain benchmarks, beginning with the Early Childhood Certificate (Child Care Services Association, 2005). The average teacher turnover rate in North Carolina is now 24%, a drop from 31%, with turnover in some participating counties as low as 10 to 12% (Child Care Services Association, 2005). The Alameda County Child Development Corps (Whitebook et al., 2004), which is a professional incentive program that encourages early childhood educators to remain in the field by giving them stipends based on their level of education, as well as leadership training and professional advice, is yet another effort that shows promise in reducing turnover.

It should be said that there can be positive aspects to staff turnover. Supervisors, especially in programs employing low-income staff, can be proud if they have supported the personal and professional growth of caregivers so that they continue their education, take advantage of promotions in the early childhood field, or even move on to new careers in other fields. The involvement of parents, senior citizens, high school students, and volunteers brings diversity to the lives of both children and permanent staff. When a program has contributed to the training of student teachers and job trainees, it has contributed to the profession and to a better life for young children. What we do not want is for skilled and promising practitioners to leave the field because of low pay, poor working conditions, and lack of support and appreciation.

STAFF AND CHILD DIVERSITY

"Cultural diversity means that the hopes and expectations that adults have for young children, as well as how they interact with young children—from comforting to disciplining to teaching—differ, sometimes dramatically" (Cohen & Pompa, 1996, p. 81). For supervisors this has implications in two areas: in their own relationships with teachers and in their work with teachers as they interact with children and parents. While we have discussed these issues to some extent in previous chapters, this section examines their implications in greater depth.

Culture, Race, and Class

There is a paucity of data describing the racial composition of staff and children in early childhood settings. However, Saluja and colleagues' (2002) large scale national survey of center-based early childhood programs of 3- and 4-year-olds does provide some recent information. They found that the great majority of teachers working with this age group were White (78%). Ten percent were African American, and 6%, Hispanic. In looking at teacher race and program type, they found that there was a smaller percentage of White teachers in Head Start programs and that there were more Hispanic teachers in public schools than in other program types.

In terms of the racial makeup of classrooms, Saluja et al. (2002) found that the average early childhood classroom is 66% White, 15% African American, 9% Hispanic, with the remainder made up of Asian Americans, mixed races, Native Americans, and others. Head Start programs tended to be more racially mixed than other program types, with a predominance of African Americans. Their study also indicated that when classrooms contain a large number of children from one racial or ethnic group (75% or more), they are likely to have a large percentage of teachers from that same group.

We all carry preconceived ideas about members of particular groups, which although often unconscious, nevertheless can affect our work. The NAEYC's *Developmentally Appropriate Practice in Early Childhood Programs* (DAP) recognizes that an understanding of culture has as much effect on how caregivers work with children as does their awareness of children's development and individual differences (Bredekamp & Copple, 1997). All of us tend to make assumptions about people based on their color, class, gender, religion, sexual orientation, or other identities. Gordon Allport (1958), one of the pioneers in examining prejudice, called this "the normality of prejudgment," stemming from the human need to mentally group things in order to make sense of them.

Talking about differences, however, usually makes us uncomfortable. To say that someone is different seems to imply inferiority. This stems from perceptions of social status that have become attached to various ethnic, religious, or racial groups. The term *class* itself is one that Americans do not like much, but classes do exist and do affect people's views of one another. Differences are not deficits, though, and denying their existence does not make them or their effect on our own and others' lives go away.

It often seems safer to rely on a basic sense of fairness and good will, to say "I don't see color," than to attend to differences and examine their implications, especially when it seems that to do so may offend someone. But understanding and communication do not happen automatically. A true atmosphere of openness and trust is based on knowledge of another's life experiences and values and a sensitivity to the ways one is perceived. A middle-class White head teacher, for example, may have developed a good understanding of Hispanic culture and have been able to communicate well with her Hispanic staff, but a new low-income Hispanic aide who has experienced much discrimination has no way of knowing this. This aide's emotional survival requires that she proceed cautiously and perhaps defensively in her relationship with her supervisor. This head teacher must proceed from an awareness not only that the aide might have such feelings, but also that, because of her role and because she is a member of the majority culture, she possesses power and authority that affect their relationship (Delpit, 1995). In fact, class and cultural stereotypes are often reinforced when a supervisor or director is from the dominant culture or from a middle-income background and staff members, especially those in lower-status jobs, are people of color or from low-income families, not an uncommon situation.

The most difficult task is to accept and understand differences when they conflict with personal and professional values. The values of the mainstream culture are generally reinforced in schools, so those who are born or socialized into the mainstream culture may have had no opportunity to question them. They may assume that others have the same values, or perhaps that if they differ they should be corrected. This can lead to the values of teachers and parents from African American, Native American, Asian, and Hispanic cultures, and those of the poor, being devalued or stereotyped (King, Chipman, & Cruz-Jazen, 1994).

Powell (1994) notes that what has been considered developmentally appropriate practice in child care and education is in "stark contrast with the images of appropriate settings for young children generally held by lower income and ethnic minority parents" (p. 171). They are likely to believe that adults should act as limit-setting authorities and should direct and guide children. Middle-class parents, on the other hand, tend to feel they should help the child to become self-disciplined and autonomous. Since the goals of a developmental early childhood program include autonomy and independence, along with nondirective adult-child interactions, middle-class, and especially White, supervisors and caregivers are more likely to be comfortable with these goals because they do not conflict with their values. On the other hand, they may find that their own indirect style leaves children and even adults from other ethnic and income groups confused as to what is expected.

We need, then, to acknowledge that people's differing ways of interacting with one another are not necessarily wrong, even when they seem to be at odds with developmentally appropriate practice. Lisa Delpit (1995) shows, with numerous examples, that teachers of color often feel that their experiences are discounted in discussions of ways to work with children. An African American teacher's or aide's reluctance to follow a recommended way of working with children, for example, may represent a legitimate concern about the children based on personal knowledge of their cultural or family expectations. In such an instance, a supervisor's role is to do lots of listening, allowing "the realities of others to edge themselves into her consciousness" (p. 47), and thus learn and consider changes in program implementation. To have a goal of actively affirming the cultures of both school and home without devaluing either means that supervisors must become aware of others' views and be willing to negotiate or come to an accommodation with teachers or parents where behavior expectations are in conflict.

Sexual Orientation

In discussing diversity, a topic that is often swept under the rug is that of sexual orientation. As some states make civil unions or marriage among gay and lesbian couples legal and as adoption among gay and lesbian couples becomes more widespread, the reality is that more children with same-sex parents will enroll in early care programs. Supervisors are encouraged to engage staff in gaining a greater understanding of alternative families and in discussing how to sensitively and sensibly work with children and parents. It is important to develop a mission statement declaring that diversity is a value, and to create nondiscrimination policies that welcome gay and lesbian staff and that celebrate all families (Gelnaw, 2005).

Helpful resources for supervisors and staff exploring this issue include *Gay Parents, Straight Schools: Building Community and Trust* (Casper & Schultz, 1999), and *Families Like Mine: Children of Gay Parents Tell It Like It Is* (Garner, 2004). *ABC—A Family Alphabet Book* (Combs, 2001) and *And Tango Makes Three* (Richardson & Parnell, 2005) are among a growing number of children's books on alternative families. The Web site of the Family Pride Coalition (www .familypride.org) offers a series of resources and publications that may also prove useful.

Language

The supervisory issues involved when even one child speaks a language other than English can become dauntingly complex when several home languages are present in the same classroom. The issues are important whether the children are recent immigrants or members of long-established Spanish-speaking, Native American, or other communities in the United States who see their native language as an important part of their culture.

Teachers and parents often have strong feelings about encouraging the use of a child's first language in school. Many fear that it will interfere with the learning of English. Or they may believe that speaking English is a symbol of being, or wanting to be, truly American and that the use of another language emphasizes what is different about each child and leads to divisiveness rather than unity. Others may feel equally strongly that children should begin school entirely in their first language, gradually moving into English, or that both languages should be used equally.

Supervisors have to acknowledge the highly personal and emotional meaning that language has in people's lives, while also becoming knowledgeable about second-language acquisition. There is considerable evidence, for example, from several countries, that a second language is learned best when students are both literate and fluent in their first language (Cazden, 1995). Garcia (1997) reports that successful teachers of second-language learners understand and value the home language, culture, and values; recognize that children come to school with some knowledge about language and how it works; and understand that children develop higher language skills through socially meaningful activities and that development and learning occur in the "interaction of linguistic, socio-cultural, and cognitive knowledge and experiences" (p. 12).

We support the view stated in the NAEYC (1996) position statement on cultural and linguistic diversity that " because knowing more than one language is a cognitive asset, early education programs should encourage the development of children's home language while fostering the acquisition of English" (p. 5).

Building a Culturally Responsive Program

A supervisor's attitudes and willingness to deal openly with the issues of culture, race, class, sexual orientation, and language are crucial to the creation of an atmosphere of understanding, trust, and responsiveness to children's needs. Only by bringing these "tender topics" to the surface, Elizabeth Jones (1994) cautions, can we "open the way for those with less power but greater understanding to speak out with authority about their personal experiences with inequity" (p. 30). This is by no means an easy task, especially as we are all at different stages in awareness of and openness to these issues.

The first step toward intercultural competence is to create the time and space to find out who *we* are, how we feel about it, and "how we are connected and disconnected to one another" (Delpit, 1995, p. xv). "We" means *all* staff, including supervisors. Connie Sturm (1997) started a group for this purpose when she and other teachers realized that some of their parents were approaching child rearing very differently from the ways that they considered developmentally appropriate. After exploring their own previously unexamined values, they began a series of parent-teacher dialogues, structured so as to be open to mutual sharing by parents and teachers. Through these experiences they gained new insights about commonalities as well as differences, and began to develop the intercultural communication skills that carried over to their classroom interactions.

Valuing the recruitment of a diverse staff, especially for teacher or supervisory positions, even if your program is relatively monocultural, is another way that you as a supervisor can address issues of culture, race, and class. Become committed to the education, mentoring, and promotion of people in lower-status positions, while allowing for flexibility regarding credentials and English proficiency when looking for staff who speak the children's home languages. Use caregivers', parents', and volunteers' knowledge as a resource for others and as a connecting link between home and school, especially if the administration and/or staff of your program are not from the same background as the families.

Know yourself, your values and goals, and your fears and discomfort regarding issues of diversity. Be flexible, strive for dialogue, and enjoy the challenge and stimulation of cross-cultural communication. Lastly, learn more about cultures that are different from your own. Foreign travel is a wonderful way to gain a greater understanding and appreciation of other races and cultures; but if this is not possible, just visiting neighborhoods in your own city that practice different customs and traditions can be a wonderful and inexpensive educational opportunity for you and your staff.

We encourage supervisors to build programs where diversity in race, culture, and language is honored. Even when children and staff are relatively homogeneous, this can be an exciting way to begin to initiate them into a world of diversity. Three books to consider for background reading and practical suggestions include *Diversity in Early Care and Education Programs: Honoring Differences* (Gonzalez-Mena, 2005); *The Skin That We Speak: Thoughts on Language and Culture in the Classroom* (Delpit & Dowdy, 2002); *Teaching and Learning in a Diverse World: Multicultural Education for Young Children* (Ramsey, 2004); and *What If All the Kids Are White? Anti-Bias Multicultural Education with Young Children and Families* (Derman-Sparks & Ramsey, 2006).

CONCLUSION

The issues discussed in this chapter present challenges to supervisors and staff alike, but thoughtful supervisory and staff development practices, those we have described and others, can have an impact. It will also take concerted, long-term efforts by professional groups and individuals to have an impact on the views of the public at large about the value of well-trained and adequately compensated early childhood staff. As research about the importance of children's early years continues to be publicized in the popular press, the public at large will become better informed, and early childhood professionals will be better able to interpret to them how training and improved compensation of caregivers contributes to quality care and education for young children. Closer to home, parents can be educated through involvement in classrooms, by getting to know and respect staff members through a variety of means. As a supervisor in a program with a strong multicultural emphasis said, "So *many* things are solved by including parents."

Staff meetings and staff development are essential elements of the supervisory process not only for improving staff skills but also for their positive effect on morale. The community building that results can be especially important where the staff and the children served are from diverse backgrounds. In Part IV we explore these issues further, including some specific suggestions for implementation.

PROGRAM ACCREDITATION

The following criteria for program accreditation from *NAEYC Early Childhood Program Standards and Accreditation Criteria: The Mark of Quality in Early Childhood Education* (NAEYC, 2005) represent a sampling of those related to staff morale and diversity:

    3.A.01 Teaching staff, program staff, or both work as a team to implement daily teaching and learning activities, including Individualized Family Service Plans (IFSPs), Individualized Education Programs (IEPs), and other individual plans as needed. (p. 28)

    3.B.04 Teaching staff are active in identifying and countering any teaching practices, curriculum approaches, or materials that are degrading with respect to gender, sexual orientation, age, language, ability, race, religion, family structure, background, or culture. (p. 29)

    4.B.01 Programs use a variety of assessment methods that are sensitive to and informed by family culture, experiences, children's abilities and disabilities, and home language; are meaningful and accurate; and are used in settings familiar to the children. (p. 35)

    7.A.02 Program staff actively use a variety of formal and informal strategies (including conversations) to become acquainted with and learn from families about their family structure; their preferred child-rearing practices; and information families wish to share about their socioeconomic, linguistic, racial, religious, and cultural backgrounds. (p. 56)

    7.A.04 To better understand the cultural backgrounds of children, families, and the community, program staff (as part of program activities or as individuals), participate in community, cultural events, concerts, storytelling activities, or other events and performances designed for children and their families. (This criterion is an Emerging Practice.) (p. 56)

7.A.07 Program staff ensure that all families, regardless of family structure; socioeconomic, racial, religious, and cultural backgrounds; gender; abilities; or preferred language are included in all aspects of the program, including volunteer opportunities. These opportunities consider each family's interests and skills and the needs of program staff. (p. 56)

10.B.09 The program has plans and policies to attract and maintain a consistently qualified, well-trained staff and reduce staff turnover. (p. 56)

EXERCISES

1. As a new supervisor, you discover that there has been a lot of staff turnover in your center in the past few years. Using the information presented in this chapter as a beginning, how would you analyze this problem, and how would you work with staff to develop a strategy for combating it?

2. Duplicate standard 3.B.04 above and distribute it at a staff meeting. Use it as a basis for discussion at the meeting to review how staff are addressing this standard.

3. Brainstorm strategies for advocating higher pay, increased benefits, or other quality issues, such as lower staff-to-child ratios, with the person or group that has control over funds for your program. Sort these through, and try out the most promising.

4. *A Problem for Discussion.* (Note: You may wish to substitute an actual example from your program that deals with the same kinds of issues.) Rosa is a new aide in the child care program of which you are the director. It has a high percentage of Portuguese children. She is a Portuguese immigrant who has been in this country for about 3 years and speaks English fairly well, although she has an accent and her speech is not always grammatically correct. She has had no previous experience in group care, although she has two children of her own.

   Elaine, the teacher in whose room Rosa works, has come to you with concerns about Rosa's interaction with children, which she finds overly directive. She thinks that Rosa speaks too much Portuguese with the children and that her "broken" English presents a poor model for them.

   How do you feel about Elaine's concerns? What supervisory issues are apparent? What do you need to know? How would you approach these issues with each caregiver individually, and what kinds of supervision or training might you plan in response for (1) Elaine, (2) Rosa, and (3) the staff as a whole?

PART IV

STAFF RECRUITMENT, DEVELOPMENT, AND EVALUATION: A CONTINUUM

THE CAREER LADDER/LATTICE: A FRAMEWORK FOR STAFF RECRUITMENT, DEVELOPMENT, AND EVALUATION

THE MOST COMMON IMAGE that comes to mind when thinking of a lattice is that of a garden trellis (INCCRRA, 2006) with a climbing vine, such as a clematis, that grows vertically and yet branches across the trellis at various points. The concept of a career lattice works much the same way. It enables employees to see the career development options available to them and the qualifications needed to advance within the employee's area of specialization or move to another within the broad field of early care and education. For example, a staff member might take a job as an assistant teacher and move up the ladder to become a head or mentor teacher. Or at some point, that staff member might decide to move across the career lattice to meet the qualifications of a family advocate, home visitor, or nutritionist.

The lattice forms a network of strands connecting the various sectors within the early care and education field, ranging from child care in homes to child care centers (infant-toddler, preschool, and kindergarten) and Head Start programs, from public and private school-age programs, including out-of-school programs, to family services. Caregivers may enter a lattice at any point to pursue a particular path. Competency areas that describe the core knowledge and skills and the education and training necessary for a role at a specific level are identified, accompanied by a statement of salaries and benefits. Oftentimes, each level of a lattice is divided into smaller steps so that individuals can be rewarded—personally, professionally, and financially—as they make progress.

Staff members are thus able to see the big picture, the variety of opportunities available to them, and the steps they need to take to attain their professional goals.

STATE INITIATIVES

The concept of the career lattice was first introduced in 1993, when NAEYC's governing board formally adopted the framework (Willer, 1994). Then, recognizing the importance and connection between professional development and the quality of early childhood programs, the Committee on Early Childhood Pedagogy was established by the National Research Council in 1997. It called for each state to develop standards for early childhood programs and to establish a career ladder to include teaching assistants, teachers, and supervisors, with differentiated pay levels (Bowman, Donovan, & Burns, 2000).

At the state level, during the decade from 1992 to 2002, comprehensive planning efforts among key early care and education stakeholders developed initiatives in a range of key areas with the goal of establishing a high-quality early childhood workforce. The areas for improvement included raising standards for practitioners, increasing access to training toward professional credentials and degrees, and creating registries to document the training of individuals (Morgan & Costley, 2004).

By 2001, 29 states were in the process of implementing a career lattice, 31 states were establishing core competencies for teachers of young children, and 34 states were developing core knowledge areas (Wheelock College Institute for Leadership and Career Initiatives, 2002). By October 2005, 21 states had implemented some type of early childhood practitioner registry, with others in the planning stages (NCCIC, 2005).

Career lattices vary from state to state, but they share the goals of ensuring that early care and education practitioners are well prepared and of stabilizing the early childhood workforce by offering higher pay for increased education and responsibility. Common elements of lattices across states are a progression of levels from entry level to a master's or doctoral degree and a list of the education, experience, and training requirements for entry into each level.

Introductory levels have minimal requirements, such as a high school diploma or GED, CPR and first aid training, and/or specified hours of training in core competencies as in South Dakota (South Dakota Pathways, n.d.). As individuals move up the ladder, they are often required to hold a professional credential such as a CDA or equivalent and eventually an associate's degree and higher.

The scope of career lattices may also vary from state to state. The Illinois Early Childhood Career Lattice, for example, is quite broad in that it encourages professionals to explore multiple areas ranging from infant and toddler care to administration/leadership, to family support (INCCRRA, 2006). And the State of Maine has a social service professional lattice for family child care specialists, home visitors, and other support staff; a direct professional care lattice for child care practitioners, teachers, and group leaders; and an administration lattice and a management/coordination lattice for program directors, managers, and coordinators, enabling individuals to become aware of a broad range of opportunities (*Maine Roads to Quality*, 2006).

State Registries and the Career Ladder

As we noted above, many states have or are developing practitioner registries. In a nationwide survey, Bellm and Whitebook (2004) found that registries had several purposes: (1) to track and validate training of the workforce and to collect data on the ECE workforce, (2) to increase the recognition and status of the ECE workforce, and (3) to create a coherent professional development system.

Registry models are different from state to state (Bellm & Whitebook, 2004). In some states, registration is voluntary while in others, it is a requirement for licensure or for work in a state-funded program. Some states issue transcripts each time training is completed, while others update data every 2 years or more. And some offer stipends, tuition assistance, certificates, and recognition events as incentives for participants who raise their levels on the career ladder. Caregivers are required to pay for membership in some locations, while in other states membership is free.

Implications for Supervisors

How can supervisors in homes, centers, or schools take advantage of a state's career development program? An obvious first step is to learn about their state's career lattice program and support it by becoming a member of their state's registry, using it for their own professional development. Making staff members aware of the registry and lattice program so they also can take advantage of the opportunities provided is an important means of augmenting professional development offered at the program level. A representative from the state might in fact be willing to come to a program to present an overview. Sample packets of the state's plan and resources should be available in a program's professional resource library. When hiring new staff, a supervisor can ask prospective employees for registry transcripts and certificates that document their professional development. To further support the work of a state registry, staff can be encouraged to include these transcripts in their professional portfolios to reinforce the notion and the expectation of continuing one's professional education.

CAREER LADDER/LATTICE AT THE PROGRAM LEVEL

The idea of a career ladder/lattice can be incorporated at the center or program level. It supports the concept of developmental stages, which we described in Chapter 5, and the value of having a mix of ages, experience, and education levels among staff, and it motivates staff.

For years the careers of teachers in public school programs have been unstaged; that is, teachers have had few opportunities to assume new roles within teaching. Their options have been to move into administration or, for some, to risk stagnation within the teaching role. This situation is changing with the creation of mentor teacher and other teacher-leader positions as evidenced by plans in such districts as Rochester, New York (see Chapter 16).

The field of early care and education, however, is leading the way with the rapid advancement of the career ladder/lattice concept. At the program level, supervisors and staff can design a career ladder (see Table 13.1) as a basis for staff recruitment, development, and evaluation.

A way to begin is to identify about five levels such as teacher aide, assistant teacher, teacher, head teacher, and director. Write clear job descriptions for each role and the prerequisite qualifications for entry to that position. It is important to check state licensing requirements for each role. By becoming familiar with a state's career development system and resources, supervisors can link with that system and use it as a guide for determining levels, qualifications, and salaries and for helping staff to become aware of training opportunities, career advisement services, and scholarships. Incorporating a state's core knowledge and skill competencies into a program makes a great deal of sense, too, although a program may have its own competency statements based on its mission and funding source.

Lastly, working with staff in establishing recruitment goals and policies, in designing development and learning opportunities, and in determining approaches to staff evaluation and learning builds commitment to a program and ownership of the career development concept.

Staff Recruitment

The fact that a program has a thoughtful, articulated, public plan for staff recruitment, development, and evaluation is a recruitment tool in and of itself. Prospective employees are likely to be impressed by the fact that they have the opportunity to enter a setting that is professional and that has its own infrastructure for supporting staff.

A policy that describes how compensation is connected to education and training and promotion and how staff members may take advantage of career-advancement opportunities is helpful in making a program run smoothly. Graphic portrayals—perhaps in a handbook or on a Web site—which illustrate the various positions within a program and pathways to advancement, assist staff and prospective staff to clearly see career possibilities. And, of course, designing ways to communicate a program's career development plan internally as well as to parents, community members, partner organizations, and the public is critical to effective recruiting and to making a program's career ladder work (Manter, 2002).

Table 13.1. Program Career Ladder

Position	Job Description	Job Qualifications and Competencies	Salary and Benefits	Staff Development and Learning Opportunities	Staff Evaluation and Learning Opportunities
Director					
Head Teacher					
Teacher					
Assistant Teacher					
Teacher Aide					

Staff Development

Staff development is a term that can be applied to all experiences that aid staff in improving their work with children. It is a growth-oriented concept, based on the assumption that the quality of early childhood programs can be maintained and improved only through a well-planned and continuing program of experiences designed to foster practitioners' personal and professional development.

All staff, including administrators and highly competent teachers, can benefit from staff development opportunities. However, because of the many different paths through which early childhood practitioners come to their work, it is a challenge to find ways to serve all of their professional development needs. The career ladder can provide a framework for planning as staff members think about their career goals, where they fit within the ladder, and what their next step for development and learning might be.

Of course, staff members who are at novice or survival stages will most likely require different training and support than those who are at consolidation or mature stages (see Chapter 5). Some staff members may have little education, training, and experience working with young children, while others may hold a college degree and be very experienced. The funding source of a program may in fact mandate that a certain percentage of staff members have an associate's or bachelor's degree.

As supervisors work with staff to design a career ladder, they may also wish to think about the ways in which the professional development opportunities reinforce the knowledge and skill competencies required for staff members in each role. Since the content of the education or training and the follow-up support will vary at each stage of the career ladder, supervisors need to ask, which professional development options make sense for each step? Who should provide these? Are there professional development experiences that will be mandated for all staff? Which staff development options will be voluntary?

Similar questions can be asked of staff evaluation practices.

Staff Evaluation

The career ladder concept provides a program with the opportunity to offer a differentiated staff evaluation plan (Danielson & McGreal, 2000). Rather than have all staff evaluated on the identical competencies, in a similar fashion, by the same individual, evaluation practices can vary for staff who have various experience and education levels and who are in different roles.

It may make sense to evaluate staff with less experience and education more frequently than staff who have been in a program for a substantial amount of time. Some staff may be evaluated by the director, while the head teacher or peers may be involved in evaluating others. Evaluation procedures and tools used may be different at each step on the ladder; for example, portfolios might be used with some staff, while it may make more sense for other individuals to be asked to identify and plan how to achieve long-range goals (see Chapter 16).

CONCLUSION

We have identified some of the issues that need to be explored as supervisors work out the details of a program's career ladder plan. In the chapters that follow, we will offer some ideas for consideration in constructing a program career ladder. This is a process that will take a considerable amount of thought and time; in fact, it can be completed over time, perhaps a section or two each year.

PROGRAM ACCREDITATION

The criterion below for program accreditation is one of several from the *NAEYC Early Childhood Program Standards and Accreditation Criteria: The Mark of Quality in Early Childhood Education* (NAEYC, 2005) related to career ladders/lattices:

10.E.1 The program has written personnel policies that define the roles and responsibilities, qualifications, and specialized training required of all staff
and volunteer positions. The policies outline nondiscriminatory hiring procedures and policies for staff evaluation. Policies detail job descriptions
for each position, including reporting relationships; salary scales with
increments based on professional qualification, length of employment, and
performance evaluation; benefits; and resignation, termination, and grievance procedures. Personnel policies provide for incentives based on participation in professional development opportunities. The policies are
provided to each employee upon hiring. (p. 79)

EXERCISES

1. Obtain a copy of the early care and education career or professional development packet from your state and become familiar with its contents.
2. Review the child care staff licensing regulations in your state.
3. Work with staff members in completing Table 13.1. As you read the remain-
   ing chapters of this book, jot down ideas that might be useful in your program.
   a. Identify the positions that will form the basis of your career ladder.
   b. Write clear job descriptions for each role.
   c. Determine the qualifications and indicate the basic licensing requirements
      for each position.

   d. List the knowledge and skill competencies for each position.

   e. Name the salary and benefits for each position.

   f. List the professional development and learning opportunities for individuals in each role; take advantage of the statewide resources included in your state's career ladder plan.

   g. Determine the evaluation options for each role, the frequency of evaluation, and who the evaluators are.

STAFF RECRUITMENT, SELECTION, AND ORIENTATION

W E BELIEVE THAT STAFF RECRUITMENT and selection, staff orientation, on-the-job development and learning, and ongoing assessment and
evaluation for learning and career advancement are part of a professional continuum. The pieces of this continuum fit together to make up a whole. Supervisors and staff will want to keep the big picture in mind as they plan each segment.

In this chapter, we raise some questions and issues and make some suggestions for consideration in staff recruitment, selection, and orientation. These make
up the initial component of the continuum and set the stage for developing a culture of professionalism in a program as prospective and new staff are introduced
to and inducted into that culture.

PLANNING AND RECRUITING

Planning

A number of issues need to be considered before the recruitment process actually
begins. If a program is new, planning will involve a determination of the number
of staff needed, what the positions should be, and the requirements for each position, in light of state licensing regulations. If a program is already in operation,
planning may include a revision of job descriptions. Supervisors might want to
reconsider the present staff structure and configuration; perhaps a team concept
would be more effective than what exists. It may also make sense to revise the
current staff schedule, given the number of hours the program is in operation and
the emotional and physical demands placed on staff members throughout the day.
The approach to hiring substitutes might be looked at as well, and whether or not
a program needs a new position such as a mentor or coordinator.

Before establishing salaries and benefits, it might be useful to learn about neighboring programs and what they offer so as to be competitive. Benefits that prospective staff find attractive include on-site professional development, financial support for attending conferences, parental leave, tuition reimbursement, health insurance, social security contributions, career ladder salary increments with increased education, a retirement plan, scholarships for staff children, and paid time for staff preparation and meetings (Battersby, 2005). Of course, low staff-child ratios are a key incentive for joining any program.

Providing a staff handbook describing personnel policies such as grievance procedures, staff evaluation requirements, vacation and sick leave policies, salary schedules, and dismissal procedures conveys a message to prospective employees that a program is organized and that staff are taken seriously. Clear personnel policies, in print and public for all to see, let them know what the rules are in advance. The policies also provide guidelines to administrators and staff, which help avoid unpleasant confrontation when dealing with difficult problems.

The development of an application form that requests basic information about each applicant, such as educational background, job history, professional memberships, and names of individuals who can provide references, will enable members of the interviewing team to more easily compare candidates, even if resumes are also provided by applicants.

In this planning stage, professional child care associations, state registries, and local child care resource and referral agencies can be of assistance. A director's support group can also be an important resource for the exchange of information about staffing issues, job descriptions, salary schedules, and job application forms.

These are all examples of nitty-gritty planning issues, but a critical, overarching need is to be clear about the goals of a program and what it values. Prospective employees, particularly those with some experience and training, will want to make an informed choice. They will want to feel a sense of compatibility between their own philosophy and values and those of the program in which they will be working. A program's Web site and printed material are excellent media for conveying what a program stands for. The environment of a center or home and the images prospective staff and parents see in published materials or on a Web page convey a program's values; these images can extend an invitation or turn people away.

Values, reflected in a program's mission statement, also affect the composition of the staff to be recruited. For example, is there a value placed on staff diversity? Will an attempt be made to broaden the applicant pool to include males, individuals with diverse racial and linguistic backgrounds, and/or those who can who can act as links to the cultures represented in the community served by a program? Is it a priority to have different generations represented among staff?

The needs of a program and its particular challenges, the children being served, and the strengths and personalities of existing staff will serve as guidelines for determining the qualities and qualifications sought in new staff. Directors, then, will want to be clear about priorities when hiring staff and be able to articulate their program's vision in order to successfully recruit future employees.

Recruiting

Once a time frame is established for the recruiting, interviewing, and selection process, getting the word out about the job vacancy to the widest possible audience is one of the great challenges in finding the best qualified staff.

Writing a job announcement for advertising and postings is a first step. Existing announcements in the local paper or in a state registry provide some ideas of what an announcement might contain. The components of an effective job advertisement usually include the job title, qualifications, and description; the work schedule and scope (full- or part-time); the program's location and particular features; contact information; when and how to apply; and a policy statement of nondiscrimination (Albrecht, 2002).

Professional contacts and community connections are important in disseminating information about an opening. Local organizations such as the Chamber of Commerce, Rotary, Kiwanis, and Junior League; parks and recreation centers; nearby high schools, community colleges, and universities; nonprofits such as the United Way and YMCAs; state and national professional associations; and registries and referral agencies are all sources for posting job announcements. Bulletin boards in coffee shops, laundry mats, and grocery stores are also excellent places to post listings as well.

Creating a large, diverse talent pool of applicants means thinking about sources for applicants that do not normally come to mind. Houses of worship and religious institutions as well as senior groups can be a rich source for recruiting staff as well (Moore, 1999). Also, NAEYC's Web site (www.naeyc.org) includes an Early Childhood Career Forum, which brings job seekers and employers together, as does the Employment Opportunities Exchange of Childcare *Exchange* (www.childcareExchange.com).

Costs will be associated with some advertising. Daily and local newspapers, student newspapers, specialty papers which target specific groups, professional publications, and the Internet sell space for advertisements. Fees are associated with radio advertising, but perhaps these can be shared with other programs, unless local stations offer public service announcements that include job listings for free. Some state registries may charge a small fee for listing announcements.

A large applicant pool will increase the chances of finding individuals who fit best within a program. The hiring process, selecting the right person for the job, is the next stage of this professional continuum.

STAFF SELECTION

A systematic, organized hiring process that involves staff members already employed as well as parents is educational for those taking part and presents an image to candidates and a message to employees that collegiality and staff and community input are valued.

Again, planning ahead pays off. The interview committee, however small, will benefit from a review of the steps in the hiring process and their role in it. Reexamining job requirements and criteria so that there is consensus as to the skills and qualities they are looking for in a candidate is also worthwhile.

Once applications have been received and the deadline date closed, a review and ranking of all of the applications by committee members is a sensible next step. Some committees find it useful to develop a form with criteria listed and questions for reviewers to serve as a guide as they examine applications. Individual committee members often rank candidates first, privately, before coming together as a group to determine who will be invited for an interview.

Interviewing

Once a decision has been made as to which candidates to invite for an interview, committee members may wish to construct a list of questions that will be asked of each candidate during the group interview. This will enable them to better make comparisons among the applicants. Permitting the candidates to do most of the talking is a way to learn more about them and their thinking about the job. It is important to leave time for them to ask questions at the end; the kinds of questions they ask is also revealing.

Taking notes during an interview can be helpful in recalling key points for a follow-up discussion about each individual; however, note taking can also be distracting to a candidate, who is under pressure, responding to a multitude of questions. Beginning an interview with a brief informal chat about noneducational issues can relieve tension and set the candidate at ease. It is helpful to be aware of time and to keep to the schedule of the day so the candidate will have an opportunity to tour the center, work with children, and be interviewed individually by other staff and perhaps a small group of parents.

Teaching

Giving candidates an opportunity to interact with children and other staff is a wonderful way to get a sense of their strengths and lets them shine in the arena where they are most comfortable. Candidates will need to know ahead of time that they will be expected to work in a classroom for a short period of time or teach a minilesson, depending on the age level of the group. The demonstration teaching will enable supervisors and staff to gain a sense of the match between the candidate and the program and to assess whether a personal connection has been made.

Screening

Checking references to verify past employment and educational credentials is a critical part of the hiring process. Some directors find it beneficial to prepare questions ahead of time for previous employers. The interview held with the candidate may suggest certain issues to be followed up on during this stage. Criminal background checks are required of child care employees in many states; state licensing agencies provide information about the necessary procedures for obtaining these.

A summary of each candidate and a ranking of the applicants against the identified criteria is a final step before an offer is made. Input from all those who participated in the hiring process is essential before the committee makes its ultimate decision.

With the hard work of recruiting and selecting colleagues now complete, the process of inducting new employees into a program can be one of the most rewarding aspects of staff support and development.

STAFF ORIENTATION

The quality of an individual's first few days on the job can have a lasting effect on a program, children, and staff. The orientation experiences provided lay the foundation of a professional development program. A well-thought-out orientation plan enables supervisors to establish standards of professionalism from the very beginning and to induct new employees into the organization's culture. By laying out the framework of the orientation program in writing, it can be used as needed throughout the year since new staff members and volunteers do not always begin their employment at the start of the school year.

Supervisors and mentors may wish to organize the content and structure of the orientation program into modules or phases, making it easier to administer within different time frames. New staff can suffer from "information overload" if everything is presented at once. The format can also be varied so that individuals have opportunities to absorb and process new information through listening and interacting. Possible components that may be spread out over several days include a welcome and overview, a description of the program's philosophy and values, a tour, some time to observe in classrooms with follow-up questions, and laws and regulations.

Particular topics within modules might include a review of some foundations of a good developmental program for young children as well as certain key ideas that require continued emphasis and reinforcement—for example, the place of play in young children's lives, respect for children, policies concerning speakers of other languages, the importance of communicating positively with parents, and the need for objectivity and confidentiality.

It is also advantageous to set forth clearly and simply the program's point of view about discipline right from the start. For staff with little training, very specific examples—even explicit dos and don'ts—are more effective than general statements that can be misinterpreted. The reasons behind these procedures can be explored when the new person has had a variety of experiences to build on.

Volunteers, students, and job trainees who work only a few hours a week are often not aware that their roles in the classroom are important and affect other members of the staff as well as the children. Clarification of responsibilities, presented in a positive way, enhances the person's role, while at the same time making clear that the expectations are real.

At the end of this chapter is a list of basic information about the organizational aspects of a program, including an orientation, that is required by NAEYC accreditation.

Developing Relationships with Staff

A major objective of the orientation period is to help each new staff member feel comfortable with colleagues. Introductions to all staff, including secretaries and custodians, should not be overlooked. The staff member assigned to do this becomes a key person in facilitating the new person's transition to becoming a member of the staff. If there are trained mentors on the staff, this would be a time for them to initiate their relationship.

An introduction to parents can take place informally, when they leave their children and pick them up, and through a newsletter, e-mail, or announcement on a bulletin board. Notices can include brief background information about the new caregiver and his or her special interests and role at the center. Similar information can also be placed on a program's Web site. Supplemental staff members such as job trainees, students, and foster grandparents should also be introduced. Parents can be given a list of names, the times they will be working, and the rooms to which they are assigned, along with some information about how their presence helps the program.

If possible, have new people take part in setting up the rooms and in planning at the beginning of the school year. This gives them a stake in what will be happening with children and helps them understand what is needed to make it work.

Other Activities

Having new caregivers, especially those with little early childhood background, observe in classrooms before they begin work is an especially effective means for helping them understand what a program for young children is all about. At this stage, observations can focus on such things as becoming familiar with children's names, identifying areas of the room and what goes on in each, and noting some aspects of the roles of the teaching staff. Allowing time for observation also helps more experienced teachers get to know children and staff, and the "personality" of the particular program.

Group sessions provide opportunities for sharing perceptions and for becoming acquainted with others with whom they will be working. When more formal workshops are held for volunteers and trainees, information should be directly related to the experiences in which they will be involved during their first few weeks at the center, and active learning techniques should be used.

When orientation is designed so that it can be carried out on an individual basis, it can combine independent experiences with supervisory conferences, which allow supervisors to understand how the new staff member is perceiving the work environment and processing the new experience and to respond to the individual's questions and concerns.

Supervisors often become aware of particular areas that cause problems for new staff members. One Head Start supervisor, who noticed that the paperwork in her program can be confusing, has developed a packet of forms she finds useful in orienting new staff members. As she "walks through" each form with the staff members, different facets of Head Start's components and regulations and their implications for children and staff are revealed. Such creative solutions to specific problems can make a supervisor's job more interesting and provide important learning for new staff members.

There is sometimes a temptation to teach everything at orientation time. The purpose of an orientation, however, is to lay the foundation for a continuing process of professional development that builds as it goes on. It is usually most effective, therefore, to be very specific and present the most basic ideas, using examples wherever possible, even with sophisticated people if they are beginners. The general tone of this initial training period and the use of active learning principles can make it a model of the kinds of attitudes and, to some extent, the techniques that are to be used with children.

Taking time to orient new staff pays off, even if it places a burden on other staff members for a while. Staff orientation can be included in the Professional Development category of a program's career ladder. Leading orientation activities and participating in the process of recruiting and selecting staff are very appropriate professional development experiences for veteran staff members. These can also be designated on the career ladder.

CONCLUSION

The process of staff recruitment, selection, and orientation is one that will be repeated over time. Directors may want to create a map, blueprint, or checklist that will serve as a resource guide, enabling them to easily re-create the essential steps of the process each time.

The Right Fit (Albrecht, 2002) and *Leaders and Supervisors in Child Care Programs* (Sciarra & Dorsey, 2002) are two books which include ideas and many sample forms that can be used in the process of recruiting, selecting, and orienting staff.

PROGRAM ACCREDITATION

The following criteria for program accreditation from *NAEYC Early Childhood Program Standards and Accreditation Criteria: The Mark of Quality in Early Childhood Education* (NAEYC, 2005) represent a sampling of those related to staff recruitment, selection, and orientation:

6.A.03 Before working alone with children, new teaching staff are given an initial orientation that introduces them to fundamental aspects of program operation including
- program philosophy, values, and goals;
- expectations of ethical conduct;
- health, safety, and emergency procedures;
- individual needs of children they will be teaching or caring for;
- accepted guidance and classroom management techniques;
- daily activities and routines of the program;
- program curriculum;
- child abuse and neglect reporting procedures;
- program policies and procedures;
- NAEYC Early Childhood Program Standards;
- regulatory requirements

Follow-up training expands on the initial orientation. (p. 52)

6.A.04 Substitutes, volunteers, and other adults are given a preliminary orientation that introduces them to fundamental aspects of program operation before they begin working with children. The orientation includes health, safety, and emergency procedures; accepted guidance and classroom management techniques; child abuse and neglect reporting procedures and regulatory requirements.

These adults work with children under the direct supervision of qualified teaching staff. Follow-up training expands on the initial orientation. (p. 53)

7.A.01 As part of orientation and ongoing staff development, new and existing program staff develop skills and knowledge to work effectively with diverse families. (p. 56)

8.C.04 Program leadership builds mutual relationships and communicates regularly with close neighbors, informing them about the program, seeking out their perspectives, involving them in the program as appropriate, and cooperating with them on neighborhood interests and needs. (p. 61)

EXERCISES

1. Make a list of the characteristics and special qualities or abilities that you are looking for in a future employee of your program.
2. Cut out and review job advertisements from a local newspaper and then make up a mock ad for each of the major staff positions in your own program. Keep these on file.
3. Brainstorm and make a list of the advertisement and recruiting strategies that you plan to use to attract potential employees.
4. Make up a candidate summary sheet that allows committee members to easily see the strengths and weaknesses of each candidate interviewed.

CHAPTER 15

STAFF DEVELOPMENT
AND LEARNING

THE SUPERVISORY ROLE HAS MANY dimensions, ranging from being a listener and support person to being a manager and evaluator. It also includes being a facilitator of learning. It is the perspective of the supervisor as a facilitator of learning, as a learner, and as an adult educator that we will consider in this chapter. We will describe different views of adult learning, explore the role of the supervisor in fostering a community that encourages learning, and offer some staff development and learning options that might be included in a program's career ladder.

APPROACHES TO ADULT LEARNING

We wish to emphasize the connection between staff development and learning because all too often experiences and activities intended to bring about change in staff and improve their effectiveness in working with children, colleagues, and parents are offered for their own sake and have little impact on staff performance. Although there are many theories of adult learning, we have selected andragogy, transformative learning, and social constructivism as approaches that supervisors will find to be particularly useful in thinking about and planning meaningful and effective professional development.

Andragogy

The best known model of adult learning, called andragogy, was developed by Knowles and associates (1984) who identified five characteristics or assumptions about adults as learners. Although Knowles's theory has stimulated debate and controversy over the years (Merriam & Caffarella, 1999), practitioners have found his concepts useful in their work with adults. These assumptions and their implications for supervisors are described below.

Need for Self-Direction

As an individual matures, his or her self-concept changes from being a less dependent personality to a more independent one. Of course, the pace of moving toward independence varies for different people, and adults may be dependent some of the time in new or temporary situations. However, most adults have a need to be self-directing.

Although it seems contradictory, supervisors who are committed to helping teachers develop independence in children often have difficulty supporting the independence of their staff members. Teachers may be given a good deal of autonomy about the ways in which they work with children, but sometimes this is "benign neglect," resulting from the supervisor's need to juggle time between teaching, administrative duties, and conducting observations, conferences, or staff meetings. When this happens, supervision may become a rescuing, crisis-oriented operation where a directive approach is almost inevitable. Perhaps the major reason may be that supervisors themselves have not had role models who supported this adult need. They are, therefore, likely to imitate supervisory styles based upon experience as students or teachers or their views of what an administrator or supervisor is "supposed" to do.

Even when supervisors feel comfortable in encouraging independence, staff members may not have had much experience asserting themselves and may have been socialized or conditioned to be dependent. Many schools reward convergent thinking rather than problem solving, and for many staff members, "learning" may be associated with school experiences where the learner is the receiver, rather than the generator of knowledge. Also, caregivers who were not very successful in school may be reluctant to risk further failure by voicing ideas they fear may not be "right." Or supervisees may see the supervisor as the one who is supposed to tell them what to do. Thus supervisors and supervisees may need to learn how to be part of a collaborative process of problem exploration and joint inquiry where risks can be taken and mistakes made.

A Reservoir of Experiences

A staff member's life and work experiences are rich resources for learning. One of the satisfying aspects of teaching and supervising adults is that even when they have a limited education, have not taken early childhood courses, or are not fluent readers, their knowledge gained through their experience with children and with the world in general can be brought to bear on their day-to-day work.

The other side of this, of course, occurs when a supervisee holds onto personal experiences as being the only valid source for teaching behavior. A need to maintain stability and a sense of adequacy can prevent them from accepting the implications of new situations and may foster a reliance on meanings, skills, values, and strategies that have developed from past experiences. A certain amount of unlearning may be necessary as understandings and values are changed and new meanings are discovered and integrated within the context in which they are working. Of course, some new ideas may be rejected as they are tested out in the classroom.

Providing opportunities for staff members to contribute to each other's learning is a way that supervisors can tap into the rich and varied backgrounds and experience levels that staff bring to the workplace. When staff development and learning activities include mixed groups of teachers, aides, and other personnel, each person can contribute to the group from his or her own experiential and cultural perspective. Assumptions, understandings, and values may be challenged, significant insights furnished, and theoretical and practical knowledge shared during group discussions that can bring about a shift in thinking and new learning.

Interest in Application of Learning

Adults are ready to learn those things that they have a need to know. This need is often expressed by teachers who want to know how new information will help them in their work tomorrow. That is, they are ready for new learning when it will help them be more effective in their roles. Although this emphasis on immediacy of application can narrow the scope of learning, it can be viewed as a starting point for working with staff. Supervisors need not wait for this readiness stage to develop naturally. It can be induced in learners by helping them assess their work so they can set performance and career goals and by exposing them to more effective role models (Knowles, 1980).

A Problem-Centered Focus

Adults tend to have a problem-centered approach to learning. That is, they are more likely to be motivated to learn when the new learning can help them perform a task or solve a problem. For supervisors, this means that learning experiences should be organized around real teaching situations. For example, staff can be asked to describe a teaching dilemma in one or two paragraphs to be used as the basis for discussion in a staff meeting. In this way supervisors and colleagues might assist each other in solving problems related to their everyday work.

A problem-centered approach can also be used in individual staff conferences. This allows staff members to learn to look at teaching as problem solving and discover that, by working together with their supervisor, they may be able to find the best ways to resolve issues that confront them. A problem-centered approach shifts the focus away from the teacher and toward the situation, removing a sense of blame that either teacher or supervisor may have otherwise felt.

Internal Motivation

Internal factors, rather than external ones, motivate adults to learn. For example, being more effective on the job or raising one's self-esteem are more motivating than receiving a gift certificate for a job well-done.

Supervisors can provide learning and work experiences that are related to the aspirations and goals of staff members. They might assist staff in the process of self-evaluation and in diagnosing learning needs by encouraging staff to set their own learning goals and conferring with staff regularly to assess their progress toward meeting them.

An effective professional development and learning program in a center that helps staff grow and develop is likely to provide these internal motivational factors.

Transformative Learning

A second view of adult learning that has taken center stage in the field of adult education is transformative learning or transformational learning. First proposed by Mezirow (1991), transformative learning is less concerned with the characteristics of adults and more focused on how adults interpret and make meaning from their experiences (Merriam & Caffarella, 1999). It is "big learning" in that it involves changing the perspectives that have served to filter our understanding of ourselves and the world around us. These perspectives or meaning schemes include specific knowledge, beliefs, value judgments, assumptions, expectations, and feelings that we use in interpreting our experience (Mezirow et al., 2000). They are derived from our personal histories and culture and form our habits of mind as we attempt to make meaning.

Mezirow and colleagues (2000) believe that learning is often set in motion by a disorienting dilemma or event. The birth of a child, the death of a loved one, or perhaps even moving to another country may cause us to critically examine our long-held assumptions, biases, and values. This self-reflection, coupled with constructive discourse with others, enables us to justify or to shed taken-for-granted ways of thinking and to develop new interpretations, understandings, and opinions, representing a fundamental change in our perceptions. As a result, we view ourselves and the world around us through a different lens. We try out new roles and behaviors, negotiate new relationships, and reintegrate these into our daily lives. Thus transformative learning implies both change, as we are freed up from old ways of thinking and behaving, as well as development, as we act on our new set of assumptions and beliefs.

It is not uncommon for some early childhood staff members to undergo major changes in their thinking about themselves and about the care and education of children. Caregivers hired as teacher aides, for example, may enroll in Head Start or Child Development Associate training programs. This step, which may open up a whole new world for them, can have a major effect on their perceptions of themselves as knowers and as individuals with skills and abilities who can make a significant impact on a program, thus becoming a transformative experience. With new awareness and greater confidence, these staff members often move up the career ladder, taking on roles of increased responsibility.

The use of questioning techniques by supervisors and mentors as they work with staff on a one-to-one basis to stimulate critical reflection and examination of underlying beliefs is central to supporting a staff member's journey. Staff development that provides opportunities for group dialogue where assumptions can be challenged and other viewpoints heard is also essential to reflective learning. Fostering this discourse means the authority of staff members is recognized and that supervisors need to become collaborators in the process.

Additionally, role-playing, multiple-perspective taking, journal writing, storytelling, and even videotaping of teaching can assist individuals as they undergo this process of change. Of course, the freedom and encouragement to test out new meanings, roles, and behaviors is critical to the process of reintegrating these into daily activity. Timing of supervisory support is an important consideration as such major shifts in thinking cannot be forced and such disorienting events cannot be artificially induced.

Social Constructivism

The basic notion of constructivism is that learning is a process of constructing meaning. It recognizes individuals as knowers and as owners of the process of constructing knowledge. Social constructivists believe that knowledge creation is a social process that takes place through dialogue and reflection with others (Merriam & Caffarella, 1999).

Much has been written about constructivism in terms of children's learning, but how might this notion apply to adult learning, specifically to working with teachers? Hannay (2004) argues that we need to rethink the ways in which we foster professional learning in schools. She distinguishes between professional development and professional learning. In her view, professional development is associated with information delivery or transmitting knowledge, while professional learning is "an 'internal' mental process through which individuals create professional knowledge" (p. 7). She urges us to shift our emphasis from delivery to assisting individuals in constructing and reconstructing their personal/professional knowledge.

As professionals, we have developed considerable knowledge through practical experience. Oftentimes, we take this knowledge for granted, rarely even thinking about it as we carry out our roles. This knowledge, usually unarticulated, is called *tacit knowledge* (Hannay, 2004). When we meet with colleagues and engage in discussions about our work, reflect on and share our practices, our tacit knowledge becomes *explicit* knowledge.

As we articulate our practical knowledge in a group, our colleagues have opportunities to challenge us and to offer alternative perspectives. Sometimes, we are called upon to justify our practices. As a result of this collective interchange, we reconstruct what is now our explicit knowledge, which is shared and sanctioned by the group. This reconstructed knowledge becomes tacit knowledge when it is tested out in the classroom and incorporated into our practice (Hargreaves, 2002). The process of constructing and reconstructing personal/professional knowledge, then, involves an interplay between tacit and explicit knowledge and between the individual and the group (Nonaka & Takeuchi, 1995).

If this notion of learning is used as the basis of a staff development and learning plan for a center, then that plan will look quite different from what has been traditionally employed in many schools, such as workshops offered by outside consultants or prepackaged commercial professional training programs. The focus will be on staff members and their expertise, on collaboration among colleagues and dialogue about practice, and on the work context.

Fostering Cultures That Promote Professional Learning

We have described three views of adult learning that have implications for supervisory practice. What is the role of a supervisor in supporting professional learning?

First, as a supervisor, you need to be a learner too. As a role model, you set the tone for your program, greatly influencing its culture. By setting an example as a risk taker and by participating as a coinvestigator in the learning process, you can show that the creation of knowledge in your setting is valued.

Second, in the theories of learning described above, the learner plays a key role in driving the learning process, as does the personal experience of the learner. Clearly, connecting learning opportunities to problems, issues, and concerns about actual practice, about real-life situations, can have a major impact on the motivation of the learner and increase the possibility for changes in practice. Although taking teachers out of the work setting clearly has value, learning on-site enables them to study current practice and to experiment with new behaviors to see firsthand the impact they have on children.

Third, as we emphasized before, a work environment characterized by an atmosphere of openness and emotional safety enables teachers to freely discuss long-held values, to share their working knowledge, and to experiment with new practices without fear of pressure or disapproval from supervisors or colleagues.

Fourth, the role of critical reflection and analysis, of questioning existing understandings, is key to both the transformative and constructivist views of learning. Collaboration among colleagues in a shared space fosters an exchange of ideas and practices, stimulates dissonance that can trigger transformations in thinking, and, most important, allows new practices to be sanctioned by the group and incorporated into a program's culture without reprisal. Disseminating new practices within a program and outside a program validates and helps sustain the learning process.

Finally, learning takes time. If real change is to take place, it is essential that you arrange the organizational variables in your setting so that learners have time to process and internalize new ideas, to reflect, to discuss, and then to implement new practices at a reasonable pace.

TEACHER-DIRECTED PROFESSIONAL DEVELOPMENT

What are some specific strategies and experiences that incorporate some or all of the elements described above? Teacher-led study groups, action research, and lesson study/group supervision are three approaches that we describe in this section. Later in the chapter we discuss mentoring, informal modeling, and observing peers and children. These approaches, along with Child Development Associate training and National Board Certification, as well as resources such as the use of technology, professional reading, and involvement in professional associations and advocacy groups can form the basis of a coherent and ongoing professional development plan that includes many options. The career ladder can provide a framework for creating such a plan as supervisors work with staff members to develop a consensus as to the content and timing of learning experiences. Other inquiry-based strategies such as portfolio development, long-range goal setting, critical friends groups, and storytelling will be discussed in Chapter 16.

Teacher-Led Study Groups

A study group is a community of teachers who take charge of their own learning. This may be a small group of staff members within your program who would like to investigate and study a particular topic related to their practice. They might, for example, like to explore the theme of "Learning through play" or "Assessing young children in mathematics," or a theme related to one of NAEYC's accreditation standards. The group might meet monthly, discussing a different article at each session, examining children's work , and/or even viewing a videotape or photographs of their classrooms related to the designated topic of study. Follow-up activities might be developed and field-tested in classrooms and brought back to the group for discussion.

An individual or a pair of teachers could be assigned to coordinate the group's agenda, select readings, prepare critical questions for discussion, arrange for space, maintain communication, and assemble needed materials. Some programs develop simple, one-page, study group proposal applications in which prospective members are asked to name their topic and describe their goals and questions for study, the proposed procedures, the materials and resources needed, ways of documenting meetings, and expected outcomes. Reviewing these proposals can help the group to clarify its purpose. Minutes of each meeting could be kept or some type of log maintained, and the group's progress could be assessed with the use of a rubric. Although teacher accountability is important, we think that it makes sense to keep bureaucratic paperwork to a minimum. Study group members sometimes use e-mail as a means of supporting communication among members.

Study groups have the potential to be very meaningful professional development and learning experiences. They build a sense of community, use and strengthen expertise among staff within a program, and focus on practice.

Action Research

Individual Teachers' Action Research

When Vivian Paley, whose insightful observations are contained in *The Girl with the Brown Crayon* (1997) and many other books about life in classrooms, realized that being curious was a missing element of her teaching, she started using a tape recorder. She began to discover a lot about children's thinking and about her own responses to children, realizing that they were not necessarily the best ones.

Experienced teachers or providers often want to find their own answers to questions about the effectiveness of classroom practice, children's behavior and development, or family interactions. Perhaps they are curious about something that did work, but they don't know why. These caregivers are ready to do action research in their own classrooms.

Action research is a process in which practitioners systematically reflect on their work and as a result change their practices. They use qualitative and sometimes even quantitative methods or combinations of both to observe and reflect, plan an intervention, collect data, and then make changes. They may use tape recorders to collect data as do teachers in the preschools of Reggio Emilia, or an array of other ethnographic techniques, such as interviewing children, parents, or others individually or in focus groups; keeping journals; or using photographs or portfolios.

Schoolwide Action Research

Although action research is often undertaken by individual teachers, groups of teachers within a school can also carry out research by collecting evidence about a particular phenomenon that is of interest and concern to members of their school.

The Coalition of Knowledge Building Schools in Sydney, Australia, has been experimenting with the notion of schools as places where research and inquiry are embedded into the culture of schools. Here, as a normal part of their professional work, groups of teachers collect and discuss evidence that informs them about teaching and learning and contributes to school improvement (Groundwater-Smith, 2002). In one school, for example, a researcher in residence is assigned to support teachers in their research efforts and a research advisory committee receives research recommendations from teachers, students, or parents and decides which questions will be studied. Participants in the Coalition learn to use a variety of ways to collect evidence about their research questions, including images and metaphors, photographs and drawings, focus groups, and surveys and questionnaires (Groundwater-Smith & Mockler, 2003). The idea is that the entire school becomes a knowledge-building organization (Hargreaves, 2002). Not only do members acquire knowledge through reading journals or attending professional conferences and through other sources, but the school constructs knowledge itself (Groundwater-Smith, 2002).

The idea of an early childhood program generating and articulating knowledge about early childhood practice poses some exciting possibilities for professional learning. Supervisors can lead staff in exploring issues that are of concern to parents and teachers in a program. Even with little experience as formal researchers, supervisors and teachers together can informally experiment with studying particular issues using their common sense as a guide, coupled with a willingness to take risks. Helpful resources for getting started are books about action research, such as *An Educational Leader's Guide to School Improvement* (Glanz, 2003) and *The Art of Classroom Inquiry: A Handbook for Teacher-Researchers* (Hubbard & Power, 2003). Other steps that supervisors can take to lay the groundwork for learning through teacher research include finding a university-based partner who could serve as a research facilitator; identifying an action research study group, perhaps through public schools, training centers, or local professional organizations; or arranging for an action research course to be given on site.

Lesson Study/Group Supervision

Lesson study is an approach to professional development used in Japan that has elements of group clinical supervision developed by Goldhammer (1969) and described in Chapters 9 and 10.

In Japan small groups of teachers jointly plan a lesson together based on a specific goal that they wish to achieve with their students (Fernandez & Chokshi, 2002). One teacher teaches the lesson using the plan developed by the group, while the others observe the class, collecting data based on the research questions identified. The group comes together to discuss their observations and to reflect on the lesson. Sometimes they revise the lesson based on their research, and then it is taught by another teacher in the group. Oftentimes, an outside observer or advisor, called a "knowledgeable other" serves in a support role to the group by offering a different perspective when reacting to the work of the group, by providing additional information about content or new ideas, or by sharing the work of other lesson study groups. Teachers document their work in lesson study sometimes in the form of published research about their practice (Watanabe & Wang-Iverson, 2002).

We believe that groups of teachers planning lessons together, observing each other, and talking about their observations afterward is one of the most sensible, pertinent, and powerful forms of staff development and learning. Supervisors and mentors can facilitate this process by juggling organizational variables so that groups of teachers can have the time to meet together and to observe each other; providing some structure and practice for a group such as working with teachers to create a sensible lesson plan format or offering some workshops on communication skills; providing copies of curriculum and accreditation standards that can be helpful in determining goals and research questions; and serving as "knowledgeable others." Documentation of the lesson study process could be one of a program's career ladder professional development requirements. Additional information about lesson study can be obtained from the Lesson Study Research Group (LSRG) of Teachers College, Columbia University (http://www.tc.edu/lessonstudy/research.html).

Teachers Helping Teachers

In addition to teacher-directed professional development and learning activities, teachers can also have a major impact on teacher learning and change by working directly with colleagues in classrooms as mentors, coaches, and consultants.

Mentors are skilled and experienced teachers or providers who serve as guides or coaches for novice teachers. They may work in the same programs as their protégés or in a different one. Their role differs from that of a supervisor in two ways: They are peers of the people they guide; and while they support, give feedback, and counsel them, they do not evaluate them.

Many knowledgeable and skilled caregivers find this role fulfilling. It provides opportunities for new challenges and learning, both through formal training in such areas as communication skills and adult learning and through opportunities to learn from their less experienced proteges. Not all advanced teachers, however, make good mentors. Not all advanced teachers, however, make good mentors. They should be people who are interested in helping adults, as well as children, learn and grow; who see themselves as learners; who are creative, flexible, and reflective; and who have good interpersonal skills with adults, and a respect for diversity (Bellm, Whitebook, & Hnatiuk, 1997).

The training that is required for mentors includes many of the approaches described in this book. There are a number of formal training programs, the oldest of which is the state-supported California Early Childhood Mentor Program. The Early Childhood Mentoring Alliance at the Center for the Child Care Workforce, American Federation of Teachers Education Foundation (see Appendix) can provide information on many aspects of mentoring. *The Early Childhood Mentoring Curriculum* (Bellm, Whitebook, & Hnatiuk, 1997) is a comprehensive resource for mentors in center-based and family child care programs. Those in Head Start programs will find many helpful suggestions in *Putting the Pro in Protégé: A Guide to Mentoring in Head Start and Early Head Start* (2001).

In addition to mentors, some early childhood programs have created other teacher consultant positions such as curriculum coaches or advisors who provide on-site technical assistance to teachers in classrooms to help them learn new instructional techniques and/or how to adapt curriculum and teaching to meet the needs of children with special needs. These are usually very skilled teachers, familiar with the setting and children, who model new teaching strategies, assist with management and organizational issues, and give feedback to other teachers who are testing out and practicing new methods in their classrooms.

The use of mentors, coaches, or consultants to support professional learning incorporates colleagueship as teachers are working with their peers. The relationship and dialogue between teacher and consultant and respect for the staff member's knowledge and experience, is particularly important as are a mentor's questions in fostering the reflective process that is central to learning (Mezirow et al., 2000). Although consultants may engage in administrative activities dealing with screening, enrollment, and district paperwork (Ryan, Hornbeck, & Frede, 2004), we believe that their hands-on work with teachers in classrooms and ongoing support has the greatest potential for innovation and lasting change.

STRUCTURED STRATEGIES
FOR PROFESSIONAL DEVELOPMENT

Teachers at all stages of development can benefit from inquiry-based professional learning opportunities. Novices, who may be very analytical despite their lack of a knowledge base, can assume responsibility for their own learning and become investigators of their practice. Sometimes, however, beginning teachers as well as experienced teachers who are trying something new require a different kind of structure and support. Strategies used by mentors, coaches, and supervisors include modeling teaching behaviors and providing staff with opportunities for observing peers and children.

Informal Modeling

Modeling goes on all the time when there are two or more people working together in the same space with the same children. Directors, coordinators, and head teachers model behavior constantly by the way they organize staff meetings, interact with staff in classrooms and during conferences, write memos that capture a tone of colleagueship, and work with parents and children. The trust and mutual respect for adults and children that is communicated by directors and other supervisors sets the stage for the way staff members are expected to interact with children, families, and colleagues.

Caregivers are most likely to learn from the modeling of teaching behaviors when they are helped to focus on significant aspects of what is taking place. It is not easy to recognize, for example, the importance of the ways in which a teacher reacts to small incidents during the day, spontaneously picking up on what a child says or does, preventing trouble by anticipating problems, and then keeping activities moving or changing pace.

One preschool director-teacher models reflective teaching by thinking out loud, describing what she is doing as she does it. She might say, "It's beginning to cloud up outside. The children seem to be getting restless. Let's go sit with them for a minute." Or perhaps to illustrate that few decisions are clear-cut, "Activity in the house corner seems to be beginning to break down. I wonder, shall we wait a little to see if it will work out, or take a group and read a story?"

Nonteaching supervisors who visit a classroom during a free-play period can model appropriate behaviors in the role of temporary assistant on the classroom team. This form of supervision is especially effective when the lead teacher or the classroom team as a whole is the focus of training.

Staff members also benefit when teachers or supervisors talk about children—their styles, likes and dislikes, and skills—as they work together in the classroom. This helps caregivers see the individuality of each child and understand teachers' actions in relation to specific child behaviors. This can be especially useful when a class includes children with special needs or those from a variety of cultural or linguistic backgrounds.

Commenting when a child is misbehaving (or seems to be) can be especially instructive, since views about discipline are so bound by one's own experiences. The supervisor might say, "We're letting Tommy stay out of the group for the time being, since he becomes overwhelmed by sitting with so many people." Or "I wasn't sure whether to intervene in that little squabble or not. I'm glad to see they've worked it out themselves. It can be valuable when they do, but I try to keep an eye out."

These situations become a rich source of material for individual or group conferences, which should follow important incidents as closely as possible. They can be discussed and related to other experiences, to readings, or to other kinds of training in which caregivers have taken part, and staff can be encouraged to try out effective techniques themselves.

There are some cautions about modeling by supervisors, especially if they are not members of the classroom team. Sensitivity to the roles of other adults in the classroom, particularly in participant supervision situations, is essential. It is helpful to make clear to all members of the team, especially the lead teacher, that your role is to fit in with the ongoing program, not to take over responsibilities that teachers, assistants, or volunteers see as their own. The message "You're really not doing it right; super-teacher will show you how" is less likely to be conveyed when supervisors respond in a natural way to children's real needs within the context of the particular activity.

Taking advantage of informal modeling opportunities helps new staff and volunteers see that "teaching" includes everything that goes on in the classroom and discover that teaching involves an attitude of continually questioning and learning from one's experiences.

Planned Observations of Peers

Planned observations of other caregivers provide a different kind of learning opportunity. These observations work especially well when based on a specific need identified by the supervisor or a staff member. A particular setting, behavioral focus, or time of day can then be selected to best accomplish that purpose. The caregiver thus takes part in the decision about what to observe and why.

Beginning Teachers

During orientation or the first months on the job, caregivers can be assigned to observe teachers at different parts of the day, especially times such as free play or transitions when the teaching role is not so clearly identifiable. A discussion beforehand about what to look for or an observation sheet with focus questions narrows what is to be examined to manageable proportions. For example, instead of suggesting that a caregiver "observe transitions," a series of observations might be set up. One could focus on how teachers prepare children for change (e.g., going from free play to snack), another on what they do to make it easier for children who don't function well during transitions, and a third on how teachers work together to take care of stragglers. An observation sheet for free-play time might include this series of questions:

> How do teachers help children make choices?
> What do they do when a child seems to be wandering around?
> What seems to help children learn from their play?
> What seems to interfere?

Eventually, as caregivers develop observation skills, they will be able to function with much more open-ended guidelines.

Experienced Teachers

More experienced caregivers may respond better to ideas for changes in teaching strategies when they can examine alternatives to help them determine what method would work best for them. For example, in a supervisory conference a concern may be raised about keeping the children's attention while reading aloud. Through a problem-solving process, the teacher may be able to come up with some causes for their inattentiveness but still be unsure of what to do about it. It could then be

suggested that she observe several other teachers as they read to children and identify some alternative strategies for keeping the children involved.

Frequently, teachers are stimulated by workshops to try new techniques or
activities but do not feel confident enough to actually attempt them. In such situations, the supervisor or a skilled teacher can demonstrate the technique in the classroom. Art, cooking, and creative movement are types of experiences that lend
themselves well to this type of demonstration, since they are more easily shown
than explained. If at all appropriate to the activity, classroom team members should
take part in it. These observations are most effective when they begin with a planning session in which all participants are actively involved and when they are
followed by a feedback session during which perceptions, questions, and opinions are shared.

Lesson-study described earlier in this chapter and group and peer supervision
are other examples of professional development that incorporate peer observation.

Observing Children

When teachers—whether they are new to the job or have been teaching for years—
really begin to look at children, new worlds open up to them. Observing increases
caregivers' understanding of developmental age or stage characteristics and of
how children construct learning through their own play. They gain insight into
some of the very real differences children show in their interactions with adults,
with other children, and with equipment and materials. And they develop an awareness of changes in individual children over time, an ability especially important
for those who work with infants, speakers of other languages, or children with
special needs. Objective observation of children is also, of course, a skill in itself
that should be acquired and used by anyone who works with young children.

Caregivers may keep *anecdotal records* of one or two children over a period
of several weeks, which can help them gain an understanding of children's behavior over time. Or they might make *running records*, describing everything that
they hear or see during a brief, designated time interval. This technique is especially valuable in revealing children's ability to be self-directing, to explore and
learn from their explorations, and to learn through their play. In working with
infants, such direct observations often result in surprising insights when caregivers
see that every gesture provides some information about a child's development and
personality.

When care is taken to make records descriptive and nonjudgmental, they can
be shared among staff members and even with parents to assist in making decisions
about a child or the program. Assignment of observations of children, of course,
must be accompanied by a discussion of professionalism and confidentiality.

There are many resources for tools and methods for observing young children.
Among these are Cohen, Stern, and Balaban's classic book, *Observing and Recording
the Behavior of Young Children* (1997), which provides guidelines and questions

for looking at classroom behavior in a variety of settings, and the *Preschool Child Observation Record* (High/Scope Educational Research Foundation, 2003).

Because young children's behavior reveals so much about their abilities and about how they learn, observation is an especially valuable tool for staff learning. It makes available a reality base that is hard to find in any other way.

CAREER DEVELOPMENT

Career development can be described simply as opportunities that are part of an early childhood staff development and learning plan designed to promote upward mobility within a program and perhaps beyond. Opportunities for staff to obtain credentials that verify their acquired knowledge and skills are important elements of such programs. It is here that the career-ladder concept and state career development initiatives, including state registries, which we described in Chapter 13, can be especially useful.

Such efforts may be focused on staff members who are at the lower job levels and who do not have degrees as well as those who may be interested in preparing for new roles such as head teacher, educational coordinator, or director; or in changing direction from preschool to infant care, or toward social services, parent education, or special-needs education.

Supervisory Assistance

There is considerable range in the extent of involvement of supervisors in career development. In a large program with a commitment toward such opportunities, it is best to have someone on the staff who has the major responsibility for coordinating contacts with state agencies and educational institutions and keeping up with staff members who are taking part. Problems with finding transportation or baby sitters, choosing appropriate courses, taking courses online, and working through a college bureaucracy can quickly discourage a staff member whose self-confidence is low. The coordinator can field such problems and help caregivers find ways to solve them.

In smaller programs, the involvement will be more informal, with supervisors acting as encouragers and facilitators for staff who wish to pursue formal education. A third role for supervisors is to act as a field advisor or trainer for CDA candidates, which could include supervising field experiences and taking part in the assessment process.

College Preparation Programs

The simplest and most helpful part supervisors can play in encouraging formal study is to gather and disseminate information about colleges that have early childhood courses, CDA training, and/or degree programs that are appropriate to the needs of their staff. A college or university that has provided CDA and other training for Head Start staff may also be able to serve staff from other early childhood programs. Institutions that show an understanding of the special strengths and needs of adult learners and that assess previous work or life experience for credit are preferable. External degree programs, which provide course work through independent studies or online and distance learning, are readily available.

It is often possible to negotiate for courses on special topics and even for new degree programs if sufficient numbers of students can be guaranteed. On-site courses are also sometimes an option. Working together with other early care and education programs or public schools helps develop evidence that there will be a continued market for such courses or programs in that location. State registries and research and referral agencies can be very helpful in these efforts. So that formal study programs will affect more than a few highly motivated staff members with enough money to pay for their own courses, every effort should be made to provide or seek out some kind of tuition subsidy.

The CDA Credential

The Child Development Associate credential has a number of advantages as a career development goal. This system allows people with varying amounts of formal or informal education, with or without degrees, to focus on the same goals and reach them at their own pace and in a way that is most appropriate for them. The requirements are flexible, both in time and in the type of training needed. And, because the CDA competencies are based on sound developmental principles and the credential is awarded on the basis of a caregiver's actual work with children, there is a direct relationship with the quality of teaching and the care of children.

The CDA assessment and credentialing system was developed in the early 1970s to provide a nationally recognized, validated standard of competence for early childhood practitioners. It is administered by the Council for Professional Recognition, a nonprofit corporation in Washington, D.C. (see Appendix).

At the heart of the CDA system there are six major competencies, which are subdivided into 13 functional areas (see Council for Professional Recognition, n.d.). These define the standards by which individuals are assessed and the credential awarded. Assessment is a six-stage process that includes the collection of documents, a verification visit by a Council representative, and a review of documentation of competence. There are some variations based on where the candidate for the credential works; that is, in a center-based preschool, center-based infant/toddler program, family child care home, or bilingual or special needs setting, or as a home visitor. CDA is an especially attractive alternative for those who do not feel ready to pursue a degree and to those with degrees but without early childhood course work. For a full description of CDA requirements and the process for obtaining a credential, see the Council's Web site (http://www.cdacouncil.org).

National Board Certification

The National Board of Professional Teaching Standards (NBPTS) offers National Board Certification in many teaching specializations, including Early Childhood Generalist, for teachers of children ages 3–8. This is a voluntary certification process that requires extensive documentation, analysis, and reflection of practice based on high performance standards. Teachers who have a baccalaureate degree, 3 years of experience working with children ages 3–8, and a valid teacher license or certificate, if required by their state, are eligible to apply. There is a substantial fee associated with the process, which takes almost a full school year to complete.

At the heart of the process are the standards for Early Childhood Generalist (see NBPTS, 2004). Teachers are asked to demonstrate these standards through a portfolio that contains videotapes of their teaching, products of student learning, and other teaching artifacts, as well as documented work with families and the larger school community. Reflective statements about their practice are also included.

In addition, teachers must complete an assessment-center component which focuses on a candidate's content knowledge. The exercises are computer-administered at statewide testing centers. The candidates write answers to questions based on materials that have been sent to them in advance or are presented on-screen. Teachers who meet the performance standard receive a certificate for 10 years, which can be renewed.

The National Board Certification process is a rigorous one and a wonderful professional development experience. It is based on what teachers actually do, why they do it, and how they think. We recommend that you review the Board's Web site (http://www.nbpts.org) to obtain a full description of requirements and procedures for obtaining this certificate.

RESOURCES FOR PROFESSIONAL LEARNING

We have described several possible components of a professional development and learning program. Computer and digital technology, a professional library, and professional associations are other important resources that can lend support to a staff member's growth and development.

Technology Resources

The use of technology in the field of early care and education continues to grow very rapidly. In a survey of child care programs, including family child care,

Donohue (2003) found that programs use technology for accounting and market-ing purposes; communicating with parents and staff; Internet access; purchasing books, supplies, and equipment; and security systems. Digital and video cameras are also used for parent conferences and staff training. Assistive technology for use with children with special needs is another important application.

Many of the professional development and learning options described above can be enhanced with the use of technology. A few possible applications are using a digital camera in preparing portfolios, a video camera to record teaching epi-sodes for group supervision or lesson study, the Internet for investigating topics for action research projects, e-mail for staff to stay in touch with each other and to network with other professionals, and online discussion groups and chat rooms for support purposes. In addition, the list of organizations, universities, agencies, and other providers delivering online courses for child care professionals is greatly expanding.

The NAEYC Technology and Young Children Interest Forum (www.tech andyoungchildren.org) is one of a number of sites that include online resources for staff development and training programs as well as examples of best educa-tional practices of using technology with young children and families, including a bibliography of articles and research studies on this topic.

It is clear that the use of technology in the early childhood field is expanding and that child care staff will need access to computers and other technology tools as well as ongoing training in how to use them. Technology training for supervi-sors is especially critical because they will need to display a comfort with tech-nology and background knowledge so that they can support, advise, and guide staff as they learn and benefit from the use of technology in their work with chil-dren, colleagues, and parents.

Professional Reading

Even though the Internet brings a world of professional resources to staff, easy access to a well-stocked library of professional materials has an essential place in any child care setting in which a culture of learning is valued.

Staff may be asked to read particular articles for discussion at staff meetings and might be encouraged to read during children's nap times or, when working with older children, at times set aside when everyone in a program reads silently.

Supervisors serve as models when they share their own reading experiences in staff meetings on a regular basis and make the reading materials available afterward. Staff members can be invited to share books or articles they have recently read. Individual conferences and meetings with classroom teams also provide opportuni-ties for supervisors to suggest readings related to a specific area of concern.

Some staff members, perhaps those involved in study groups, may be inter-ested in researching books and articles to recommend to colleagues or parents or writing short reviews for the center newsletter or Web site. The greatest value in professional reading comes when staff have opportunities to discuss with each other ideas from their reading in terms of relevance to their work with children, families, and each other.

Supervisors are sometimes surprised to discover that some members of their staff are not proficient readers. For these caregivers, materials that are both appropriate and not too difficult must be searched out. For those for whom English is a second language, readings in native languages can be made available. Connecting staff members with courses in reading and writing improvement can make a great difference in enabling all to become full participants in the field.

Professional Associations

Participating in professional associations such as the National Association for the Education of Young Children (NAEYC), the National Association for Family Child Care (NAFCC), Association for Childhood Education International (ACEI), and the Council for Exceptional Children (CEC), and their state and local affiliates is an important means for staff to see themselves as part of a large profession. These and other organizations (see Appendix) offer opportunities for staff to participate in their chosen field beyond the confines of their program. Through membership in professional associations, they can meet new colleagues, extend their professional education, and assume new leadership roles.

Through their Web sites, publications, conferences, and workshops, professional organizations offer a multitude of learning opportunities. Directors of programs may wish to send staff members to conferences on an alternating basis and/or provide some form of membership reimbursement as a program benefit. It is important for directors to take an active role in professional associations themselves so they are up-to-date on the latest developments in the field.

MAKING THE WORKPLACE ENJOYABLE

In concluding this chapter, we'd like to offer a few suggestions for setting an upbeat tone to a program. Of course, if staff members are challenged, if they have opportunities to collaborate, and if they are learning, then chances are that there is a positive atmosphere already in a program. Here are some additional small steps that can be taken to make a difference in the work environment:

1. Highlight staff accomplishments through your program's Web site, newsletter, and bulletin board.
2. Make teaching "fun." Plan centerwide special days for the children built around a theme, a special guest, or a puppet show. Do it so it's fun for the teachers as well as the children, without so much work that the enjoyment is lost.
3. Have social events periodically in which staff have a chance just to get to know

each other as people. When people discover and rediscover that they can have fun together, tensions can be relieved and even dissipated. Include families and friends in some events. Plan them with sensitivity to financial and family needs, and help staff to accept individual's lack of participation without resentment.

4. Add food to a work session or staff meeting. It is a catalyst for informal talk and relaxation. If done only occasionally, it gives a meeting a bit of a party atmosphere. One staff found that getting together to make cookies and wrap presents for the holidays was fun in itself and also provided an opportunity to share perceptions of children on a professional level while enjoying the holiday spirit. Sometimes including parents adds to creating a community around the program.

5. Once in a while vary the place where meetings are held. This creates a change of pace for a regular staff meeting but is especially effective if you must hold an extra one. Sometimes issues arise that the staff themselves feel cannot be resolved during the regular course of the day. Perhaps tensions have developed, or time is needed just to think about a problem in a different way. A meeting at someone's house for pizza, for example, can supply the time and the atmosphere to permit staff to look at an issue as a problem to be solved rather than as a difficulty that creates hard feelings.

6. Have "catch-up days" or "curriculum refreshers." Find blocks of uninterrupted time when the staff can work on renewing skills, rearranging the learning environment, or discussing special curriculum topics. Even full-day, year-round programs can sometimes close down for one or two days, perhaps in late summer, if parents know ahead of time that they will have to make other arrangements. Also in the summer, when there are fewer children in attendance, several days to a week of full afternoons might be arranged. Hire substitutes and use job trainees and supplementary staff when needed.

7. Encourage teachers to try out things that are related to their special interests, and provide a personal day or flexible time off as a matter of policy. A half-day off on a staggered basis for holiday shopping can make a huge difference to staff who work long hours, as can pay or at least comp time to make up for an evening meeting.

8. Finally, and perhaps most important, be an advocate for better pay and working conditions for early childhood staff, to parents and to the public at large, both in your own program and in the profession as a whole.

CONCLUSION

In this chapter, we have stressed the importance of supervisors as facilitators of learning and of establishing a professional culture that supports learning. We have described three approaches to adult learning and offered a range of strategies in which colleagues can contribute to each other's learning. In addition to describing possible components of a staff development and learning program, we suggest additional resources for staff development and provide some tips for making the workplace more enjoyable.

PROGRAM ACCREDITATION

The following criteria for program accreditation from *NAEYC Early Childhood Program Standards and Accreditation Criteria: The Mark of Quality in Early Childhood Education* (NAEYC, 2005) represent a sampling of those related to professional development and learning:

6.A.07 All teaching staff have specialized college-level course work and/or professional development training that prepares them to work with children and families of diverse races, cultures, and languages. Specialized college-level course work may include core courses that cover these topics or courses addressing these topics specifically. Teaching staff adapt their teaching in response to children's differences. (p. 54)

6.A.09 All teaching staff who supervise or mentor other staff members have specialized college-level course work or professional development training and preparation in adult supervision, mentoring, and leadership development. Specialized college-level course work may include core courses that cover these topics or courses addressing these topics specifically. (p. 54)

8.B.02 Program staff connect with and use their community's urban, suburban, rural, and tribal cultural resources. (p. 61)

8.C.01 Program staff are encouraged to participate in local, state, or national early childhood education organizations by joining and attending meetings and conferences. Program staff are also encouraged to participate regularly in local, state, or regional public awareness activities related to early care and education. (p. 61)

8.C.05 Program staff are encouraged and given the opportunity to participate in community or statewide interagency councils or service integration efforts. (p. 62)

10.E.12 The program's professional development plan
- is based on needs identified through staff evaluation and from other information from program evaluation processes.
- is written and shared with staff.
- includes mentoring, coaching, and other professional development opportunities for all staff.
- includes discussion of ethical issues.
- includes training in the policies and procedures of the program.

- includes training in skills for building positive relationships, all aspects of the curriculum, teaching practices, skills for partnering with families and communities, and skills for collaborating and participating as a member of a team. (p. 81)

EXERCISES

1. What are the components of your professional development and learning program, and how do they address the various levels of education, experience, and expertise of staff members?
2. Describe some of the major problems you face in the area of staff development. Brainstorm as to possible ways that you can overcome these challenges.
3. Select one staff development option that we have described above and experiment with it. Try to document its impact on practice.
4. Describe the different ways that you encourage or might encourage group reflection and dialogue among staff in your program.

CHAPTER 16

STAFF EVALUATION AND LEARNING

E VALUATING, JUDGING, EXAMINING, appraising, and rating connote behaviors that seem contrary to the humanistic ideals dear to early childhood educators; yet probably no other supervisory process has the *potential* to affect the quality of learning experiences for children as much as what staff members learn about themselves.

The great variability in experience and education levels among professionals and paraprofessionals within early childhood programs suggests a strong need for staff evaluation. It also places great demands on directors who struggle with the dual roles of fostering the growth of staff members at different points in their professional development and making personnel decisions about them, while confronting the serious problems associated with staff turnover.

Through evaluation, directors and other supervisors acquire information about their programs and staff members that can be used to make informed decisions as they plan for the future. Also, staff members receive formal feedback about their performance, which can be useful to them in making career plans. An informal survey of early childhood program directors yielded the following purposes of evaluation:

- To improve the quality of overall services provided to children
- To make judgments about staff competence
- To ensure that program goals are being met
- To recommend that staff be rehired, fired, promoted, or reassigned
- To note the progress of staff members
- To reward staff
- To motivate staff
- To assist staff in improving their teaching or caregiving
- To meet requirements of outside funding agencies
- To set goals for the future

Although there is overlap among the stated reasons for evaluating staff and among the implied tasks, the major purpose of evaluation remains maintaining high-quality care and instruction in a program by (1) assuring that staff are effective teachers and caregivers and (2) fostering the professional development and learning of staff members.

EVALUATION TERMINOLOGY

There are several terms that are frequently used in connection with staff evaluation. These include *supervision, assessment, authentic assessment*, and *evaluation*, both *formative* and *summative*.

Throughout this text, we have equated the term *supervision* with the concept of ongoing support and professional development of staff members. Leaders in the field of supervision, however, continue to disagree over whether staff evaluation should be thought of as separate from or a part of supervision. Since evaluation can be a growth-promoting and learning opportunity and since those holding administrative and supervisory responsibility are normally expected to evaluate staff as part of their job descriptions, we believe that a legitimate aspect of supervision is the process of evaluating staff—that is, the act of judging the effectiveness of a staff member's performance.

Formative evaluation is an ongoing process that provides teachers and others with regular feedback about their performance to effect transformation and growth. Staff members do not have to wait until the end of the year to receive constructive suggestions or to know what supervisors think about their work.

Supervisors and staff members collect data in a variety of ways and from a variety of sources. These include conferences and classroom observations carried out by supervisors as well as other documents assembled by teachers, perhaps in consultation with colleagues, such as surveys, evidence of professional activities, and samples of children's work. The data are used to *assess* the presence of and the degree to which staff members possess certain qualities and teaching or caregiving competencies. Formative evaluation is comparable to ongoing assessment.

Recently, the term *authentic assessment* has been used in connection with the evaluation of both children's learning and teachers' effectiveness. By having teachers document and collect data based on the work that they actually do with children each day in their classrooms, evaluation is more authentic and is broad in its scope.

In contrast to formative evaluation, which takes place regularly and over time, *summative evaluation* takes place at the end of a specified time period, when an administrator or supervisor "sums up" and judges the effectiveness of a staff member's performance, letting that person know where he or she stands against certain predetermined standards. In summative evaluation, the "big picture" or overall performance is considered. The time established for summative evaluation may be set by a board, the director, or a funding source. Summative evaluation is a formal, legal process; it must be described in a program's personnel policy or teacher contract and is usually approved by a board of directors.

SOME GUIDELINES FOR STAFF EVALUATION

Effective evaluation programs are characterized by a culture of professionalism. Directors are sometimes reluctant to evaluate staff members for fear of creating more staff turnover, but in reality, evaluation can have the opposite effect. It enables staff to see themselves as members of a program that has high standards and values professionialism.

Evaluation processes and plans should recognize the various developmental levels of staff members. As we noted in Chapter 13, evaluation processes and procedures can vary for staff who are at different stages in their careers. Beginning teachers may be evaluated on a timeline and by individuals and by procedures that are different from those for experienced teachers or teachers who need intensive assistance (Danielson & McGreal, 2000). A program's career ladder or lattice, with defined roles and rewards, can offer a structure for designing an evaluation plan and a basis for tying it to a program's professional development plan.

Teacher involvement is essential in the design and implementation of any evaluation plan if it is to be successful. A sense of ownership of the evaluation process enables staff to perceive it as meaningful, one that can have a positive effect on practice.

Opportunities for reflection and analysis should be woven into a program's evaluation plan whenever possible. Reflective journal entries in portfolios, conferences with peers and supervisors, and completion of self-evaluation instruments are examples of activities that can assist staff members in thinking about and refining their practice.

Evaluators who are culturally responsive take into account the cultural values they bring to the evaluation process, and the cultural lenses through which they view and interpret the teaching-learning process. They strive, too, to assist staff in developing a cultural self-awareness and in becoming more cognizant of the ways that culture can impact on teaching and learning.

Time is a valuable commodity in the daily lives of supervisors and teachers. Yet if evaluation is to be taken seriously by staff and if it is to be a thoughtful process, then adequate time must be set aside for evaluation activities.

WHO EVALUATES?

Should supervisors have the sole responsibility for evaluating, or should supervisees, other staff members, parents, and children be involved? We suggest that a broad range of individuals participate in the process of evaluating staff members. In this way, data are obtained from multiple sources.

Supervisors

Whether director, educational coordinator, or head teacher, the supervisor by virtue of position has the authority and responsibility for evaluating staff. The supervisor is accountable for the program and therefore is concerned about its quality.

Effective supervisors have the experience and expertise to make judgments. They have observed and conferred with staff members over time and, most likely, have conducted training sessions with them as well. This ongoing process enables them to assess the professional development of individuals and to have a sound data base for evaluation. They are also familiar with the children, parents, and community so they understand the context in which staff members work. Supervisors may also have developed the procedures for evaluating staff in cooperation with the staff as well as with board members.

For all these reasons, supervisors are central to the evaluation process, but, as indicated earlier, they need not be the only individuals who evaluate.

Supervisees

Self-evaluation requires that individuals take time to reflect about their progress. This can be an insightful and rewarding experience, enabling them to note gains and setbacks and to set personal goals for the future.

Although all staff members benefit by evaluating themselves, our experience suggests that self-evaluation is easier for supervisees who are already analytical and reflective. Some staff members may need ideas and structure to help them think about their progress. This might take the form of an instrument in which they are asked to state goals with strategies for reaching them or a list of questions designed to stimulate self-assessment. Such a self-evaluation tool could be jointly developed with staff, who could also be introduced to readings that stimulate reflection. Another approach is to ask each staff member to interview him- or herself about his or her job performance and learning.

Supervisory conferences lay the groundwork for self-evaluation, for it is through conference dialogue that staff members practice reflecting, predicting, judging, and suggesting alternatives to caregiving and teaching behaviors. Through practice, patience, and hard work on the part of supervisors and supervisees, most staff members can learn to become skilled self-evaluators.

A drawback to self-evaluation is that supervisees sometimes underrate or overrate themselves, but individuals usually know themselves and the quality of their work better than anyone else. Also, teachers may be reluctant to make statements about what they can't do well. If they feel free from external threat, self-evaluation can empower staff. They have an opportunity to judge themselves and to respect their own judgments. They also become better at it with the help of supportive supervisors.

Peers

The idea of peer review—that is, the participation of peers in evaluating colleagues for the purpose of making decisions about their continued employment—has been controversial. However, it is gaining wider consideration, particularly when coupled with assistance for teachers who are new or who are not performing up to standard. The State of California, for example, mandates a formal peer assistance and review program for public school teachers that is tied to cost-of-living increases, and the federal government, through "No Child Left Behind," also promotes peer review (Kumrow & Dahlen, 2002).

Two public school districts that have been experimenting with peer review and assistance programs for a number of years now are those of Toledo, Ohio, and Rochester, New York. In Toledo, consulting teachers, experienced teachers given release time, work with veteran teachers who are having difficulty and with beginning teachers. After a designated period of time, they make final recommendations to a panel review board about the teacher's employment status. Due to political and contractual issues, however, only a small percentage of teachers who were found to be less than competent resigned or were terminated (Kumrow & Dahlen, 2002).

The Rochester peer assistance and review plan is based on the assumption that "nobody knows better the difference between good and bad teaching than the best teachers themselves" (Urbanski & O'Connell, 2003, p. 3). In Rochester, all newly hired teachers without experience participate in a mentor-internship program. An intervention program was also developed to support experienced teachers who are having difficulties. This program provides assistance by a peer for up to a year based on a needs assessment. At the end of the intervention, the mentor reports to a panel which, in turn, makes a recommendation to the superintendent regarding employment of the individual in question. The intervention program has been very successful in assisting teachers in meeting professional standards (Urbanski & O'Connell, 2003).

Directors and staff members of early childhood programs can explore ways to involve peers in evaluation and in providing assistance to those staff who are at risk that make sense for a program, given its size and other particular characteristics. Peers can certainly work with each other in setting long-range goals; in selecting and evaluating materials for portfolios; in reading, writing, and critiquing reflective statements; and in helping each other improve their teaching.

Parents

Parents informally evaluate early childhood programs: They judge staff members and programs by continuing to send their children to a center or by withdrawing them. Parents can be asked to evaluate staff more formally by completing anonymous questionnaires as is done in the Child Development Associate (CDA) credentialing process (see Chapter 15).

Soliciting the views of parents can increase their support and enthusiasm for a program and can enhance its climate. Critical to their successful participation, however, is the method used to involve them as well as the ways in which staff members are prepared for parental involvement. Parents need to be informed about why their help is requested, to understand the nature of the actual power they have, and to know appropriate protocol and behavior for participating in the evaluation process.

Children

Measures of children's growth and learning comprise another source of data to assess effective teaching. Children's portfolios, which may contain examples of writing, artwork, and digital photographs of them at work and play over time, are wonderful ways to demonstrate their language, mathematical, social, and artistic development to themselves, parents, and others.

SOURCES OF EVALUATION CRITERIA

In developing instruments for assessment and evaluation, program administrators, supervisors, and staff members will need to determine the criteria upon which individuals in each role will be evaluated.

Rather than re-creating what has already been developed by various researchers and other experts funded by professional organizations and governmental agencies, it makes sense to tap into what represents current thinking about effective teaching and caregiving and support that work by integrating it within your own program. For example, core and knowledge competencies identified by a state's career lattice program or at the public school level by the state department of education can be incorporated into a local evaluation plan. Other sources of criteria are the Child Development Associate (CDA) Competency Goals and Functional Areas (see Council for Professional Recognition, n.d.), the Early Childhood/Generalist Standards of the National Board of Professional Teaching Standards (NBPTS) (see NBPTS, 2004), and certainly the accreditation criteria of the National Association for the Education of Young Children (NAEYC, 2005).

Additional sources for identifying criteria for evaluation specific to a program's particular context are administrators and staff members themselves. Asking staff members to keep track of their time, to describe their daily activities and their perceptions of their roles, and to identify the qualities, knowledge, and skills they believe to be important in carrying out their jobs is a worthwhile staff development endeavor as well as a practical source for evaluation criteria and job descriptions.

APPROACHES TO EVALUATION AND THE CAREER LADDER

In designing evaluation that is based on stages of career development, there are several questions to consider:

1. Which evaluation practices make sense for staff given their needs and experience levels?
2. Which evaluation practices should be required and which should be optional given staff stages of development?
3. How do the roles of the evaluator(s) and staff members change at different points of the career ladder?
4. As staff members acquire experience and expertise, should the criteria on which they are evaluated change?
5. As one moves up the career ladder from teacher aide to head or master teacher, should the frequency of evaluation vary?
6. At what point should evaluation focus less on determining the presence of competencies and more on professional development?

An Expanded Definition of Teaching

Shulman's work (1987), in connection with teacher certification for the NBPTS, has had a major impact on teacher assessment standards and practices. His definition of teaching focused not just on what teachers know, but on how they think and their decision making, reasoning, and new understandings in preparing for instruction, and during and after instruction. This conception of teaching has brought assessment strategies closer to practice and broadened data collection for national certification to include multiple sources of documentation collected over time.

In recent years, assessment practices in school settings have also begun to change by going beyond the evaluation of teachers based solely on supervisory observation of instruction, to include aspects of planning for teaching and reflection during and after teaching. Teachers are asked to reveal their thinking about their teaching and to document how they have changed their practice and what they have learned as a result of it. The collection of artifacts in portfolios, the writing of personal narratives and reflective statements, and the carrying out of action research projects are strategies now more commonly associated with teacher assessment. These approaches are more inquiry-oriented, place more responsibility in the hands of staff members, and more closely reflect a broad definition of teaching. We consider them to be evaluation approaches that are more closely linked to professional development and learning. You may want to use some of them in combination with each other and with traditional approaches, keeping in mind the career stages of staff members.

Tools and Reports

As you and your staff members design an evaluation plan within the career-ladder concept, you might wish to consider some of the tools and approaches to evaluation described below. Using tools such as *rating scales*, *rubrics*, or *narrative reports*, described in this section, are traditional summative evaluation practices in which supervisors tend to have major responsibility and control. They are often used in conjunction with a series of classroom observations by evaluators.

Rating Scales

Rating scales have a quantitative emphasis. The quantitative approach is based on specific criteria that researchers, practitioners, and policy makers have deemed essential to professionals in a field. These criteria or competency statements, such as the CDA standards mentioned above, can be modified to create scales that ask evaluators to indicate the presence of specific competencies and to rate the extent to which a staff member manifests them by placing a check on a scale representing a minimal to a high level of performance.

Rating scales can be administered with relative ease, depending on their length. The competencies to be evaluated are explicit and available to supervisor and supervisee at the beginning of the evaluation period. Those with numerous competency statements can seem overwhelming and perhaps a bit unrealistic to the supervisee, yet they can be useful as both formative and summative evaluation tools. Teacher rating scales do not provide the reader with personal or specific examples and illustrations of a staff member's behavior, and they should not be used as instruments for observing teaching in the clinical supervision cycle.

Rubrics

Unlike a traditional rating scale, a rubric is a set of criteria that *describe* specific behaviors to be expected at various levels of performance. Such levels might range from beginning to accomplished or unsatisfactory to exceptional. Criteria focus on the performance of teachers, and may include the results of their work with children. A rubric could, for example, be constructed using one of the criteria from the NAEYC's (2005) accreditation standards, as in Figure 16.1.

The advantage of a scale that includes descriptors of performance levels is that it gives teachers a clear idea of what is expected. It can take into account the developmental stages of teachers' professional growth and promote discussion between the teacher and supervisor about the teacher's practice. Evaluators, for

Figure 16.1. Rubric Based on NAEYC Criterion

3.G.01   Teachers have and use a variety of teaching strategies that include a
broad range of approaches and responses.

Beginning 1	Developing 2	Proficient 3	Distinguished 4
Teacher tends to feel comfortable with and to rely on one or two basic teaching strategies regardless of the needs of the children and the goal of the lesson.	Teacher is learning alternative teaching strategies and shows a willingness to try different approaches and to take risks. Teacher is beginning to see which strategies work best with this particular class and which make sense given the purpose of the lesson. Teacher is starting to use a greater range of instructional materials.	Teacher demonstrates a knowledge and use of a variety of teaching strategies, including cooperative learning, learning through play, guiding children individually, direct instruction, and others. Teacher varies strategies based on curriculum goals and the children's responses. Teacher uses a range of instructional materials.	Teacher employs a broad repertoire of teaching strategies including cooperative learning, learning through play , guiding children individually, direct instruction, and others. The use of these strategies depends on the curriculum goals and the children. Teacher varies strategies frequently to maintain a high interest level among the children. Approaches are altered, even within a single lesson, based on the response and input of the children. Teacher uses exceptionally interesting instructional materials.

Note: Criterion 3.G.01 is reprinted from *NAEYC Early Childhood Program Standards and Accreditation Criteria: The Mark of Quality in Early Childhood Education,* by National Association for the Education of Young Children (NAEYC), 2005, Washington DC: Author. Copyright 2005 by National Association for the Education of Young Children. Reprinted with permission by National Association for the Education of Young Children.

example, can cite specific events from classroom observations, and teachers can
point to evidence from practice to demonstrate criteria and performance levels
(Danielson & McGreal, 2000).

Examples of rubrics and rubric templates are readily available on the Internet.

Descriptive Reports

Descriptive evaluation reports, often called narratives, are qualitative in nature.
A greater emphasis is placed on the meaning and quality of the experiences that
children and staff members have in classrooms. Rather than rating a teacher on
specific competencies, supervisors are more concerned with context and setting,
with understanding and describing how teachers and children engage each other,
and with discovering the assumptions that underlie classroom practices.

These narrative reports are statements that describe what a supervisor has observed over a period of time rather than during a single observation, as discussed in Chapter 11. As summative reports, they include a supervisor's judgments and recommendations with regard to a staff member's performance. The format of this report can be open-ended, but some narrative instruments provide evaluators with more structure by asking for comments on such general areas as knowledge of child development, planning, behavior management, establishing classroom learning environments, teacher-child interaction, interpersonal communication, professional development, personal qualities, relations with parents and community, and nonteaching responsibilities. Some supervisors and supervisees like this type of instrument because it can help them sort out the important issues to be considered and what needs to be done.

The advantage of this type of evaluation approach is that it gives the evaluator(s) space to set a context and to describe and illustrate with examples; and it can be very thorough, offering the reader a substantial amount of specific information. Descriptive or narrative evaluation reports provide a lasting record, highlight patterns of behavior, and encourage evaluators to be thoughtful. On the other hand, writing a summative report is time-consuming. Its open-ended quality may not provide enough structure for the evaluator(s), who may over-emphasize some areas and leave out others just as crucial. The narrative report is compatible with a naturalistic view of evaluation, but some believe it is simply too open-ended and relies on the evaluator's values to a greater extent than need be.

Following is an example of a summative evaluation written by the director of a program whose goals include a strong emphasis on play and child-initiated learning and on parent participation, including volunteering in classrooms and active board membership. Kate is a kindergarten teacher in her second year in this program.

> Kate has been intrigued by open education and sees her most important goal as what she calls community building. As she is aware, at the beginning of this year, there were complaints from parents about Kate's methods of guidance of children's behavior, and that she was not doing enough to prepare children academically.
>
> As I observed Kate during the year, I found some real strengths in terms of her loving and nurturing interactions with children, her very special ways of developing positive communication among the children, and her work with individual children, especially those with problems. In the latter case, she worked all year with a child who had had a traumatic experience at home, developing relevant classroom experiences, and including his parents in her plans. In addition, her classroom has indeed become a community in terms of children's social exchanges and their gaining respect for one another.

It was evident, however, that the parents' concerns had some merit. I have been working with Kate to help her understand the need to set expectations for children and to follow up on them. She is beginning to see that doing this helps children to become more self-disciplined, rather than pressuring them, as she feared. She no longer takes the phrase "open classroom" literally. For example, instead of sitting and waiting for long periods of time for children to pay attention at the beginning of circle time, she has found ways within her own style to let them know what she expects them to do.

Kate also needs to think about how to build in more specific ways to develop literacy and math skills. Her fear of overstructuring has made it hard for her to work in this area. She is beginning to see that children need to be challenged, and that this is different from pushing them. We have been discussing ways for her to arrange the room environment so that each area can contribute to the educational program.

Kate has moved a long way in her relations with parents. She has had a hard time understanding the legitimacy of the parents' concerns, especially in their wanting more academic preparation for children. She said that she didn't feel it was necessary to explain why she was doing what she was doing. She has developed a good system for sharing developmental information with parents, for example, but she is so indirect with them that they don't always understand what she means. Recently, Kate has begun to share her goals and methods with parents, and to respond to their questions, rather than telling them what she thinks they want to hear when she is criticized. This process has forced her to articulate her philosophy and has given her confidence, and the parents love it!

Kate and I have agreed on four goals for her to pursue next year: to improve her skills in guidance of children's behavior; to find developmentally appropriate ways for children to acquire literacy and math skills; to design a more comprehensive means of documenting assessment, such as using portfolios; and to continue to improve her skills in parent communication.

In the above summative evaluation report, the supervisor described Kate's strengths with specific examples. She was positive and supportive throughout. She also laid out areas of concern, being very specific, and noting if progress was being made on these areas. The supervisor concluded by identifying mutually agreed upon goals that established expectations for the next evaluation cycle. The evaluation is written in a very understandable and straightforward manner.

Inquiry-Oriented and Collaborative Approaches

Long-range goal setting, the use of personal narrative, the establishment of learning communities such as critical friends groups, the use of individual and schoolwide portfolios, the creation of dossiers, and the program accreditation process are other approaches that can be part of the evaluation process.

Long-Range Goal Setting

Long-range goal setting can be used effectively with both novices and experienced staff, but novices will require more specific and more frequent supervisory input. Individuals with experience, however, will have most likely attained a comfort level with their teaching and a program's expectations so that they may want to work on more specialized areas as they move up the career ladder. As they are more experienced and competent and do not require assessment as frequently as they did at earlier stages of their careers, they are likely to benefit greatly from long-range goal setting.

The notion behind long-range goal setting, which is very compatible with Knowles and colleagues' (1984) view of adult learning, is that teachers set their own goals for themselves and their classrooms in cooperation with their supervisors. Goals may be related to the attainment of specific competencies, to curriculum, and/or to children's and teacher's learning. At the end of an agreed-on time period, the teacher and supervisor jointly write what has been accomplished, reflect about the experience, and plan the next steps. A unique aspect of this evaluation strategy is that there are no summative reports or ratings.

Teachers may also be paired with coworkers, who confer with them regularly to discuss, review, reflect, and plan. These conferences may take place between scheduled meetings with supervisors. Another variation of this approach is to encourage teachers who work with a particular age or at a specific grade level to meet in groups to establish goals for the group. The entire group can meet periodically with the supervisor to review progress. Teachers sometimes complete a form in which they identify goals, action steps, assistance and resources needed, and data collected to document the experience. A very simple conference guide can also be used to describe meetings between colleagues. These two options build in collaboration, dialogue, sharing, and reflection.

Storytelling

Storytelling is a powerful communication tool that encourages reflection on practice and professional growth and development. Stories, whether oral or written, are a means of sharing our personal versions of the world around us. By telling our stories or writing them down and engaging in dialogue with ourselves or others, we can clarify our thinking about particular issues, about people or contexts, and refine our behavior.

Storytelling is a way of learning (Egan, 1987). Bruner (1996) describes narrative as a mode of thinking and a structure for organizing our knowledge. In certain oral cultures, storytelling is an art form, and important messages are embedded in stories. Stories also serve to strengthen relationships among community members and to transmit cultural values.

Rossiter (2002) enumerates a number of ways that stories foster learning. Stories are a source of knowledge and make information more memorable. They encourage the involvement of the learner. Listeners fill in the blanks of what has not been said and raise and answer questions from their own sources of knowledge, thus creating new meaning. Learner engagement in stories encourages empathy and multiple-perspective taking. And stories also have the potential to be transformative since they can be motivational and lead one toward new paths of learning and growth.

Personal narratives or stories, in the form of case studies, role-playing, and simulations have been used as a means of teacher preparation to help develop professional ways of thinking. By reading and writing case studies, students learn to "think like a teacher," to frame problems, to design strategies, and to explore moral and technical issues that are a part of everyday teaching (Kleinfeld, 1988). Case studies have been used to successfully train cooperating teachers (Caruso, 1998), as have short stories or vignettes in supervisor preparation to encourage thinking about successful elements of teacher collaboration. Learning journals, logs (including videos and electronic forms), and reflective diaries are other forms of narrative that facilitate independent learning and reflection that is associated with deep learning (Centre for Teaching and Learning, 2005).

It is exciting to think about how to incorporate personal narrative or stories into the assessment process. Certainly autobiography as a form of self-assessment, short vignettes about daily teaching experiences, and even photo stories about life in classrooms, all of which can be shared and discussed with others, offer simple yet potentially effective possibilities for helping staff gain confidence, discover their own knowledge, and reflect on their work. These, and some of the other forms of narrative mentioned above, can be incorporated into portfolio assessment and can also serve as the basis for stimulating staff meetings.

Learning Communities

Another vision of an inquiry-oriented and collaborative approach to assessment and professional development is the concept of teacher learning communities. In addition to helping teachers be more effective (Lieberman & Miller, 1992; Little, 1990), learning communities offer teachers the possibility of being part of a caring and interconnected culture in which values are shared. Key ideas in the concept of learning communities are that the agenda of such groups arises from the needs and interests of teachers, that there is an emphasis on inquiring about and learning from practice, and that teachers have control over such groups.

Learning communities take a variety of forms and may include a range of people. Some groups might consist of staff members within the same program or from several programs. Others might include supervisors, advisors, and university professors. Communities might come together to conduct action research on a topic of mutual interest or simply to engage in "story swapping" (Little, 1990), that is, sharing anecdotes about their work with children. Communities might also take the form of study groups and lesson study/group supervision, which were described in Chapter 15.

Learning communities called Critical Friends Groups are described as "a model of collective inquiry that champions the co-construction of knowledge through talk" (Meyer & Achinstein, 1998, p. 6). It is one that builds on the notion of friendship. Our friends, after all, are our advocates. They care about us, and we have a shared history with them. Because we trust them we can accept criticism and advice from them and offer the same in a relationship that is reciprocal. In groups of friends one is able to obtain multiple perspectives on an issue. Central to Critical Friends Groups are critique that takes the form of probing and questioning that fosters serious reflection and change regarding beliefs and practice.

In a study of Critical Friends Groups of novice teachers at Stanford University, Meyer and Achinstein (1998) describe a structure for group meetings, which last from 20 to 90 minutes. Groups begin with a *check-in* followed by a *charrette*. Check-in is a time for group members to get to know each other and to eventually form a bond of friendship. This activity is one in which all members of the group give a brief update of their personal and professional lives. Charrettes, often used by architects or city planners when beginning new projects, are group-process brainstorming sessions, in which many new ideas are generated. During the charrette process in Critical Friends Groups, a teacher-presenter brings an artifact for discussion and sets the context for it. At the conclusion of often-dynamic discussions around the issues, ideas, and experiences connected with the artifact, the meeting is summarized and sometimes members write in their journals.

Critical friendships may take place as an exchange between individual teachers who come together around a common goal or theme as described above or when teams of educators visit partner schools to be of service to that school. In this case, the host school requests assistance with a specific focus, identifying questions and problems with which they are struggling and need help. (For more information on Critical Friends Groups and how they function, see the Coalition of Essential Schools Northwest Web site at www.cesnorthwest.org/cfg.php)

Critical Friends Groups, which meet outside of the school day and which consist of staff from a variety of settings, could be sponsored by a local professional association, a consortium of early childhood programs, or a college or university partnership. Neighboring early childhood programs could form critical friends teams for exchange visits, becoming a valuable source of help for each other, as they offer an outsider's perspective, a "fresh eye" when looking at a program.

Portfolios

Portfolio development, long used in the Child Development Associate credential program, is a means by which staff members can learn more about themselves, their teaching, and the children with whom they work and advisors and evaluators can gain a more complete picture of teaching, caregiving, and learning in a particular setting. Anderson (2002) describes the portfolio as "a thoughtfully organised compilation of artefacts and evidence, developed over time and in collaboration with others, that provides a record of goals, growth, achievements, learning, and professional attributes" (p. 2).

There are different types of portfolios each with their own purpose. Professional development portfolios describe and document professional growth and learning, promoting the teacher's ownership of the learning process, evaluation portfolios validate teacher effectiveness usually in connection with a performance review, and employment portfolios showcase a teacher's strengths and accomplishments to a prospective employer (Retallick, 2002). Thus the content and structure of a portfolio will vary depending on the type.

A professional development portfolio might include a teacher's professional growth and learning plan, a log of professional development activities, evidence of how the plan was implemented, and reflective statements about various entries. On the other hand, a professional development portfolio with a focus on a particular question identified by the teacher for investigation might feature entries that describe how the problem was studied, the results obtained, what the teacher has learned, and its impact on the teacher's practice.

An evaluation portfolio might be based on specific competencies and contain evidence that the teacher is working toward or has attained them. It might include a self-assessment and lesson plans, a video, samples of children's work, and brief reflective statements intended to address each competency area.

An employment portfolio could include a resume, letters of recommendation, statement of personal philosophy and goals, evidence of specific career accomplishments, and examples of successful teaching activities.

An examination of portfolio materials should enable supervisor, staff member, and peers to raise questions and draw inferences about the teacher's assumptions of how young children learn, what the teacher values, how children spend their time, and the ways in which teacher and children interact. These inferences can be validated by classroom observations and by engaging in dialogue with classroom teachers in portfolio conferences. The portfolio will also provide information about the teacher as a learner.

Portfolio evaluation conferences between teachers and supervisors give the teacher voice. Teachers have an opportunity to take the lead, to describe what is important to them, to highlight strengths. The supervisor becomes a listener and learner and raises questions. Portfolio conferences, however, can be very time-consuming. Some ground rules may have to be set to give the conference a clear focus and to set some limits. There probably will not be time to discuss each entry. Supervisors will need to have an opportunity for input and will want to know what they can do to support the teacher's ongoing learning.

Supervisors can serve as facilitators in portfolio development by establishing a means for staff members to assist each other in the creation of portfolios and in the assessment of portfolio contents and by providing the time for them to do so. Supervisors, for example, might lead group sessions with staff in which they discuss how they are going to illustrate a specific competency in their portfolios, create teams of staff members who assist each other in the selection of portfolio entries, or facilitate collaborative-assessment conferences in which teachers come together to describe, discuss, and interpret a portfolio entry, such as a sample of children's art work or writing (Seidel, 1998).

Most undergraduates have had considerable experience in developing portfolios in relation to teacher preparation courses; however, portfolios as a form of assessment once a teacher is hired will have a purpose, format, and structure that is geared to the workplace context. In creating evaluation plans using portfolio development, supervisors and teachers will have to address a number of concerns and issues:

- Should the development of portfolios be voluntary or required, and at what stage of the career ladder might they best be used?
- Should evaluation portfolios have a specific focus each year on a few competency areas that represent a program's priority?
- Does it make sense to manage the size of portfolios by requiring a limited number of entries?
- Should rubrics be developed to assess entries that demonstrate competency areas that apply to all staff?
- Should more experienced or tenured staff have greater flexibility in the focus and design of their evaluation portfolio?

Portfolios may undervalue the strengths of effective teachers who excel in areas such as personal interactions with children (Peterson, 2000), an area that is difficult to represent in the form of materials. On the other hand, portfolios provide a rich data source for personal reflection and for dialogue on the quality of classroom events and experiences and shift the locus of control of the assessment process from supervisors to teachers.

The School Learning Portfolio

In Chapter 15, we described the work of the Coalition of Knowledge Building Schools in New South Wales, Australia. There the collaborative action research projects carried out by teachers is combined with the concept of learning portfolios in their work on school improvement (Groundwater-Smith & Kemmis, 2004).

Instead of creating individual portfolios, as groups of teachers collect evidence about the challenges and problems they face, they document their work in school learning portfolios, the idea being that schools themselves are learning organizations. The *school learning portfolio* is defined as "evidence-based documentation of organizational and collegial learning regarding a workplace's transformation" (Groundwater-Smith & Kemmis, 2004, p. 38). In other words, the school learning portfolio provides documentation on how the school as an institution changes, adapts, innovates, copes, and learns (Beveridge, Groundwater-Smith, Kemmis, & Wasson, 2004).

Portfolios contain statements describing the goals, philosophy, and context of the school and the specific strategies used in the study of identified problems as well as the steps taken to solve them. They also contain evidence of what was learned about teaching, student learning, and the school and community. Reflective statements by collaborative team members describing their professional learning are also included (Groundwater-Smith & Kemmis, 2004).

As we noted in Chapter 15, an early childhood director interested in this approach might seek assistance from a critical friend through a college or university, professional association, or state agency and may wish to become familiar with principles of action research by enrolling in a course at a nearby institution or agency.

Dossiers

An alternative to a teacher evaluation portfolio is the dossier (Peterson, 2000). This is a document which is limited in size, perhaps up to 12 or 14 pages. At least four data sources are selected by a teacher for inclusion in the dossier from a range of possibilities including parent surveys, peer reviews, administrator reports, teacher tests, professional activities, action research projects, student achievement data, participation in school improvement activities, and other data that are unique to the teacher. The data are intended to present the teacher in the most favorable light and are used for summative evaluation purposes. The teacher may remove contents from the dossier at his or her discretion. Dossiers may be used in place of formal classroom visits by those conducting the summative evaluation. For more on this process, see Teacher Evaluation: New Directions and Practices online (http://www.teacherevaluation.net).

Program Accreditation

The self-study process for the NAEYC and other accreditation systems (see Chapter 2) can become an effective context for staff learning as well as program evaluation. The decision to work toward accreditation is a statement of a commitment to quality, and thus to the improvement where needed of all aspects of the program. Although accreditation focuses on programs and not on individuals, one cannot critically examine a program without looking at one's practices. Because all staff members are working toward the same goal, and using the same criteria as they work through the self-study, they gain a sense of community and ownership of a program, as well as an opportunity for self-examination.

The self-study criteria of the NAEYC accreditation system provide concrete outside standards against which staff members can measure their work. Like the CDA, the process is self-affirming when strengths are validated, which helps caregivers feel more comfortable in pinpointing areas of concern. When supervisors build training around these identified areas, staff members have a strong incentive to apply the newly acquired information and skills. As a consequence, they often find that their jobs are made easier, because their new knowledge and skills support their everyday work (S. Connor, personal communication, April 2, 1998).

The accreditation process takes a strong, significant, and sustained commitment from administration and staff. Studies have indicated that centers that have intensive on-site assistance are much more likely to complete their self-study. The assistance includes regular mentoring, paid staff release time for training, and support groups for administrators ("What Centers Need," 1997). State and other funds can often be obtained to support training and fees.

We have described a range of evaluation practices that can be used to promote professional growth and learning in teachers. Dialogue between supervisor and supervisee, and/or among staff, is a key component in each of them in helping staff to examine their practices and to plan for change.

SOME CULTURAL CONSIDERATIONS

Culturally sensitive assessment is dependent on supervisors' being aware of classroom cultural patterns as well as the cultural perspectives that they bring to the evaluation process.

In Chapter 10, we described cultural variables that have a bearing on communication. These and others are likely to come into play as supervisors observe teachers for evaluation purposes, communicate with them about their observations, and nurture teachers in learning about how cultural patterns affect children's learning. We offer several examples from the research literature to illustrate possible cultural misunderstandings and their effect on teacher assessment, since what constitutes good teaching varies across different cultural communities (Delpit, 1995).

Many cultural groups, particularly Native American communities, place great value on social, interdependent relationships versus the individual achievement prevalent in mainstream culture. A principal way of connecting with others in many Native American groups, for example, is through storytelling. In a case study of one Lakota master teacher, Kathleen Jeanette Marsh (1998) found that there was a pattern in the ways in which the teacher used personal narrative to help her students learn. In each of her lessons, she created a context for the discussion of the material she presented, shared some personal stories and perspectives related to the concepts being taught, and questioned and encouraged questions for clarification. While some evaluators might marvel at the way in which she connected with the students and their family and community values, a culturally insensitive evaluator or one with different values or a lack of knowledge of Lakota values might perceive the context building and personal sharing aspects of her lessons as not a good use of classroom time.

Among examples of cultural difference that might affect teacher assessment that Delpit (1995) points out is the level of emotion displayed by teachers. She refers to a study by Foster (1987) that revealed that African American students view assertive, aggressive, and even angry behavior as acceptable teaching behavior for communicating intentions as long as the emotions are genuine. Students perceived subtle messages or messages lacking sufficient emotional quality as noncaring. Delpit notes, however, that in assessment situations, African American teachers who display strong emotions are often viewed by evaluators as teachers who are too harsh, too authoritarian, too "pushy" with their students, and thus receive poor ratings.

Jacqueline Jordan Irvine (1991) expresses concern that culturally responsive teachers often do not meet the expectations of traditionally trained supervisors. She describes some of the characteristics of these teachers:

> Responsive teachers . . . spend a great deal of classroom time developing a personal relationship with the minority children they teach. These relationship-building exchanges are recurrent and spontaneous daily events. These teachers understand that teaching is a social interaction involving affect as well as cognition. They listen nonjudgmentally and patiently to their students and allow them to share personal stories and anecdotes during classroom time. Students often express themselves openly and with high affect and emotion violating mainstream rules about turn taking and raising one's hand to be recognized. These teachers also share their personal lives and experiences. These teachers report, however, that their behaviors are often misinterpreted by supervisors as time off task, unnecessary delays and digressions, or inappropriate relationships between students and teachers. I have noticed that these teachers wait longer for their minority students to respond, and they probe, prompt, praise and encourage lavishly. These teachers use an abundance of interactive techniques, and the pace is brisk and the activities varied. They move about the classroom and use their bodies, voices, and facial gestures as teaching instruments. (p. 7)

As supervisors observe and interpret teaching and assist teachers in becoming culturally responsive, they should think about the cultural patterns of understanding they bring to an observation. Bowers and Flinders (1990) provide us with an example of how a supervisor, Karen in this case, uses her cultural knowledge to interpret an observation. She summarizes her observation of Glen's class by noting that he began his class by giving two Japanese pupils an individual writing assignment. While they worked diligently at this task, he carried on a discussion with the class as a whole.

Using her cultural understanding of language, Karen thinks about Glen's intentions and how the students may be interpreting his behavior. Glen, unsure of the students' ability to speak English, may have seen himself as supporting the two students by giving them individual attention, standing close to them, smiling, and having direct eye contact with them. The students, however, based on their cultural patterns, may view being separated from the large group as a form of rebuke and may interpret Glen's nonverbal signals as either rapport or reprimand.

Bowers and Flinders (1990) believe that Karen, as a culturally responsive supervisor, should make explicit her own cultural frameworks for interpreting the observation as she nurtures Glen to explore new ways of seeing and hearing by introducing a cross-cultural perspective.

Supervisors, then, must be willing to learn about cultural and racial groups different from their own and even to study other languages if they are going to assist teachers in thinking about their interactions from a cultural perspective and in creating learning environments that are responsive to the cultures of children and families in a program. They must consider that the supervisory relationship could also be affected by factors such as racial identity, the ways in which people from different races perceive each other, and the worldview that individuals from various cultures have regarding concepts of time, self-disclosure and discussion, and the purpose of the supervisory process itself (Page, 2003).

Being a good listener and observer, putting oneself "into another's shoes," learning from staff members and parents who can serve as "cultural brokers," and spending time to get to know the workplace and its community are some ways that supervisors can learn about cultural values and patterns and become more culturally sensitive as they carry out their work.

A SPECIAL CONCERN: THE MARGINAL PERFORMER

As a result of formative or summative evaluation, supervisors will occasionally have to deal with a staff member whose performance is marginal. Marginal performers may frequently be absent from their work or simply avoid responsibilities while on the job; they may exhibit inappropriate behavior toward children; they may be moody or aggressive; or they may offer many excuses for not performing up to par. Marginal performers are individuals who are not working up to their capabilities. They inconsistently meet program standards and supervisory expectations.

In working with such individuals, determine the seriousness and the source of the individual's unsatisfactory performance. When conferring with staff members who are at risk, be very specific and clear as to what the problem is and what needs to be done to correct it. If the source is job related, it may be possible to spend more time with the staff member and alter certain job conditions to improve the situation, setting goals and a timeline. If the problem is of an instructional nature, offering assistance through a mentor for a specified period of time gives the staff member the opportunity to improve.

Supervisors may have to correct or change their own behavior if they are the source of the problem—for example, if they do not give complete and clear directions for accomplishing a task. Sometimes a direct, take-charge approach is needed, whereby the supervisor sets up a very structured schedule for the individual or moves the staff member from one team to another. If the source of the problem is outside the program, the supervisor may have little control over its solution but may be of some help by listening to the supervisee and offering suggestions.

Firing

As every supervisor knows, it is sometimes necessary to terminate an employee. This is a very difficult and unpleasant supervisory responsibility. The decision to fire someone should come after careful thought, after the collection of solid data over time, and after a sincere effort has been made to examine the problem from different angles and to solve it. The collection of descriptive and relevant data is essential not only to make the reasons for the decision clear to the employee but as backup in case of a grievance or legal challenge to the firing.

There are many reasons why it may be necessary to terminate the employment of a staff member. Directors point to sub-par performance, poor work habits, unacceptable behavior and policy violations as major reasons that may lead to the firing of a staff member (Thirty Directors, 1981). In order to avoid many negative consequences of firing, directors make the following recommendations:

1. Establish a grievance procedure, which includes a means for appealing personnel actions.
2. Review staff performance on a regular basis. Let staff know when there are problems, provide support and set goals for improvement.
3. Avoid surprises by giving adequate warning; be specific as to the problem and what is required to correct it.
4. Keep written records, documenting conferences with the individual, written warnings, and so forth.
5. Keep the executive director, sponsoring agency, owner, or regional director informed.
6. Make the decision objectively when emotions are held in perspective.
7. Notify the employee directly and as soon as possible once the decision has been made.
8. Announce the action honestly and directly without violating the employee's confidentiality.

In many cases, although certainly not all, firing someone can be in that person's best interest. Sometimes an employee who is unhappy, frustrated, or unfulfilled in the job simply cannot make the decision to "get out of a rut" and into a new job, routine, or lifestyle. In those cases, supervisors actually relieve pain by making the decision for the individual. Also, keeping someone on staff whose performance is not up to par can lower staff morale and take away from a sense of professionalism in a program.

Staff members in programs with effective systems for self-evaluation and frequent communication between supervisor and supervisee are usually not surprised by such actions, as they have been working with their supervisors to address problems over time. Suggesting ways that the person might find another job, redirecting the person to another career, and reminding the individual of the skills that he or she does have can be helpful. This is especially important for low-income persons who have few alternatives. Firing an employee can be almost as painful for the supervisor as for the staff member. You should assume, however, that you are in a supervisory position because you have expertise and sound judgment and that your decision, not taken lightly, is in the best interest of the program and the children it serves.

CONCLUSION

Our emphasis in this chapter has been to address the changing landscape of staff evaluation and learning by acknowledging its dual nature. We have described several approaches that link evaluation with professional development and learning. These include making portfolios, telling stories, participating in learning communities, conducting action research, and setting long-range goals. We have set evaluation within the context of a program's career ladder, encouraging supervisors and staff to jointly design and implement evaluation programs and processes. We have also suggested that evaluation should be culturally sensitive. This is a topic that needs greater attention in the field of supervision. Finally, we offer directors some guidelines for working with staff who may not be performing up to standard and for firing staff, in those rare cases when such action may be necessary.

PROGRAM ACCREDITATION

The following criteria for program accreditation from *NAEYC Early Childhood Program Standards and Accreditation Criteria: The Mark of Quality in Early Childhood Education* (NAEYC, 2005) represent a sampling of those related to staff evaluation:

6.B.01 All teaching staff evaluate and improve their own performance based on ongoing reflection and feedback from supervisors, peers, and families. They add to their knowledge and increase their ability to put knowledge into practice. They develop an annual individualized professional development plan with their supervisor and use it to inform their continuous professional development. (p. 55)

10.E.09 All staff are evaluated at least annually by an appropriate supervisor or, in the case of the program administrator, by the governing body. (p. 81)

EXERCISES

1. Discuss the notion of the teacher portfolio with your staff members. Ask if one or two teachers would be interested in experimenting with the idea of developing a portfolio and discussing its artifacts with you. After reasonable time intervals, confer with the staff member(s) using the portfolio entries as a basis for discussion. You and the teacher(s) can practice analyzing the material in terms of your program's goals for young children. Carry this idea a step further by asking groups of teachers who work with a particular age or grade level to develop a joint portfolio.

2. Review your program's evaluation policy and procedures in light of the principles discussed in this chapter. If revisions are needed, begin by involving your staff members in a process of describing the competencies they believe are necessary to do their jobs effectively.

3. As you consider developing an evaluation plan with staff based on the concept of the career ladder, discuss which approaches described in this chapter are suitable for novice staff, staff with moderate experience, and staff with considerable experience and expertise.

4. Practice observing classrooms through a "cultural lens." Think about how you can assist staff in becoming more aware of the cultural implications of their teaching.

ORGANIZATIONAL RESOURCES

Center for the Child Care Workforce
A Project of the American Federation of
Teachers Educational Foundation
555 New Jersey Avenue, NW
Washington, DC 20001
T 202-662-8005
F 202-662-8006
www.ccw.org

Compensation, working conditions,
education, training, publications;
Worthy Wage Campaign, Early
Childhood Mentoring Alliance.

Council for Professional Recognition
2460 16th Street, NW
Washington, DC 20009-3575
T 800-424-4310
F 202-265-9090
www.cdacouncil.org

Child Development Associate (CDA)
competency standards, assessment,
and training.

Council for Exceptional Children
1110 North Glebe Road, Suite 300
Arlington, VA 22201-5704
T 888-CEC-SPED or 888-232-7733
F 703-264-9494
www.cec.sped.org

An international professional
organization dedicated to improving
education outcomes for individuals

with exceptionalities, students with
disabilities, and/or the gifted.

National Association for Family Child
Care
5202 Pinemont Drive
Salt Lake City, UT 84123
T 800-359-3817
F 801-268-9507
www.nafcc.org

Affiliates; newsletter, publications,
insurance, accreditation.

National Association for the Education of
Young Children
1313 L Street, NW, Suite 500
Washington, DC 20005
T 800-424-2460
F 202-232-8777
www.naeyc.org

Also state, regional, and local
affiliates; accreditation, conferences,
journals, publications, position
statements.

National Association of Child Care
Resource and Referral Agencies
3101 Wilson Blvd., Suite 350
Arlington, VA 22201
T 703-341-4100
F 703-341-4101
www.naccrra.org

Membership organization for
community-based child care resource

and referral agencies; publications, technical assistance, training, and advocacy for families, providers, and community.

National Black Child Development
  Institute
1101 15th Street, NW, Suite 900
Washington, DC 20005
T 202-833-8220
F 202-833-8222
www.nbcdi.org

  Publications, affiliates, direct services, newsletters, conferences, African American Parent's Project, Cross Cultural Partnership Program.

National Board of Professional Teaching
  Standards
1525 Wilson Blvd, Suite 500
Arlington, VA 22209
T 703-465-2700
F 703-465-2715
www.nbpts.org

  National teacher certification, standards.

National Child Care Information Center
10530 Rosehaven Street, Suite 400
Fairfax, VA 22030
T 800-616-2242
F 800-716-2242
www.nccic.org

  A service of the Child Care Bureau, Administration for Children and Families; a national clearinghouse and technical assistance center providing a link to early care and information.

National Institute on Out-of-School Time
[Formerly School-Age Child Care
  Project]
Wellesley College
106 Central Street
Wellesley, MA 02481
T 781-283-2547
F 781-283-3657
www.niost.org

  Research, education and training, consultation, and curriculum and program development; publications, self-study process (ASQ).

National Latino Children's Institute
1325 N. Flores Street, Suite 114
San Antonio, TX 78212
T 210-228-9997
F 210-228-9972
www.nlci.org

  A national network of endorsers, supporters, and experts on Latino children's issues; promotes the National Latino Children's Agenda; clearinghouse/resource center; training and technical assistance; special events.

World Organization for Early Childhood
  Education
www.omep-usnc.org
www.omep.org.uk

  Worldwide nongovernmental organization which focuses on children 0–8, UN Convention Rights of the Child; represented at UNESCO, UNICEF, and Council of Europe; annual meeting, newsletter.

REFERENCES

Acheson, K. A., & Gall, M. D. (1997). *Techniques in the clinical supervision of teachers: Preservice and inservice applications* (4th ed.). New York: Longman.

Albrecht, K. (2002). *The right fit: Recruiting, selecting, and orienting staff.* Lake Forest, IL: New Horizons.

Albrecht, K. (2006). *Social intelligence: The new science of success.* San Francisco: Jossey-Bass.

Alfred, M. V. (2001). Expanding theories of career development: Adding the voices of African American women in the White academy. *Adult Education Quarterly, 51*(2), 108–127.

Allport, G. W. (1958). *The nature of prejudice.* Garden City, NY: Doubleday Anchor Books.

Anderson, T. (2002). *Current trends and issues in portfolio development.* New South Wales Department of Education and Training. Retrieved November 6, 2005, from http://www.schools.nsw.edu.au/edu_leadership/prof_read/portfolios/anderson.php

Arin-Krupp, J. (1981). *Adult development: Implications for staff development.* Manchester, CT: Adult Development and Learning.

Arredondo, D. E. (1998, April). *Enhancing cognitive complexity through collegial supervision.* Paper presented at the annual meeting of the American Educational Research Association, San Diego, CA.

Barnett, W. S., Hastedt, J. F., Robin, K. B., & Shulman, K. (2004). *The state of preschool: 2004 preschool yearbook.* New Brunswick, NJ: National Institute for Early Education Research, Rutgers University.

Barnett, W. S., Lamy, C., & Jung, K. (2005, December). *The effects of state prekindergarten programs on young children's school readiness in five states.* New Brunswick, NJ: National Institute for Early Education Research, Rutgers University.

Battersby, M. (2005, January/February). Find, attract, and retain workers with affordable benefits. *Exchange, 161,* 14–18.

Beers, C. D. (1993). Telling our stories: The CDA process in Native American Head Start. In E. Jones (Ed.), *Growing teachers: Partnerships in staff development* (pp. 2–19). Washington, DC: National Association for the Education of Young Children.

Belenky, M. F., Clinchy, B. M., Goldberger, N. R., & Tarule, J. M. (1997). *Women's ways of knowing: The development of self, voice, and mind.* New York: Basic Books. (Original work published 1986)

Bellm, D., Burton, A., Whitebook, M., Broatch, L., & Young, M. P. (2002). *Inside the pre-k classroom: A study of staffing and stability in state-funded prekindergarten programs*. Washington, DC: Center for the Child Care Workforce.

Bellm, D., & Whitebook, M. (2004). *State registries of the early care and education workforce: A review of current models and options for California*. Berkeley: Center for the Study of Child Care Employment, Institute of Industrial Relations, University of California.

Bellm, D., Whitebook, M., & Hnatiuk, P. (1997). *The early childhood mentoring curriculum* (vols. 1–2). Washington, DC: Center for the Child Care Workforce.

Bents, R. H., & Howey, K. R. (1981). Staff development—change in the individual. In B. Dillon-Peterson (Ed.), *Staff development: Organization development* (pp. 11–36). Alexandria, VA: Association for Supervision and Curriculum Development.

Bernhardt, J. L. (2000). A primary caregiving system for infants and todddlers: Best for everyone involved. *Young Children, 55*(2), 74–80.

Beveridge, S., Groundwater-Smith, S., Kemmis, S., & Wasson, D. (2004, November 28–December 2). *Professional learning that makes a difference: Successful strategies implemented by Priority Action Schools*. Paper presented at the annual conference of the Australian Association for Research in Education, Melbourne.

Binh, D. T. (1975). *A handbook for teachers of Vietnamese students*. Arlington, VA: Center for Applied Linguistics.

Bloom, P. J. (1995a). Building a sense of community: A broader view. *Child Care Information Exchange, 114*, 7–14.

Bloom, P. J. (1995b). The quality of worklife in early childhood programs. In S. Bredekamp & B. Willer (Eds.), *NAEYC accreditation: A decade of learning and the years ahead* (pp. 13–24). Washington, DC: National Association or the Education of Young Children.

Bloom, P. J. (1997). Decision-making influence: Who has it? Who wants it? *Child Care Information Exchange, 114*, 7–14.

Boller, K., & Sprachman, S. (2001). *The child-caregiver observation system (C-COS-R) instructor's manual* (Rev. ed.). Princeton, NJ: Mathematica Policy Research.

Bond, J. T., Galinsky E., & Hill, J. E. (2004). *When work works: Summary of Families and Work Institute research findings*. Retrieved February 7, 2005, from http://familiesandwork.org/3w/research/3wes.html

Bowers, C. A., & Flinders, D. J. (1990). *Responsive teaching: An ecological approach to classroom patterns of language, culture, and thought*. New York: Teachers College Press.

Bowers, C. A., & Flinders, D. J. (1991). *Culturally responsive teaching and supervision: A handbook for staff development*. New York: Teachers College Press.

Bowman, B. T., Donovan, M. S., & Burns, M. S. (Eds.). (2000). *Eager to learn: Educating our preschoolers* [Executive summary]. Washington, DC: National Academy Press. Retrieved June 11, 2005, from http://www.ciera.org/library/instresrc/eagertolearn/index.html

Boyatzis, R., McKee, A., & Goleman, D. (April, 2002). Reawakening your passion for work. *Harvard Business Review, 80*(4), 86–94.

Boyd, B. J., & Schneider, N. I. (1997). Perceptions of the work environment and burnout in Canadian child care providers. *Journal of Research in Childhood Education, 11*, 171–180.

Bredekamp, S., & Copple, C. (Eds.). (1997). *Developmentally appropriate practice in early childhood programs* (Rev. ed.). Washington, DC: National Association for the Education of Young Children.

Brown, J. (2002, June). *Washington State early childhood education career and wage ladder pilot project: Evaluation report of year 1-summary of findings, June 2002*. Retrieved May 31, 2006, from http://www.econop.org

Brundage, D. H., & Mackeracher, D. (1980). *Adult learning principles and their application to program planning*. Toronto: Ontario Institute for Studies in Education.

Bruner, J. (1996). *The culture of education*. Cambridge, MA: Harvard University Press.

Burton, A., Whitebook, M., Young, M. P., Bellm, D., Wayne, C., Brandon, R. M., & Mahler, E. (2002). *Estimating the size and components of the U.S. child care workforce and caregiving population*. Washington, DC: Center for the Child Care Workforce; Seattle, WA: Human Services Policy Center.

Bushnell, D. (2004, December 6). By choice or necessity, retirement yields to reinvention. *The Boston Globe*, p. G6.

Cadwell, L. B. (1997). *Bringing Reggio Emilia home: An innovative approach to early childhood education*. New York: Teachers College Press.

Carter, M. (1995). Building a community among teachers. *Child Care Information Exchange, 101*, 52–54.

Caruso, J. J. (1998). What cooperating teacher case studies reveal about their phases of development as supervisors of student teachers. *European Journal of Teacher Education, 21*(1), 119–132.

Caruso, J. J. (2000, January). Cooperating teacher and student teacher phases of development. *Young Children, 55*(1), 75–81.

Caruso, J. J., & Graham, C. (1994). *Collaborative supervision handbook*. Unpublished manuscript, Framingham State College, Framingham, MA.

Casper, V., & Schultz, S. B. (1999). *Gay parents, straight schools: Building community and trust*. New York: Teachers College Press.

Cazden, C. L. (1979). *Language in education: Variation in the teacher-talk register*. Paper presented at the 30th annual Georgetown University Round Table on Languages and Linguistics, Washington, DC.

Cazden, C. L. (1995). A different road to English. *Harvard Graduate School of Education Bulletin, 39*, 12.

Center for the Child Care Workforce. (2004). *Current data on the salaries and benefits of the U.S. early childhood education workforce*. Washington, DC: Author.

Centre for Teaching and Learning, University College Dublin. (2005). *Good practices in teaching and learning*. Retrieved March 19, 2005, from http://www.ucd.ie/

Child Care Services Association. (2005). *Child care WAGE$ project: An education-based salary supplement program for child care teachers, directors and family child care providers*. Retrieved May 27, 2006, from http://www.childcareservices.org/ps/wage.html

Children's Foundation. (2004). *Child care licensing study* [summary]. Retrieved October 19, 2004, from http://www.childrensfoundation.net/research/htm

Christensen, C. R., & Hanson, A. J. (1987). *Teaching and the case method*. Boston: Harvard Business School.

Cogan, M. L. (1973). *Clinical supervision*. Boston: Houghton Mifflin.

Cohen, D., Stern, V., & Balaban, N. (1997). *Observing and recording the behavior of young children* (4th ed.). New York: Teachers College Press.

Cohen, N. E., & Pompa, D. (1996). Multicultural perspectives on quality. In S. L. Kagan & N. E. Cohen (Eds.), *Reinventing early care and education: A vision for a quality system* (pp. 81–98). San Francisco: Jossey-Bass.

Combs, B. (2001). *ABC: A family alphabet book.* Ridley Park, PA: Two Lives Publishing.

Copple, C., & Bredekamp, S. (2005). *Basics of developmentally appropriate practice: An introduction to teachers of children 3 to 6.* Washington, DC: National Association for the Education of Young Children.

Cost, Quality, and Child Outcomes Study Team. (1995). *Cost, quality, and child outcomes in child care centers: Technical report.* Denver: University of Colorado at Denver.

Council for Professional Recognition. (n.d.) *The Child Development Associate assessment system and competency standards: Preschool caregivers in center-based programs.* Washington, DC: Author. Retrieved December 2, 2005, from http://www.cdacouncil.org

Danielson, C., & McGreal, T. L. (2000). *Teacher evaluation to enhance professional practice.* Alexandria, VA: Association for Supervision and Curriculum Development.

Darn, S. (2005, February). Aspects of nonverbal communication. *The Internet TESL Journal, 11*(2). Retrieved December 19, 2005, from http://iteslj.org/Articles/Darn-Nonverbal/

Deal, T. E., & Kennedy, A. A. (1982). *Corporate cultures: The rites and rituals of corporate life.* Reading, MA: Addison-Wesley.

Delpit, L. (1995). *Other people's children: Cultural conflict in the classroom.* New York: New Press.

Delpit, L., & Dowdy, J. K. (2002). *The skin that we speak: Thoughts on language and culture in the classroom.* New York: Norton.

Derman-Sparks, L., & Ramsey, P. (2006). *What if all the kids are white? Anti-bias multicultural education with young children and families.* New York: Teachers College Press.

Dodge, D. T., Colker, L. J., & Heroman, C. (2002). *The creative curriculum for preschool* (4th ed.). Washington, DC: Teaching Strategies.

Donohue, C. (2003, November/December). Technology in early childhood education. *Child Care Information Exchange, 154*, 17–20.

Dyson, A. H., & Genishi, C. (2005). *On the case: Approaches to language and literacy research.* New York: Teachers College Press.

Education Commission of the States. (2002). *ECS Education Policy Issue Site: Early Learning, Pre-Kindergarten Database.* Retrieved May 12, 2006, from http://www.ecs. org

Education Commission of the States. (2004a). *Brain research.* Retrieved October 8, 2004, from http://www.ecs.org/html/issue.asp?issueid=17/

Education Commission of the States. (2004b). *Class size: Overview.* Retrieved September 24, 2004, from http://www.ecs.org/html/IssueSection.asp?issueid=24&s=Overview/

Education Commission of the States. (2006). *ECS Education Policy Issue Site: Kindergarten.* Retrieved May 12, 2006, from http://www.ecs.org

Egan, K. (1987). Literacy and the oral foundations of education. *Harvard Educational Review, 57*(4), 445–472.

Eisner, E. (1982). An artistic approach to supervision. In T. J. Sergiovanni (Ed.), *Supervision of teaching* (pp. 60–65). Alexandria, VA: Association for Supervision and Curriculum Development.

Erikson, E. H. (1980). *Identity and the life cycle.* New York: Norton.

Erikson, E. II. (1982). *The life cycle completed.* New York: Norton.

Families and Work Institute. (2002). *Generation and gender in the workplace* [Issue brief]. Retrieved December 15, 2005, from http://familiesandwork.org/eproducts/genandgender.pdf

Family Child Care Accreditation Project (Wheelock College). (2005). *Providers self-study workbook: Quality standards for NAFCC accreditation* (4th ed.). Salt Lake City, UT: National Association for Family Child Care.

Fernandez, C., & Chokshi, S. (2002, October). A practical guide to translating lesson study for a U.S. setting. *Phi Delta Kappan, 84*(2), 128–34.

Fields, J. (2004). *America's families and living arrangements: 2003* (Current Population Reports No. 20-553). Washington, DC: U.S. Census Bureau. Retrieved December 16, 2005, from http://www.census.gov/prod/2004pubs/p20-553.pdf

Folkman, S., Moskowitz, J. T., Ozer, E. M., & Park, C. L. (1997). Positive meaningful events and coping in the context of HIV/AIDS. In B. H. Gottlieb (Ed.), *Coping with chronic stress* (pp. 293–314). New York: Plenum.

Foster, M. (1987). "It's cookin now": An ethnographic study of the teaching style of a successful Black teacher in a White community college. In L. Delpit (Ed.), *Other people's children: Cultural conflict in the classroom* (pp. 135–151). New York: New Press.

Foundation for Child Development. (2003). *Mapping the P–3 continuum (MAP): P–3 as the foundation of education reform.* New York: Author.

Fredrickson, B. L. (2000). Cultivating positive emotions to optimize health and well-being. *Prevention and Treatment, 3*(1). Retrieved May 9, 2005, from http://content.apa.org/journals/pre/3/1/1/

Fredrickson, B. L. (2001). *Leading with positive emotions.* Ann Arbor: Regents, University of Michigan. Retrieved May 9, 2005, from http://www.lsa.umich.edu/psych/peplab/leading/

Freedman, M. (2006). *Making policy for an aging century: Civic Ventures.* Retrieved May 28, 2006, from http://www.civicventures.org/articles.cfm

Freire, P. (1972). *Pedagogy of the oppressed.* New York: Herder & Herder.

Fuller, F. (1969). Concerns of teachers: A developmental conceptualization. *American Education Research Journal, 6*(2), 207–226.

Fuller, F., & Bown, O. H. (1975). Becoming a teacher. In K. Ryan (Ed.), *The 74th yearbook of the National Society for the Study of Education* (Part 2, pp. 25–52). Chicago: University of Chicago Press.

Garcia, E. (1997). The education of Hispanics in early childhood: Of roots and wings. *Young Children, 52*(3), 5–14.

Gardner, H. (1993). *Frames of mind: The theory of multiple intelligences.* New York: Basic Books. (Original work published in 1983)

Gardner, H. (2003). *Multiple intelligences after twenty years.* Paper presented at the annual meeting of the American Educational Research Association, Chicago.

Garman, N. B. (1982). The clinical approach to supervision. In T. J. Sergiovanni (Ed.), *Supervision of teaching* (pp. 35–52). Alexandria, VA: Association for Supervision and Curriculum Development.

Garner, A. (2004). *Families like mine: Children of gay parents tell it like it is.* New York: HarperCollins.

Gelnaw, A. (2005, May/June). Belonging: Including children of gay and lesbian parents—and all children—in your program. *Exchange, 163*, 42–45.

Gilliam, W. S., & Marchesseault, C. M. (2005, March 30). *From capitols to classrooms, policies to practice: State-funded prekindergarten at the classroom level. Part 1: Who's teaching our youngest students? Teacher education and training, experience, compensation and benefits, and assistant teachers*. The National Prekindergarten Study. New Haven, CT: Yale University Child Study Center.

Gilligan, C. (1982). *In a different voice: Psychological theory of women's development*. Cambridge, MA: Harvard University Press.

Givens, D. B. (2005). *The nonverbal dictionary of gestures, signs and body language cues*. Spokane, Washington: Center for Nonverbal Studies Press. Retrieved January 3, 2006, from http://members.aol.com/nonverbal2/diction1.htm

Glanz, J. (2003). *An educational leader's guide to school improvement* (2nd ed.). Norwood, MA: Christopher Gordon.

Glassberg, S. (1980, April). *A view of the beginning teacher from a developmental perspective*. Paper presented at the annual meeting of the American Educational Research Association, Boston.

Glickman, C. D., Gordon, S. P., & Ross-Gordon, J. M. (2004). *Supervision and instructional leadership: A developmental approach* (6th ed.). Boston: Pearson Education and Allyn & Bacon.

Goldberg, R. J., & Steury, S. (2001, December). Depression in the workplace: Costs and barriers to treatment. *Psychiatric Services, 12*(52), 1639–1643.

Goldhammer, R. (1966). *A critical analysis of supervision of instruction in the Harvard-Lexington summer program*. Unpublished doctoral dissertation, Graduate School of Education, Harvard University, Cambridge, MA.

Goldhammer, R. (1969). *Clinical supervision: Special methods for the supervision of teachers*. New York: Holt, Rinehart & Winston.

Goleman, D. (1995). *Emotional intelligence*. New York: Bantam Books.

Gonzalez-Mena, J. (2005). *Diversity in early care and education programs: Honoring differences* (4th ed.). Boston: McGraw-Hill.

Gould, R. L. (1978). *Transformations: Growth and change in adult life*. New York: Simon & Schuster.

Gratz, R. R., & Boulton, P. J. (1996). Erikson and early childhood educators: Looking at ourselves and our profession developmentally. *Young Children, 51*(5), 74–78.

Greene, M. (1988). What happened to imagination? In K. Egan & D. Nadaner (Eds.), *Imagination and education* (pp. 45–56). New York: Teachers College Press.

Greene, M. (1995). *Releasing the imagination: Essays on education, the arts, and social change*. San Francisco: Jossey-Bass.

Greenough, K. (1993). Moving out of silence: The CDA process with Alaska native teachers. In E. Jones (Ed.), *Growing teachers: Partnerships in staff development* (pp. 21–35). Washington, DC: National Association for the Education of Young Children.

Grimmett, P. (1983, April). *Effective clinical supervision conference interventions: A preliminary investigation of participants' conceptual functioning*. Paper presented at the annual meeting of the American Educational Research Association, Montreal, Canada.

Groundwater-Smith, S. (2002, November). *Evidence based practice in school education: Some lessons for learning in museums*. Paper presented at Why Learning? Seminar,

Australian Museum/University of Technology, Sydney, Australia. Retrieved November 5, 2005, from http://www.amonline.net.au/amarc/pdf/conferences/susangs.pdf

Groundwater-Smith, S., & Kemmis, S. (2004, January). *Knowing makes the difference: Learnings from the NSW priority action schools program.* New South Wales Department of Education and Training. Retrieved November 5, 2005, from http://nla.gov.au/nla.arc-45897

Groundwater-Smith, S., & Mockler, N. (2003). *Learning to listen: Listening to learn.* Sydney, Australia: MLC School & Faculty of Education and Social Work, University of Sydney.

Guba, E. G., & Lincoln, Y. S. (1981). *Effective evaluation.* San Francisco: Jossey-Bass.

Gullo, D. (Ed.). (In press). *K today: Teaching and learning in the kindergarten year.* Washington, DC: National Association for the Education of Young Children.

Hannay, L. M. (2004). *Rethinking professional learning: Engaging the little grey cells.* Toronto: National College for School Leadership, Ontario Institute for Studies in Education, University of Toronto.

Hargreaves, D. (2002). The knowledge-creating school. In B. Moon, J. Butcher, & E. Bird (Eds.), *Leading professional development in education* (pp. 224–240). London: Routledge & Farmer.

Harms, T., Clifford, R. M., & Cryer, D. (2005). *Early childhood environment rating scale* (Rev. ed.). New York: Teachers College Press.

Harms, T., Cryer, D., & Clifford, R. M. (2006). *Family child care rating scale* (Rev. ed.). New York: Teachers College Press.

Harris, P. R., & Moran, R. T. (2000). *Managing cultural differences* (5th ed.). Houston: Gulf Publishing.

Head Start Bureau. (2001). *Putting the pro in protégé: A guide to mentoring in Head Start and Early Head Start.* Washington, DC: Author. Retrieved January 3, 2006, from http://www.headstartinfo.org/pdf/mentoring/pdf

Heathfield, S. M. (2006). *Managing your human resources: How to mediate and resolve conflict.* Retrieved January 5, 2006, from http://humanresources.about.com/od/managementtips/a/conflict_solue_2.htm.

Helburn, S. W. (Ed.). (1995). *Cost, quality, and child outcomes in child care centers* [Technical report]. Denver: University of Colorado at Denver.

High/Scope Educational Research Foundation. (2003). *Preschool Child Observation Record (COR)* (2nd ed.). Ypsilanti, MI: High/Scope Press.

Hirsh, E. (1996). *The block book* (3rd ed.). Washington, DC: National Association for the Education of Young Children.

Hohmann, M., & Weikart, D. (2002). *Educating young children: Active learning practices for preschool and child care programs* (2nd ed.). Ypsilanti, MI: High/Scope Press.

Hubbard, R. S., & Power, B. M. (2003). *The art of classroom inquiry: A handbook for teacher-researchers* (Rev. ed.). Portsmouth, NH: Heinemann.

Hunt, D. E. (1971). *Matching models in education.* Toronto: Ontario Institute for Studies in Education.

Imel, S. (2002). *Career development for meaningful life work.* Columbus, OH: ERIC Clearinghouse on Adult Career and Vocational Education. Retrieved February 5, 2005, from http://www.cete.org/acve/docs/dig237.pdf

INCCRRA (Illinois Network of Child Care Resource and Referral Agencies). (2006).

Gateways to opportunity: The Illinois early care and education career development network. Retrieved January 10, 2006, from http://www.ilgateways.com

Irvine, J. J. (1991, November). *A response to David Flinders: Implications for culturally diverse schools.* Paper presented at the annual fall conference of the Council of Professors of Instructional Supervision, University of Houston, Houston, TX.

Jackson, M. (2004, December 5). Companies that tap older workers can profit from a wealth of experience. *The Boston Globe*, p. G1.

Jackson, M. (2005, March 13). Employers looking to help workers deal with stress of tending elder relatives. *The Boston Globe*, p. G1.

Johnson, R. G. (1979). *The appraisal interview guide.* New York: Alpine Press.

Johnson, S. M. (1990). *Teachers at work: Achieving success in our schools.* New York: Basic Books.

Jones, E. (Ed.). (1993). *Growing teachers: Partnerships in staff development.* Washington, DC: National Association for the Education of Young Children.

Jones, E. (1994). Breaking the ice: Confronting status differences among professionals. In J. Johnson & J. B. McCracken (Eds.), *The early childhood career lattice: Perspectives on professional development* (pp. 27–30). Washington, DC: National Association for the Education of Young Children.

Katz, D., & Kahn, R. L. (1966). *The social psychology of organizations.* New York: Wiley.

Katz, L. G. (1977). Teachers' developmental stages. In *Talks with teachers: Reflections on early childhood education* (pp. 7–13). Washington, DC: National Association for the Education of Young Children.

King, E. W., Chipman, M., & Cruz-Jazen, M. (1994). *Educating young children in a diverse society.* Needham Heights, MA: Allyn & Bacon.

Kleinfeld, J. (1988, June). *Learning to think like a teacher: The study of cases.* Fairbanks: Center for Cross-Cultural Studies, University of Alaska.

Kloosterman, V. I. (2003, November). A partnership approach for supervisors and teachers. *Young Children, 58*(6), 72–76.

Knowles, M. S. (1980). *The modern practice of adult education: From pedagogy to andragogy* (2nd ed.). Chicago: Follett.

Knowles, M. S., & Associates. (1984). *Andragogy in action: Applying modern principles of adult learning.* San Francisco: Jossey-Bass.

Kohlberg, L. (1984). *The psychology of moral development.* San Francisco: Harper & Row.

Kontos, S., Howes, C., Shinn, M., & Galinsky, E. (1995). *Quality in family child care and relative care.* New York: Teachers College Press.

Koplow, L. (2002). *Creating schools that heal: Real-life solutions.* New York: Teachers College Press.

Kumrow, D., & Dahlen, B. (2002, May/June). Is peer review an effective approach for evaluating teachers? *Clearing House, 75*(5), 238–241.

Lally, J. R., Young-Holt, C. L., & Mangione, P. (1994). Preparing caregivers for quality infant and toddler child care. In J. Johnson & J. B. McCracken (Eds.), *The early childhood career lattice: Perspectives on professional development* (pp. 100–105). Washington, DC: National Association for the Education of Young Children.

Levine, S. L. (1989). *Promoting adult growth in schools: The promise of professional development.* Boston: Allyn & Bacon.

Levinson, D. (1978). *The seasons of a man's life.* New York: Ballentine.

Levinson, D. (1996). *The seasons of a woman's life*. New York: Ballentine.

Levinson, H. (2005). *Feedback to subordinates* (Levinson Letter Classic). Jaffrey, NH: Levinson Institute. (Original work published 1992)

Lieberman, A., & Miller, L. (1992). *Teachers, their world, and their work: Implications for school improvement*. New York: Teachers College Press.

Little, J. W. (1982). Norms of collegiality and experimentation: Workplace conditions of school success. *American Education Research Journal, 19*, 325–340.

Little, J. W. (1990). The persistence of privacy: Autonomy and initiative in teachers' professional relations. *Teachers College Record, 91*(4), 509–536.

Loevinger, J. (1976). *Ego development: Conception and theories*. San Francisco: Jossey-Bass.

Maine roads to quality: Early Care and Education Career Development Center. (2006). Portland, ME: Edmund S. Muskie School of Public Service. Available at http://www.muskie.usm.maine.edu/maineroads/

Manter, M. A. (2002). Designing a career development and management system for Head Start. *Head Start Bulletin*, No. 72. Retrieved December 8, 2005, from http://www.headstartinfo.org/publications/hsbulletin72/hsb72_17.htm

Marsh, K. J. (1998, April). *Classroom relationships: The narratives of a Lakota high school teacher*. Paper presented at the annual meeting of the American Educational Research Association, San Diego.

Mayeroff, M. (1971). *On caring*. New York: Harper & Row.

McDowelle, J. O., & Buckner, K. G. (2002). *Leading with emotion: Reaching balance in educational decision-making*. Lanham, MD: Scarecrow Press.

Merriam, S. B., & Caffarella, R. S. (1999). *Learning in adulthood: A comprehensive guide* (2nd ed.). San Francisco: Jossey-Bass.

Meyer, T., & Achinstein, B. (1998, April). *Collaborative inquiry among novice teachers as professional development: Sustaining habits of heart and mind*. Paper presented at the annual meeting of the American Educational Research Association, San Diego.

Mezirow, J. (1991). *Transformative dimensions of adult learning*. San Francisco: Jossey-Bass.

Mezirow, J., & Associates. (2000). *Learning as transformation: Critical perspectives on a theory in progress*. San Francisco: Jossey-Bass.

Modigliani, K. (2001). *A survey of family child care accreditation projects*. Arlington, MA: Family Child Care Project.

Modigliani, K., & Dombro, A. L. (1996). *There's no place like home*. Arlington, MA: Family Child Care Project.

Moore, T. (March, 1999). Bringing diversity into your center. *Child Care Information Exchange, 126*, 35–38.

Morgan, G. (2000). The director as a key to quality. In M. L. Culkin, (Ed.), *Managing quality in young children's programs: The leader's role* (pp. 40–58). New York: Teachers College Press.

Morgan, G., & Costley, J. (2004, November). *Taking the temperature of career development*. Boston: Wheelock College, and Cambridge: Lesley University, Center for Children, Families, and Public Policy. Available at http://www.lesley.edu/academic.centers/cfpp/content/taking_the_tem_report.pdf

National Association for the Education of Young Children. (n.d.). *Critical facts about young children and early childhood programs in the United States: Critical facts*

about the early childhood workforce. Retrieved November 24, 2004, from http://
www.naeyc.org/ece/critical/facts3.asp

National Association for the Education of Young Children (NAEYC). (1996). NAEYC
Position Statement: Responding to linguistic and cultural diversity—Recommendations
for effective early childhood education. *Young Children, 51*(2), 4–12. Retrieved
February 15, 2006, from http://www.journal.naeyc.org/search/

National Association for the Education of Young Children (NAEYC). (2005). *NAEYC
early childhood program standards and accreditation criteria: The mark of quality
in early childhood education.* Washington, DC: Author. Available online at: http://
www.naeyc.org

National Association of Elementary School Principals (NAESP). (1999). *After-school
programs and the K–8 principal: Standards for quality school-age child care.* Washington, DC: Author.

National Association of Elementary School Principals (NAESP). (2005). *Leading early
childhood learning communities: What principals should know and be able to do.*
Washington, DC: Author.

National Board for Professional Teaching Standards (NBPTS). (2004). *NBPTS early child-
hood/generalist standards* (2nd ed.). Retrieved February 15, 2006, from http://
www.nbpts.org/candidates/guide/whichcert/01EarlyChild2004.html

National Center for Education Statistics. (2004). *Participation in education: Trends in
full- and half-day kindergarten.* Retrieved November 21, 2004, from http://nces
.ed.gov/programs/coe/2004/section1/indicator 03.asp

National Center for Health Statistics. (2001). *43% of first marriages break up within
15 years* [News release]. Retrieved December 3, 2005, from http://www.cdc.gov/
nchs/pressroom/01news/firstmarr.htm.

National Center for Health Statistics. (2003). *Deaths: preliminary data for 2003, table 6.*
Retrieved December 16, 2005, from http://www.cdc.gov/

National Child Care Information Center (NCCIC). (2004). *Center child care licensing
requirements (August 2004): Minimum early childhood education (ECE) preservice
qualifications, administrative, and annual ongoing training hours for directors.*
Compiled by Sarah LeMoine from licensing regulations posted on the National Resource Center for Health and Safety in Child Care's Web site (http://nrc.uchsc.edu).
Retrieved November 27, 2004, from http://www.nccic.org/

National Child Care Information Center (NCCIC). (2005, October). *Early childhood education workforce practitioner registry systems.* Retrieved April 17, 2006, from http:/
/nccic.org/poptopics/practitioner-registry.html

National Institute on Out-of-School Time [NIOST]. (2003). *Training and curriculum.*
Retrieved October 18, 2004, from http://niost.org/training/index.html

National Institute on Out-of-School Time [NIOST] & Academy for Economic Development's Center for Youth Development. (2003). *Building a skilled and stable
workforce: Results from on-line survey of out-of-school professionals.* Funded by
Lucile Packard Foundation. Retrieved September 9, 2004, from http://niost.skeey
dev.net/clearinghouse/execsumbsw.asp

Neugebauer, R. (1993). Status report #1 on school-age child care. *Child Care Information Exchange, 89,* 11–15.

Neugebauer, R. (2004, July/August). Wages for early childhood professionals in North
America: Results of an Exchange insta-poll. *Exchange, 158,* 16–20.

Newberger, J. J. (1997). New brain development research: A wonderful window of opportunity to build public support for early childhood education. *Young Children*, 52(4), 4–9.

Noddings, N. (2002). *Educating moral people: A caring alternative to character education*. New York: Teachers College Press.

Nonaka, I., & Takeuchi, H. (1995). *The knowledge creating company*. Oxford: Oxford University Press.

Oja, S. N. (1981, April). *Deriving teacher educational objectives from cognitive-developmental theories and applying them to the practice of teacher education*. Paper presented at the annual meeting of the American Education Research Association, Los Angeles.

Page, M. L. (2003, Winter). Race, culture, and the supervisory relationship: A review of the literature and a call to action. *Journal of Curriculum and Supervision*, 18(2), 161–174.

Pajak, E. (2000). *Approaches to clinical supervision: Alternatives for improving instruction* (2nd ed.). Norwood, MA: Christopher-Gordon.

Paley, V. (1997). *The girl with the brown crayon*. Cambridge, MA: Harvard University Press.

Patterson, J., & Collins, L. (2002). *Bouncing back: How your school can succeed in the face of adversity*. Larchmont, NY: Eye on Education.

Peisner-Feinberg, E. S., Burchinal, M. R., Clifford, R. M., Culkin, M. L., Kagan, S. L., Yazejian, N., Byler, P., Rustici, J., & Zelazo, J. (1999). *The children of the Cost, Quality, and Outcomes Study go to school: Executive summary*. Chapel Hill: University of North Carolina at Chapel Hill, Frank Porter Graham Child Development Center.

Perry, W. G. (1969). *Forms of intellectual and ethical development during the college years*. New York: Holt, Rinehart & Winston.

Peterson, K. D. (2000). *Teacher evaluation: A comprehensive guide to new directions and practices* (2nd ed.). Thousand Oaks, CA: Corwin Press.

Piaget, J. (1961). The genetic approach to the psychology of thought. *Journal of Educational Psychology*, 52, 275–281.

Powell, D. R. (1994). Parents, pluralism and the NAEYC statement on developmentally appropriate practice. In B. L. Mallory & R. S. New (Eds.), *Diversity and developmentally appropriate practices: Challenges for early childhood education* (pp. 166–182). New York: Teachers College Press.

Ramsey, P. G. (2004). *Teaching and learning in a diverse world: Multicultural education for young children* (3rd ed.). New York: Teachers College Press.

Retallick, J. (2002). *Professional ethics and teacher practice*. New South Wales Department of Education and Training. Retrieved November 6, 2005, from http://www.schools.nsw.edu.au/edu_leadership/prof_read/portfolios/retallick.php

Richardson, J., & Parnell, P. (2005). *And Tango makes three*. New York: Simon & Schuster Children's Publishing.

Roach, M. A., Adams, D. B., Riley, D. A., & Edie, D. (2003). *Wisconsin Child Care Research Partnership Issue Brief #11: What characteristics contribute to quality in family child care?* University of Wisconsin-Extension: Madison, WI.

Rodd, J. (1998). *Leadership in early childhood: The pathway to professionalism* (2nd ed.). New York: Teachers College Press.

Rogers, C. E. (1962). The interpersonal relationship: The core of guidance. *Harvard Educational Review*, 32, 416–429.

Rossiter, M. (2002). *Narrative stories in adult teaching and learning.* ERIC Digest No. 241. Retrieved April 18, 2006, from http://www.cete.org/acve/docs/dig241.pdf

Ruden, A., & McCabe, L. (2004). *Researching universal prekindergarten: Thoughts on critical questions and research domains from policy makers, child advocates, and researchers.* New York: Columbia University Institute for Child and Family Policy; Cornell Early Childhood Program.

Ruopp, R., Travers, J., Glantz, F., & Coelen, C. (1979). *Final report of the National Day Care Study: Vol. 1. Children at the center.* Cambridge, MA: Abt Associates.

Ryan, S., Hornbeck, A., & Frede, E. (2004, Spring). Mentoring for change: A time use study of teacher consultants in preschool reform. *Early Childhood Research and Practice, 6*(1), 1–18.

Saluja, G., Early, D. M., & Clifford, R. M. (2002, Spring). Demographic characteristics of early childhood teachers and structural elements of early care and education in the United States. *Early Childhood Research and Practice, 4*(1). Retrieved January 6, 2006, from http://ecrp.uiuc.edu.v4n1/saluja.html

Schein, E. H. (1985). *Organizational culture and leadership.* San Francisco: Jossey-Bass.

Schön, D. A. (1987). *Educating the reflective practitioner: Toward a new design for teaching and learning in the professions.* San Francisco: Jossey-Bass.

Schweinhart, L. J. (2004). *A school administrator's guide to early childhood programs* (2nd ed.). Ypsilanti, MI: High/Scope Press.

Sciarra, D. J., & Dorsey, A. G. (2002). *Leaders and supervisors in child care programs.* Clifton Park, NY: Thomson Delmar Learning.

Seidel, S. (1998). Learning from looking. In N. Lyons (Ed.), *With portfolio in hand: Validating the new teacher professionalism* (pp. 65–89). New York: Teachers College Press.

Seligson, M., & Stahl, P. (2003). *Bringing yourself to work: A guide to successful staff development in after-school programs.* New York: Teachers College Press.

Sheehy, G. (1976). *Passages: Predictable crises of adult life.* New York: Dutton.

Sheehy, G. (1998). *Understanding men's passages: Discovering the new map of men's lives.* New York: Random House.

Shonkoff, J., & Phillips, D. (2000). *From neurons to neighborhoods: The science of early childhood development.* Washington, DC: National Academy Press.

Shore, R. (2003). *Rethinking the brain: New insights into early development* (rev. ed.). New York: Families and Work Institute.

Shulman, L. S. (1987, February). Knowledge and teaching: Foundations of the new reform. *Harvard Educational Review, 57*(1), 1–22.

South Dakota Pathways. (2005). *South Dakota pathways to professional development: Career lattice requirements.* Retrieved June 8, 2005, from http://www.state.sd.us/social/CCS/Pathways/Lattice.htm

Spodek, B., & Saracho, O. N. (1982). The preparation and certification of early childhood personnel. In B. Spodek (Ed.), *Handbook of research in early childhood education* (pp. 399–425). New York: Macmillan.

Strain, P. S., & Joseph, G. E. (2004). Engaged supervision to support recommended practices for young children with challenging behavior. *Topics in Early Childhood Special Education, 24*(1), 39–50.

Sturm, C. (1997). Creating parent-teacher dialogue: Intercultural communication in child care. *Young Children, 52*(5), 34–38.

Takamura, J. C. (1998). *Testimony on "The graying of nations"* Before the Senate Special Committee on Aging, June 8, 1998. Retrieved February 5, 2005, from http://www.hhs.gov/

Tennen, M. (2004). *Women's depression in the workplace.* Retrieved May 9, 2005, from http://www.healthatoz.com/healthatoz/Atoz/hl/sp/work/alert03162004.jsp

Terzi, N., & Cantarell, M. (2001). Parma: Supporting the work of teachers through professional development, organization, and administrative support. In L. Gandini & C. P. Edwards (Eds.), *Bambini: The Italian approach to infant/toddler care* (pp. 78–88). New York: Teachers College Press.

Thies-Sprinthall, L. (1980). Supervision: An educative or miseducative process? *Journal of Teacher Education, 31*(4), 17–20.

Thirty Directors. (1981, March). Overcoming the fear of firing. *Child Care Information Exchange, 18,* 11–15.

Trunk, P. (2005, February 20). From college grad to adulthood: Navigating the quarterlife crisis. *The Boston Globe,* p. G1, G10.

Urbanski, A., & O'Connell, C. (2003, September 28–30). *Transforming the profession of teaching: It starts at the beginning.* Paper presented at Summit 1, The First Three Years of Teaching, hosted by National Commission on Teaching and America's Future, Racine, Wisconsin. Retrieved June 6, 2005, from http://www.nctaf.org

U.S. Department of Education. (2004). *A description of the evaluation of the federal class size reduction program.* Washington, DC: Author.

U.S. Department of Health and Human Services. (2002, July). *Head Start 101 tool kit.* Washington, DC: Author. Retrieved January 12, 2006, from http://www.headstart info.org/infocenter/hs101.htm

U.S. Department of Health and Human Services. (2004, November). *Head Start program performance standards and other regulations.* Washington, DC: Author. Retrieved May 31, 2006, from http://www.acfhhs.gov/programs/hsb/budget/headstartact.htm#staff

U.S. Department of Labor. (1998, October 13). People average 8.6 jobs from ages 18 to 32. *MLR: The Editor's Desk.* Retrieved February 26, 2005, from http://www.bls.gov/

Vander Ven, K. (1988). Pathways for professional effectiveness for early childhood educators. In B. Spodek, O. N. Saracho, & D. L. Peters (Eds.), *Professionalism and the early childhood practitioner* (pp. 137–160). New York: Teachers College Press.

Vecchi, V. (1997, January). *The hundred languages of children: Children and art.* Paper presented at the Winter Institute, Reggio Emilia, Italy.

Watanabe, T., & Wang-Iverson, P. (2002, November). *The role of knowledgeable others.* Paper presented at the First Annual Lesson Study Conference, Stamford, CT. Retrieved September 23, 2005, from http://www.rbs.org/lesson_study/conference/2002/papers/watanabe.shtml

Wen, P. (2005, January16). The Gen X dad. *The Boston Globe Magazine.* pp. 21, 22, 30, 31, 32.

What centers need to succeed at accreditation. (1997). *Rights, Raises, Respect: News and Issues for the Child Care Work Force, 2,* 7. Available online at http://www.ccw.org/

Wheelock College Institute for Leadership and Career Initiatives. (2002, July). *Report on 2001 early childhood/school-age career development survey.* Boston: Wheelock College.

Whitebook, M. (1997, November). *Managing staff turnover in child care centers: Best practices for the field*. Paper presented at the annual meeting of the National Association for the Education of Young Children, Anaheim, CA.

Whitebook, M. (2003). *Early education quality: Higher teacher qualifications for better learning environments: A review of the literature*. Berkeley: Institute of Industrial Relations, University of California.

Whitebook, M., Howes, C., & Phillips, D. (1989). *Who cares? Child care teachers and the quality of care in America: Final report, National Child Care Staffing Study*. Oakland, CA: Child Care Employee Project.

Whitebook, M., Howes, C., & Phillips, D. (1998). *Worthy work, unlivable wages: The National Child Care Staffing Study, 1988–1997*. Washington, DC: Center for the Child Care Workforce.

Whitebook, M., Phillips, D., Bellm, D., Crowell, N., Almaraz, M., & Jo, J. Y. (2004). *Two years in early care and education: A community portrait of quality and workforce stability*. Berkeley: Center for the Study of Child Care Employment, University of California.

Whitebook, M., Phillips, D., & Howes, C. (1993). *The National Child Care Staffing Study revisited: Four years in the life of center-based child care*. Oakland, CA: Center for the Child Care Employee Project.

Whitebook, M., Sakai, L., Gerber E., & Howes, C. (2001). *Then and now: Changes in child care staffing, 1994–2000*. Washington, DC: Center for the Child Care Workforce; and Berkeley: Institute of Industrial Relations, University of California.

Whitebook, M., Sakai, L., Voisin, I., Duff, B., Waters Boots, S., Burton, A., & Young, M. (2003). *California child care workforce study: Center-based child care in Alameda County*. Washington, DC: Center for the Child Care Workforce.

Willer, B. (1994). A conceptual framework for early childhood professional development: NAEYC Position Statement, adopted November 1993. In J. Johnson & J. B. McCraken (Eds.), *The early childhood career lattice: Perspectives on professional development* (pp. 4–21). Washington, DC: National Association for the Education of Young Children.

Zill, N., McKay, R. H., & O'Brien, R. (2003). *Head Start FACES: A whole-child perspective on program performance: Fourth progress report*. Washington, DC: Child Outcomes Research and Evaluation and the Head Start Bureau, Administration for Children and Families, U.S. Department of Health and Human Services.

INDEX

Academy for Economic Development, 15
Accountability, 20, 54, 86, 147, 199, 217
Accreditation
  and career ladder, 181
  of center-based child care, 12, 16
  and evaluation, 235–36
  of family child care, 17, 18
  and learning, 212–13
  NAEYC, 12, 27–28, 36, 43, 89–91, 100–
    101, 164, 171–72, 181, 190–91,
    212–13, 230–31, 235–36
  NAFCC, 17, 18
  and National AfterSchool Association, 16
  and professional development, 212–13
  and salaries/benefits, 43
  and supervisee development, 100–101
  and supervisor development, 89–91
  and supervisor training and experience,
    36
  and turnover, 164
Acheson, K. A., 135
Achinstein, B., 227
Action research, 198, 199–200, 209, 220,
  227, 229–30, 235
Adams, D. B., 18
Adult development, 56, 57, 61, 64–69, 70–
  73, 75, 76, 89
Adult learning. *See* Learning
Adulthood
  as life stage, 64–65, 70–73
  longer transition to, 66–67
Advocacy, 43, 165, 198
After-school programs, 162
Aides/assistants, 21, 35, 36, 38–39, 42, 43,
  93, 157–58, 176, 178

Alameda County Child Development Corps,
  165
Albrecht, K., 52, 185, 190
Alfred, M. V., 67–68
Allport, Gordon, 167
Almaraz, M., 161, 165
American Federation of Teachers Education
  Foundation, 165, 201
Analysis/strategy
  as clinical supervision stage, 110–11, 135
  and closed systems, 139
  and evaluation, 216
  and learning, 197
  and open systems, 143
  overview of, 135–36
  self-, 127
  and supervisory conferences, 117, 125,
    127–28, 130, 131, 132
  See also Observation
Anderson, T., 228
Andragogy, 192–95
Arin-Krupp, J., 65, 69
Arredondo, D. E., 62
Assessment
  authentic, 215
  of child progress, 28
  and developmental dynamic, 102, 103–4
  and Head Start, 19
  and NAEYC standards, 28
  and observation and analysis, 144–45
  ongoing, 215
  as part of professional continuum, 183
  and professional development, 206, 207, 208
  self-, 20, 86, 88–89, 131, 144–45, 226
  and supervisor development, 86–87, 88–89

ABOUT THE AUTHORS

Joseph J. Caruso is a lecturer for International Education Programs, Inc., where he teaches courses in supervision to educators, government employees, missionaries, and volunteers who work in schools and other educational settings throughout the world. He lives in Boston and Wellfleet, MA. He is a landscape painter and printmaker, as well as a gardener, and does volunteer work for the Massachusetts Horticultural Society and the Provincetown Art Association and Museum. He received his B.S. degree from Boston University and his M.A. and Ed.D. degrees from Columbia University, and has published articles in many professional journals.

M. Temple Fawcett is Professor Emerita of Early Childhood and Elementary Education at Roger Williams University in Bristol, Rhode Island. She received her B.A. in music from Brown University and her M.Ed. from the Harvard Graduate School of Education in Elementary Education. She was director of the CDA pilot training program in Fall River, Massachusetts, has been a teacher and teacher educator in a variety of settings, and has been active in National Association for the Education of Young Children activities at the local, state, and regional levels.